Echoes of the Old Darkland

Echoes of the Old Darkland

THEMES FROM THE AFRICAN EDEN

Charles S. Finch III, M.D.

CONTENTS

Introduction

This book, to a large extent, can be considered an obeisance to two intellectual forces that have shaped it: Gerald Massey and Cheikh Anta Diop. Even "Old Darkland" in the title is taken from Massey's rather poetic name for Africa. Most of the contents of this book represent a continued development of lines of inquiry that emerged out of the indefatigable labors of these two men, however much their lives appear to have been separated by time and space, culture and race. Yet they were very similar in their pioneering uses of multiple levels of evidence; of appreciating the common connection among myth, history, and the human psyche.

This book is also the fruit of 19 years of private study. Like Massey and Diop, I had to create a private university in which I was both teacher and pupil because what I sought to learn and what I write about here could never be found in the curriculum of an established university. But then all true education is self-education; the completion of formal schooling should be only the beginning of learning, not the end. However, even after 19 years I am impressed by what I don't know. Diop and Massey must have felt the same way; each continued his quest for knowledge until the end of his life. However, one still tends to feel like a neophyte in the shadow cast by their achievements.

I am often asked how and why I, a physician, could devote so much of my life to such non-medical endeavors. That my consuming interest in disciplines outside of medicine should cause such astonishment is, perhaps, an oblique indictment of the profession as it now stands. From Imhotep to Osler, many doctors of old were Renaissance men; Keats was a doctor-poet; Martin Delaney was a physician and an early theoretician of Pan Africanism; William Carlos Williams, a general practitioner, was one of 20th-century America's foremost men of letters; Howard Medical School's W. Montague Cobb, a distinguished physician and anatomist, was, in addition to fluency in Latin and Greek, an accomplished violinist. Sun Yat-Sen and Franz Fanon were two physicians who left an indelible mark on the politics of liberation in this century. If this love of universal knowledge and concern for larger, global issues affecting humanity have disappeared from the medical profession, it does not bode well for its future.

The public perplexity concerning my extra-professional interests has meant that I have had to summarize my life on various occasions to help explain my immersion in these fields. Consequently, though it is a little presumptuous for a first-time author, I have resolved to incorporate a short autobiography into the Introduction of this work to help readers understand some of the forces that molded my "second career."

I was born in Topeka, Kansas, on February 25, 1948, the second son of a psychiatrist then training at Meninger Clinic. I was named after my father and grandfather, though I didn't start using the "III" after my name until my father's death in 1986. Eventually there were to be seven children in the family, six boys and a girl.

My first and most lasting influence was that of my mother, Louise Finch; in fact I attribute my abiding interest in things matriarchal (see Chapter II) to this early maternal impact. She was the true molder of our family. She, for example, was the one directly responsible for three of us following our father into the medical profession and she always insisted that our comportment exhibit qualities of strength and manliness balanced by respect for others, discipline, and good manners.

Soon after my brother Michael was born in 1949, my father re-entered the Army, where he remained until his retirement in 1963. If there ever was a possibility for an "idyllic" integrated existence in the America of the 1950's, the peacetime military service was the nearest thing. Harry Truman had desegregated the Armed Services the year I was born and officially, discrimination was "against regulations." Truthfully, my family and I experienced very little of the overt racism that characterized everyday life for most Blacks in America. Occasionally, we encountered the "N" word; minor incidents cropped up from time to time to remind us that though we were officially integrated, we were not to forget who and what we really were. But my father was an officer and a physician which did provide a buffer of sorts. We moved frequently, but far from this being troublesome, it, at the time, suited us all fine; we were never in one place long enough for anyone to "draw a bead" on us, and in the Army there were no entrenched social groups to contend against. Being a "Negro" was something that one was aware of but didn't think about too much.

In 1963, my father retired from the Army and the family moved to California. Six months later I went, for the first time, east to Massachusetts to work at a summer camp with my oldest brother (by 10 years) Arthur in 1964. I didn't know it at the time but this was to be a major turning point. I had come to the attention of Charles Merrill, founder and headmaster of the Commonwealth School in Boston, who had achieved a considerable reputation as an educator, philanthropist, and one of the largest financial backers of the civil rights movement. I interviewed at Commonwealth that summer and was admitted a week later.

There is no possible way to underestimate the profound impact of this turn of events. I moved to Boston and attended Commonwealth for the next two years. My brother was in Boston that first year involved in an organization, consciously patterned after SNCC, called the Northern Student Movement. He worked for an offshoot of that organization, the Boston Action Group, and it was at this time that I underwent a profound awakening. I became mentally and psychologically involved in the intensifying Civil Rights movement; I "discovered" Malcolm X in the political sphere and John Coltrane in the musical. I began to read Baldwin, Ellison, and Claude Brown's *Manchild in the Promised Land*. Everything that I was subsequently to become emanates from that period. My involvement with activities in Roxbury, Boston's Black community, went hand in glove with the exercises in critical thinking demanded of me at Commonwealth. Arthur had no little hand in all of this; it was he who made it possible for me to finish Commonwealth by paying my tuition my senior year. A somewhat obscure incident occurred at Commonwealth in those years that has always stuck with me: during a school assembly, the headmaster commented that the Benin bronzes were as good as anything that came out of the Renaissance. Nothing else was said, however, and I remember feeling vaguely disappointed that this remarkable statement was never elaborated on.

In 1966, I entered Yale College. Thirty-seven other black students entered with me, the largest contingent of Blacks ever admitted at one time. I cannot claim to have been a brilliant student; the latter half of the sixties was a time when protest movements were moving into a radical ideological phase and many of us rode the whirlwind. As the decade wore on, events outside the classroom proved far more compelling than the exercises inside. We "discovered" Blackness; the rhetoric of revolution and the politics of confrontation became *de rigueur.* Names like Stokely Carmichael, H. Rap Brown, Eldridge Cleaver, Huey Newton; places like Watts, Newark, Detroit, where the most violent street "rebellions" took place, crowded our fevered imaginations. Malcolm and Coltrane, by this time, had been "canonized."

One the by-products of this era of protest was a deepening interest in African history and culture. The norms of American society were being called into question on every front; legions of black students sought to delve deeper into the legacy of the first part of that new, hyphenated cognomen, "Afro-American." Existing courses in anthropology and African history were seen as woefully inadequate, taught by white teachers who, at best, evinced only the driest clinical interest in these subjects. So insistent did this demand become that in 1968–69, it brought to birth for the first time in American higher education the Black Studies movement. It was in this period that I took my initial African history and anthropology courses, encountering for the first time names like Sundiata, Sonni Ali, and Askia Mohammed and places like Ghana, Mali, and Songhay. No mention of Egypt in the context of African history, however, except once: a book entitled *Problems in African History,* edited by Robert O. Collins, contained essays by several Africanists. One such essay was an excerpt from a book by Cheikh Anta Diop. However, the published passage was not sufficient to exhibit the full Diopian thesis and though I remembered his name thereafter, I was not markedly struck by the idea that Egypt might have been a black African civilization. At the time, I did not know nearly enough.

At the end of my junior year, I took a year off. Up to that point, I had not taken any concrete steps toward a career and I began to feel somewhat adrift. Of that year, 1969–1970, it can be said that it was the best of times and the worst of times. But two things happened that set the course of my life: (1) I firmly committed myself to pursue the career that I had been "groomed" for all my life, i.e., medicine, and (2) I came across J.A. Rogers's *World's Great Men of Color.* Every so often, one comes to feel that life is a series of revelations, each one leading to the other; Rogers's book affected me that way. I had *never* imagined that all these great, historical black personages had existed. It was in this book that I was first exposed to the ideas of Gerald Massey.

I returned to Yale in the Fall of 1970 resolved to begin my pre-medical studies and to make more productive use of Yale's Sterling Library. Sure enough I began to come across books such as Massey's *Book of Beginnings,* Godfrey Higgins's *Anacalypsis,* and John G. Jackson's *Introduction to African Civilization.* However, during that year I could only scan them, serious reading would have to wait for a more opportune occasion.

In the summer of 1971, I went to work for the Black Student Summer Program of the National Urban League out of New York. It was perhaps the most pleasant summer of my life, especially important for one major discovery—Weiser's Book Store in the East Village. An Urban League co-worker had directed me there and as I started browsing I could scarcely contain my mounting excitement. Here, for the buying, were books by all of the authorities cited by Rogers and that summer I spent more than $600 on books, beginning the collection that grows to the present day. That is the summer from which I specifically date the beginning of my researches.

At the end of the summer of 1972, I took two more momentous steps: I married and then entered medical school three weeks later. I had known Ellen Joyce Nixon, daughter of a family of Philadephia educators and a student at Mount Holyoke College, since my freshman year at Yale. In a sense, we grew up together during that period in the late '60s, undergoing a parallel transformation of attitude and orientation. There was an anchoring and a balancing that my life required and I think she was the only one who could have provided it. Like other unusual women I've known, Ellen has the ability to grasp essential truths by spontaneous intuition that men seem to acquire only by long, complicated ratiocination. Ultimately, we were to have seven children.

While I was in medical school and residency training I continued my investigations. I anchored my studies in Nile Valley culture, particularly after the publication of Diop's *African Origin of Civilization: Myth or Reality?* in 1974. But early on I branched out into the related disciplines of comparative religion, cultural anthropology, and analytic (Jungian) psychology.

I was attending the wedding of my brother Mark in 1981 in San Francisco when, as I was browsing through Marcus Bookstore, I came across a thin, gold-covered periodical with the eye-catching title *Journal of African Civilizations,* edited by Ivan Van Sertima. Van Sertima was no stranger to me: in that same store I had obtained his remarkable and ground-breaking treatise entitled *They Came Before Columbus: The African Presence in Early America* in 1977. I was struck then by his marvelous gift for language as well as by his ingenious and innovative scholarly approach. Like Diop, he was well-prepared to cross disciplines to drive home his thesis. I tore through the newly-acquired *Journal* in just a couple of hours. I was so taken by what I read that as soon as I returned home, I penned him a quick letter and attached a check for a subscription. One week later the phone rang, and when I picked it up the voice on the other end said, "This is Ivan Van Sertima." To say that I was momentarily speechless is trite but true. Ivan proceeded to say that he had received my letter and was impressed enough to ask if I could write an article on the history of Blacks in medicine for the *Journal.* I stammered my assent and to this day I marvel at the whole chain of events; it was literally a bolt out of the blue. I had the good fortune to have access to Duke University's Medical Library which has an excellent history of medicine section and the result was my first article entitled "The African Background of Medical Science," published in the 1982 Spring issue of the *Journal of African Civilizations.* This was the formal beginning of a writing and lecturing career that has taken me across the country and into Europe and Africa. To the extent that I can say that I was "discovered," it was Ivan Sertima who did so. To this day I maintain a close collegial relationship with Van Sertima and 80% of my published works have appeared under his auspices.

Between 1982 and in 1985, I had the signal privilege of meeting Cheikh Anta Diop on four occasions. My sessions with him sent me off in two directions of inquiry which have culminated as chapters (I and V) in this book. It was Diop who impressed upon me the importance of studying prehistory in the effort to recover Africa's lost past. In addition, Diop, on a napkin in a restaurant in London, demonstrated to me the method by which he derived the Biblical name Abraham from the ancient Egyptian language. He already had a life overflowing with scholarly commitments so I took it upon myself to apply his method to additional Biblical names. The results were so startling that I finally realized that the Old Testament must have been derived by direct affiliation from the hoary religious symbolism of the Nile Valley cultures. Needless to say, it revolutionized my whole perspective of Judaeo-Christian religion.

In 1984, I, along with Mr. Larry Obadele Williams, co-chaired the Nile Valley Conference in Atlanta, Georgia. Other co-sponsors included Dr. Mwalimu Imara of the Department of Human Values of the Morehouse School of Medicine; Ivan Van Sertima, Editor of the *Journal of African Civilizations*; and Dr. Lawrence E. Carter, Dean of the Martin Luther King International Chapel of Morehouse College, the site of the conference. This conference represented a watershed of sorts: since then, there has developed an unprecedented level of public interest in Nile Valley culture and its impact on world civilization that continues to expand apace, leading now to ever-intensifying demands for curriculum revision in the colleges and public schools to take into account this "Nile Valley factor" in world history. No matter what the outcome, it is unlikely that American education will ever be the same.

As of this writing, I am Assistant Director of International Health at the Morehouse School of Medicine in Atlanta. My burgeoning interest in international health stems directly from my interest in traditional medicine in Africa, in time and space, and its potential role in facing down the monumental health problems plaguing Africa today. But the health of African populations is as much dependent on cultural, historical, political, and economic factors as it is medical. Like all major global problems, only a comprehensive view and a multi-disciplinary approach will prove adequate to the enormous task of resolution. Where Africa is concerned, it will be the formidable, if dormant, interior resources that she commands that will be most decisive in her rehabilitation. Until that truth is faced uncompromisingly, Africa will remain a collection of client states.

The book consists of six chapters which unfold in an "evolutionary" sequence. The more I have studied, the more I have become preoccupied with origins and sources; with getting at the root of the issue. The combined Massey-Diop influence is evident here: Massey's first book was entitled *Book of Beginnings* and Diop's paramount interest in prehistory rubbed off on me. Thus, my first chapter, "Race and Human Origins," reflects my intense interest in the issues surrounding the emergence and evolution of humanity in Africa and the subsequent appearance of the human varieties we call "races." This chapter represents an updating and revising of an earlier article I had published on the same subject but on this occasion the manuscript has benefited enormously from a critical reading by Dr. William Kimbel of the Institute of Human Origins. Having worked as an academic myself for seven years, I am keenly aware of the well-developed "territoriality" of specialists that gives them a jaundiced view of "invasions" into their fields by "outsiders." Bill evinced none of that and gave this chapter as thorough a going-over as he might a paper by a professional colleague. I will always be grateful to him for that.

Chapter II, "The Great Mother and the Origin of Human Culture," stems from my pronounced interest in the ancient matriarchy. It was something of a shock years ago when my readings made it clear that prior to the seemingly all-pervasive patriarchal social structures, most of the world's cultures appear to have been constructed along matriarchal lines. However, the works of Erich Neumann made the logic of such an evolution clear and Robert Briffault's mammoth three-volume *The Mothers* provided the empirical underpinnings for this model. But above all, the matriarchal sub-stratum undergirding virtually all culture in Africa in particular becomes abundantly evident from an analysis of Egyptian myths, language, and symbols. Some of the more imaginative might see in the contemporary assertion of women's rights a resurgence of the old matriarchy.

Chapter III, "The Emergence of the Patriarchy: Paradigm of 'Becoming,' " focuses on the genesis of partriarchal ideas and symbols out of the old matriarchal matrix. Two points are worth noting: (1) the patriarchal idea or archetype was a natural, even inevitable, step in the evolution of consciousness as shown both by Gerald Massey and Erich Neumann; (2) the archetype was equally effective in men and women so that the "battle lines" between the contending imperatives of matriarchy and patriarchy did not conform strictly to gender. The matriarchy became decadent and psychically unhealthy because it was one-sided and all-consuming; on the other hand the same indictments can now be leveled at the contemporary patriarchy which has become so overweening as to threaten the very existence of the planet itself. Seen in this way, the modern politico-ideological aspects of these questions take on a new complexion as we prepare for the new century and the new age.

Chapter IV, "Chronology, the Calendar, and the Kamite Great Year," will undoubtedly be considered the most controversial one in the book, if for no other reason than it implies that the modern way of looking at history is totally inadequate to teach us much that is meaningful about the remote past. It suggests, for example, that formal history may have actually begun nearly 13,000 years ago and that the early makers of history cycled it according to celestial events. For me, there is no sense to be made of Egyptian history at least unless the Great Year or Precession of the Equinoxes is taken into account.

Chapter V, "The Nile Valley Sources of the Old Testament," has some of the earmarks, almost, of a revelation, i.e., that hidden in the language of the Old Testament lies its true history and meaning which devolve from the Afro-Kamitic culture-complex. This gives one indication, among many, of the immense debt Western civilization owes to Afro-Kamitic culture through the fathomless influence of the Old Testament. Traditionally, historiography has seen the stream of Western civilization issuing from two primary wellsprings: Old Testament Hebrewism and classical Hellenism. As Massey would say, historiographers have not gotten at the rootage, only the first branches.

Chapter VI, "Osiris, the Egyptian Funerary Ritual, and the Birth of Christianity," shows how completely Christian sources depended on the Osiris cycle. In effect, the Christ now worshipped by 750 million people around the globe is but the latest manifestation of Osiris; virtually all the ceremonials, symbols, and rituals of Christian worship derive from that of Osiris and his Holy Family, that is Isis and Horus. There need not have been anything inherently antithetical to post-Nicean Christianity in any of this, given that all religions are derived from previous sacral forms, but the post-Nicean cult degenerated quickly into intolerance resulting in singularly brutal campaigns to liquidate the old worship. Christian fathers thus committed a kind of parricide. As a Catholic parishioner, I have never forgotten the words of Giles Conwill, then a Catholic priest, who once said to me that faith is never an excuse for ignorance.

I have structured my Introduction in such a way that I could dispense with the commonplace manner in which literary acknowledgments are usually given and yet still pay homage to those who have been instrumental in the furtherance of my work. Still I must directly express my appreciation for the efforts of Mr. Don Dehart Bronkema who proofed and edited this manuscript. To the extent that the book is readable, he can claim no little share in the credit. Also my appreciation and gratitude extend to Mr. James Brunson and Mr. Wayne Chandler who generously supplied many of the photos that grace this volume.

Charles S. Finch III
August, 1990
Atlanta, Georgia

I

Race and Human Origins

The prehuman phase of the incredibly long, unfolding drama of life on this planet begins to emerge from the hazy mists of prehistory about 40–36 mya (millions of years ago). The mammalian class of the animal kingdom had long since dominated, and its primate order was well-established by this time. The primates were largely tree-dwellers, possessing prehensile tails and hand-like appendages suitable for grasping branches. Their eyes had evolved to a forward position on the skull, providing stereoscopic vision that enhanced the hand-eye co-ordination necessary for an arboreal mode of life. Within this order there was a group, today called the monkeys, who possessed all the common characteristics of the primates, including a diet of fruits and leaves, plus, in retrospect, a potential for growth of adaptive intelligence.

The world in this period, the Oligocene, was much warmer and wetter than it is now, and a vast expanse of dense forest covered most of the earth. Monkeys were well-distributed over tropical land masses in both the eastern (Old World) and western (New World) hemispheres. The presence of such a well-demarcated primate group on two land masses so widely separated by ocean is an enigma. Either the two monkey groups represent a remarkable case of parallel evolution from prosimian, or "pre-monkey," ancestors that inhabited both hemispheres 60–80 millions years ago, or the New World monkeys are descended from early African monkeys who somehow "rafted" across the Atlantic 40 million years ago when the continents were much closer together than they are at present. There are problems with each interpretation. North and South America were not joined until five or six million years ago, yet the only Western Hemispheric prosimians who could have been ancestral to the monkeys inhabited North America. Thus, at a time when these North American prosimians could have given rise to the South American monkeys, circa 40 mya, there was a substantial gulf between the two continents. Equally important, there are no intermediate ancestral forms between the early North American prosimians and the South American monkeys. An interpretation favoring an African origin of New World monkeys is strongly recommended by the numerous African candidates for the intermediate ancestral forms at the critical time. However, the Atlantic barrier seems to weigh heavily against this interpretation since few primatologists are willing to entertain the notion that early African monkeys repeatedly rafted across to an extent that would account for their widespread proliferation in South America. The only mitigating factor is the closer proximity of the two continents then compared to now. The African origin theory appears to hold the edge, but the debate continues.

The next major development takes us to 25 mya when a new group of primates, known today as the apes, appeared. The apes derived from ancestral monkeys on the African continent and then, as now, their range was entirely limited to the Old World. The total absence of any ape species in the New World eliminates the Western Hemisphere from any further consideration in the evolutionary drama that leads eventually to human beings. The members of the ape family were also arboreal, but anatomically different from their monkey relatives. They possessed a greater cranial capacity and therefore occupied a rung or two above the monkeys on the intelligence ladder. They were bigger and stronger as well; their facial morphology shifted toward a shortened snout and a somewhat more elevated forehead height. Moreover, the apes exhibited a reduced lumbar region, a broader thorax, and longer forelimbs. As it had for the monkeys and other primates, the upper reaches of the leaf canopy of the dense, world-wide forest provided them with a home, safe from potential predators, and abundant leaves and fruits to eat at their leisure. Indeed, our own flattened molars appear to be an inheritance from the essentially vegetarian mastication patterns of our remote ape ancestors.

A drastic change in simian arboreal living patterns begins around 15 mya: the world, with the formation of the polar ice caps, began to experience significant drying and, deprived of moisture, the dense forest began to shrink. The forest gave way in many places to parkland, savannah and even desert. The apes faced their first collective challenge. Under these changed circumstances, they were perhaps at a disadvantage vis-a-vis the monkeys, because of their larger body size, lesser mobility and higher calorie requirements. Like uncounted species before them, they had to adjust or perish in the face of a drastic alteration of environment that compromises living space and food sources. This is the "call and response" pattern of evolution: nature "calls" or signals through critical changes in the climate or environment and the living species, if it is to survive, must "respond" with an array of adaptive physical and behavioral modalities which function in a seamless continuum. Sometimes the time frame of the adaptive response may be prolonged, encompassing millions of years; at other times, a new "punctuated equilibrium" may be established in a few thousand generations.

Some of the apes responded to the crisis created by the shrinking forest by literally coming down out of the trees. This process did not happen suddenly or completely, but by degrees, so that eventual adaptation to a ground habitat represented the cumulative effects of natural selection over millions of years. Nonetheless, the modification was decisive: only four ape species still survive out of the dozen or more that existed 15 million years ago and three of the four are ground-dwellers to a greater or lesser degree.[1] Particularly among the two surviving African great apes, the chimpanzee and the gorilla, ground-dwelling seems to have become the *sine qua non* of survival. Why? For one thing, ground-dwelling gave the ape the ability to exploit food sources both on the ground and in the tree-tops and the trees would still serve as a potential refuge whenever predators threatened. Ground-dwelling also gave them an ecological niche with broader adaptive opportunities. However, ground-dwelling also challenged the apes with a new set of dangers: exposure to the big cats and other predators.

In this gradual process of spending more time on the ground, the apes had to develop patterns of social co-operation so that they could more efficiently fend off predators. An individual chimpanzee or baboon is no match for a leopard or a lion, but neither of these cats would attack chimpanzees or baboons in a troop. Chimpanzees and gorillas even today do not suffer much from predation pressure, aside from human poachers, and so fearless are chimpanzees that individuals have been known to confront and drive off leopards single-handedly.[2] Suffice it to say that the ground-dwelling apes without exception live in tightly-knit, well-ordered communities; the solitary types in the ape family are to be found only among the arboreal orangutans and gibbons of the Indonesian archipelago. One may reasonably speculate that, in time, living in social communities enhanced intelligence by forcing new behaviors relating to group security, food gathering, and reproduction that in turn put a premium on, and selected for, more sophisticated means of communication. Apart from humans, the ground-dwelling chimpanzees and gorillas are the most intelligent land mammals on earth.

The disparate experiences of African versus Asian apes would prove crucial to the appearances of the hominids.* The new lacustrine regions of East Africa consisted of parkland and savannah interspersed with patches of forest. In southeast Asia, on the other hand, the climate stayed moist and the preservation of dense forests allowed the surviving apes to continue almost entirely as tree-dwellers, as gibbons and orangutans do today. The apes of East Africa, by contrast, were forced by circumstances to spend more time on the ground, even to the point of venturing into open grassland in search of food, though retiring at night to the safety of

---

* The term "hominid" means "man-like." Hominids are a true family—separate from the apes—to which all modern humans belong.

the trees. Living in this bimodal habitat was decisive, for it is here that the drama of evolution propels a particular type of ape across the hominid threshold.

We can better understand the nuances of this process by looking closer at our modern primate cousins, the chimpanzee and the gorilla. The gorilla occupies the lush low-land and mountain forests of west and east-central Africa, where, virtually free from predation, he can indulge his enormous appetite for roots and leaves. In such bountiful and unthreatening surroundings, the gorilla has developed a completely inoffensive disposition and a massive body that have limited the adaptability that might have allowed him to exploit a broader ranger of habitats. The chimpanzee is another matter. He can be found in a wide range of niches all over sub-Saharan Africa. He develops the most sophisticated of ape communities, even showing some elementary tool-using by employing sticks to extract termites from their mounds. The chimpanzee even seems to have a fairly advanced communication system, a sort of pre-language.[3] The chimpanzee has also acquired a taste for meat, hunting and eating small animals, though this forms but a fraction of his mainly vegetarian diet. Moreover, under certain circumstances the chimpanzee exhibits highly aggressive behavior toward his fellows. This is not unprecedented in the animal kingdom; competition for food, living space, and mates regularly provokes intra-group conflict. But it is unusual for competition to result in the death of a species member. It cannot be said to be commonplace among chimpanzees either, but Jane Goodall and her collaborators not only witnessed but filmed a systematic war of extermination of one chimpanzee community against another.[4] Goodall also witnessed overt acts of cannibalism among chimpanzees, recording the activities of two grown females—a mother and a daughter—who on at least four, and perhaps as many as ten, occasions attacked a new chimpanzee mother, stripped her of her infant, killed it, and ate it. Aberrant behavior to be sure, but such lethal episodes were never theretofore suspected, and persuaded Goodall that chimps were more like humans than had been surmised.

Perhaps not coincidentally, the very ape line that leads to the chimpanzee is the same one that leads to the hominids. It now appears, from good comparative biomolecular data, that the bifurcation of hominid and chimpanzee occurred a scant seven million years ago.[5] Looked at another way, modern humans are separated from the chimpanzee by only one to two percent of our genes; we and the chimpanzees are, genetically, 98–99 percent identical.

The hominid appeared as a distinct entity about four mya—a ground-dweller who had generally abandoned the forest for open savannah and parkland. He retained some residual climbing ability, but ranged farther into open country than any of the earlier pre-hominids. As always, it was the search for food that was the driving force. Like his chimpanzee cousin, he must have been a scavenger, a forager, and probably a hunter; it is likely that hunting came to occupy a larger slice of his time and effort as time passed. Still, meat accounted for less than 20 percent of his diet; the bulk of it was still adventitious vegetable food.[6]

The pre-hominid ape was hirsute, yet the emerging hominid had already lost most of his body hair. This is readily explainable. By venturing out into the open savannah in search of food, the new hominid was spending more time under the direct rays of the equatorial sun. Prolonged exposure to solar irradiation, however, posed critical problems of heat dissipation and temperature regulation within the body. The chimpanzees and other apes never faced this problem because they never ventured very far from the shade of the trees, to which they readily repaired during the heat of mid-day.

How then were the first hominids to cope with this problem of thermoregulation? Several adaptive strategies lay open to them: one was the proliferation of eccrine sweat glands in the body; another was the loss of the body's hairy coat. Sweat glands produce moisture that, upon evaporation, carries heat away from the body. The loss of body hair facilitated the process by reducing heat retention and exposing more skin surface for evaporation.[7] But this solution created a new problem: how to protect the underlying depilated skin from the destructive effects of the sun's ultraviolet radiation. We know from the fate of albinos all over Africa that unprotected skin is subject to grotesque, disfiguring cancers that are soon fatal. The problem was solved in the hominids by the natural selection of genetic lines with a higher content of dermal melanin, the substance that gives the skin a dark brown or black pigment and, by absorbing ultraviolet radiation and scattering the ions produced, protects the skin from cancer. Indeed, Gloger's Law states that the closer a warm-blooded animal is to the equator, the darker its coat.[8] The chimpanzee and the gorilla are clear examples of this, both species possessing blackish hairy coats. Our pre-hominid ancestor, who was very close to the African great apes, would also have possessed a dark coat initially; as this coat was gradually lost, the increasingly exposed skin in the species would have selected for melanin production. Thus, the hominid that emerged between five and three-and-a-half million years ago from this long evolutionary gestation absolutely required skin that was black or dark brown in color. It couldn't have been otherwise; this relatively simple adaptation allowed hominids to survive and prosper in an open, equatorial environment. It is not too much to say that without this original black pigment, there would be no human race today!

The salient issues of human paleontology are controversial because it is a discipline that has to infer much from very little. Fossil remains are few, so anthropology has had to develop numerous sub-disciplines to mine every scrap of information from the material at hand. Defining what man is and what made him has ignited some of the most volcanic and acrimonious debates in all academe.

Generally speaking, five main characteristics differentiate man and his hominid ancestors from the apes: (1) bipedality with upright ambulation; (2) cranial size and shape; (3) reduced canines; (4) use of articulated, symbolic language; and (5) construction of complex tools.[9] Bipedality in particular has provoked stormy debates. The traditional explanation is that it provided an ability to peer over the tall grass and freed the hands for the use of tools and brandishing weapons. A rather striking challenge to this scenario has arisen since 1981 from C. Owen Lovejoy.[10] It is his view that bipedalism evolved in the context of sexual division of labor.

Lovejoy begins with the premise that the transport of food and its relation to "reproductive success" is what fosters bipedal development. A male carries food to his offspring which improves his reproductive success by enhancing his offspring's survival. This food-carrying was adaptively significant because of the implied "separation of male and female day ranges," meaning that males, not burdened with the custody of a small infant, could move father afield in search of food. Lovejoy assumes that the only reason for such altruism among protohominid males was the "assurance" of biological paternity, attained by means of monogamous pairbonding. Thus, according to Lovejoy, "It appears likely that the skeletal alterations of bipedality would be under strong selection only by consistent, extended periods of upright walking and not by either occasional bipedality or up-right posture."[11] The food-carrying behavior that Lovejoy infers, particularly since it would require and encourage walking long distances, would tend to favor those individuals who would walk upright. In short, upright, bi-pedal walking was a direct outgrowth of food-carrying by the male and the monogamous pair-bonding imposed by this behavior.

Needless to say, Lovejoy's thesis, intriguing as it is, has come under furious attack, particularly from feminists who see in Lovejoy's theory an attempt to read the "patriarchal" values of the modern age back into prehistory. Ideology aside, there are nevertheless serious problems raised by Lovejoy's thesis. First of all, it is not at all clear that the food-gathering ranges of the male and female proto-hominids were as separate as Lovejoy would make them. The modern African apes, who would have been very close to the proto-hominids, do not exhibit sex differences in foraging ranges. Moreover, child-rearing did not, among apes or early hominids, relieve the mothers of the necessity of gathering food. An inkling of this comes from hunting-gathering populations such as the San ("Bushmen") of southwest Africa, among whom women procure at least 80 percent of the food even though social relations and status are determined by hunting success. We may note in passing that hunting does compel San males to travel farther afield than the women, yet the meat they bring back does *not* go merely to their offspring, but is shared by the entire group. Women in this society, far from passively depending on meat brought into the community by the males, still perform the bulk of food procurement for the entire group.

In an interview, anthropologist Tim White pointed out that since the San have a technology far in advance of the late Pliocene hominids, it may not be relevant to compare their food-gathering systems.[12] Even if this caveat is accepted, it merely means that the early hominids would have been more dependent on foraging by *both* sexes in the same range than is true today. Furthermore, even if we agree that the "typical" early hominid female with a young infant was impeded to such a degree as not to be able to move about and forage, it seems more likely that *other females* would have foraged on her behalf as an adaptive strategy instead of the putative "pair-bonded" male. We know that among the African great apes, the females groom one another and may even suckle and care for one another's babies.[13] In the remarkable series of films produced by Jane Goodall and her associates, older daughters of female chimpanzees are sometimes permitted to care for their infant siblings.[14] Perhaps the decisive step toward hominization was not male-female pair-bonding but instead the females extending and increasing their co-operative sharing behavior toward one another and their progeny.[15]

The most dangerous enemies of the young of certain species of higher primates are not outside predators but the adult males of the species. Langur male monkeys commonly attack, kill, and eat the young of a dominant male Langur who has been dispossessed of his harem. The victor who takes over the harem does not appear ever to attack his own children and this datum seems consistent with the Lovejoy scenario. Similar behavior, though not as extreme or stereotyped, can be found among certain groups of baboons and chimpanzees. Nonetheless, it is intriguing to speculate whether the danger posed by certain males to the offspring of females in higher primate societies spurred these females to evolve more co-operative behaviors as a means of "closing ranks" against these infanticides. It is impossible to say whether such infanticides were committed by males among evolving proto-hominids, though it is doubtful that they occurred on a significant scale (see the appendix at the end of this chapter). The relative paucity of children, dictated by prolonged gestation and postnatal maturation, would select against it. But in a remoter period, infanticide may have been one more factor propelling pre-hominid females toward greater social cohesion and thus full hominization. It may have been the social relationships between females, instead of the sexual link between male and female, that formed the germ of later hominid society.

As a footnote, we can point out that Lovejoy's thesis pertains only to the male of the species, since it is only he who walks around carrying food. A passive, sedentary female would not exhibit much behavior facilitating bi-pedality. Logically, then, the male alone would evolve an upright, bi-pedal posture while the female would continue as knuckle-walker—a rather bizarre, not to say unlikely, example of sexual di-morphism.* The Lovejoy scenario is hard to reconcile with a bi-pedalism affecting an entire species.

Bi-pedality—like all major issues affecting physical anthropology—is a complex phenomenon. It seems probable that it was an adaptive strategy affected by several factors: food- and child-carrying, predation, tool use, and evolving intelligence. As to the latter, we know that advanced intelligence is tied to single births, a lengthy gestation, prolonged post-natal maturation and care, and lower lifetime fertility. Infants of non-hominid primates all cling to their mothers which hominid infants could not do. Moreover, the longer period of neuro-anatomical development of hominid babies required the mothers to have free hands, instead of appendages for walking, to carry and protect their infants. Though it has been argued that an upright stance was an adaptation to spot predators, predation pressure was probably much-reduced by the time the early hominids appeared. Jane Goodall, during thousands of hours of observation, never saw a chimpanzee attacked by a big cat; Dian Fosse reported only one gorilla killed by a leopard in her many years of living among them. Chimpanzees and gorillas are both very strong, much stronger than humans, and in a troop are nearly invulnerable against the big cats or any other predator. The early hominids were also stronger, pound-for-pound, than modern humans and in a group would have been more than a match for most predators. Predators were a danger, of course, but not a threat. Moreover, no species with such a long gestation and post-natal maturation, combined with restricted birth numbers, could ever have survived had it been under high predation pressure.

Molecular biology has left a permanent imprint on paleoanthropology. Inter-species analysis of DNA and serum proteins, begun in the 1960's by Sarich and Wilson at the University of California at Berkeley, has demonstrated beyond all argument the close affinity of humans, chimpanzees, and gorillas. In fact, these three species are all closer to each other than any of them is to any other primate. The gorilla split off from the chimpanzee-hominid branch between ten and eight million years ago. Since there is every reason to believe that the very first hominid, *Australopithecus afarensis,* represented by Donald Johanson's famous "Lucy"

---

* The term "sexual dimorphism" refers to gender-specific anatomical differences within a species.

and the Laetoli fossils of Mary Leakey, had emerged by four mya, most, though not all, workers in the field believe that the chimpanzee-human split did not occur much after seven mya.[16] Between seven and four mya presumably lived a still-undiscovered proto-hominid type very much like the chimpanzee but with distinct anatomic features. "Lucy," specifically dated about 3.0 mya, was fully bi-pedal, small in stature, with a smallish, chimpanzee-like skull of 480 cc, and almost certainly black or dark-brown in color. She represents the oldest known hominid of the *Australopithecus* genus, itself first discovered in South Africa in 1925 by Raymond Dart in the person of the so-called Taung Baby. *A. afarensis,* though bi-pedal and upright, is thought to have retained some tree-climbing ability. The typical member of the species probably did not tip five feet.

Through some brilliant comparative analysis, Donald Johanson and Tim White created a hominid genealogical tree that places *A. afarensis* at the very beginning of the human lineage. This was a bold step. Previously, anthropologists, particularly in the influential Leakey circle, were not disposed to admit any connection between the four species of Australopithecus and the specifically human line of evolution. The four Australopithecus types are identifiable as *afarensis,* the oldest and most primitive of the genus and therefore ancestral to all the others; *africanus,* lightly-built and "gracile"; *robustus,* heavy-featured and massive; and finally *boisei,* hyper-robust. It was the original belief of Johanson and White that *afarensis* gave rise to two lines: one line leading progressively to *africanus,* then to *robustus,* then hyper-robust *boisei* who died out completely; and the other to the *Homo* branch, the genus of modern man. However, a recently discovered skull, with the name of KNM-WT 17000 and dated at 2.6 mya, shows features of marked robusticity. Thus, there was a robust Australopithecus older than *robustus* and *boisei,* and very close in antiquity to the earlier *africanus.* It is unlikely, therefore, that KNM-WT 17000 is descended from *africanus.* This development, in effect, puts more branches on the tree, but it does not displace *afarensis* from the "root" of the tree. As Tim White has said, "What they found was perhaps the best evidence of human evolution that we yet have. They have found a perfect link between *A. afarensis* and *A. boisei,* the robust *Australopithecus....* This black skull is the missing link between *A. afarensis* and the robust *Australopithecus* form that later evolved and went extinct in East Africa."[17]

Australopithecus dominates human evolution from about four mya to two mya, dying out altogether by one mya. Though they vary from small, lightly built to heavy, robust types, they are all upright, bi-pedal, diminutive in stature, forager-scavengers by occupation, scant of body hair, and black or dark brown in skin color. They use sticks and stones as tools but are not true tool makers. They do not seem to have been fire-builders either and their range was confined to their original habitats in East and

Southern Africa. Unlike many of the great apes before them, and some of their more advanced *Homo* successors afterwards, they do not appear to have left Africa. Genealogically, they were very close to their chimpanzee cousins and, from about two mya, share their habitat with *Homo habilis,* who is a descendant of either *afarensis* or *africanus* and the first of the genus that leads directly to modern humans.

The type specimen of *H. habilis* was discovered by Mary and Louis Leakey in Olduvai Gorge, Tanzania in 1960. It was the most shocking fossil brought to light since Dart's Taung Baby 36 years before. The Taung Baby had established incontestably Africa's primacy in the unfolding story of human evolution; the Olduvai find fixed the date of the human ancestral line back to two mya, ages older than anyone had ever dreamed. Acceptance of the Leakeys' interpretation of the Olduvai bones was a little while in coming, however. Though the dating was good, the Leakey camp had unearthed mere fragments with which to reconstruct the skull, and reconstruction was crucial because skull size would be the primary determinant differentiating the Olduvai fossils from the Australopithecines. Upon completing the reconstruction, the Leakey team estimated the skull's capacity at 682 cubic centimeters (cc's) or about 200 cc's more than the average Australopithecine cranial capacity. Immediately, a storm of controversy arose over two things: (1) the accuracy of the reconstruction and (2) the designation of this skull as the earliest of the *Homo* genus. It was not until 1972 that a younger Leakey, Richard, found a skull in the Lake Turkana region of northern Kenya which was nearly complete, though reconstruction took a painfully long time, and which, at 752 cc's, was clearly large by early hominid standards. The Lake Turkana skull was more rounded than that of the typical Australopithecine and was dated at two mya. Here then was a type that was significantly different in skull size and configuration from the Australopithecine and, considering significant variations in dental morphology, could clearly be differentiated from its predecessor. The new skull shared enough traits with the Olduvai *habilis* find to be classified with it. Thus Richard, the son, vindicated the work of his parents, Mary and Louis. His find, known simply as skull "1470," definitely established *Homo habilis* as a distinct species on the road to modern man.

In light of recent findings, *Homo habilis* can be seen to have arisen directly from *A. afarensis* as the *Homo* branch of that ancestral hominid family. He was clearly a tool-maker, not just an opportunistic tool-user, hence his species name *habilis,* which identifies him as "handy man" or "man with ability." He and the Australopithecines shared the East and Southern African habitat for a million years, but with his undoubted intelligence and tool-making ability, he had the competitive edge. He, too, would have been heavily pigmented, diminutive, and fully bi-pedal, but significantly different in dentition from his hominid ancestors. His cranial capacity ranged from 600–800 cc's and with him, *Homo* becomes an established hominid lineage.

By one million years ago, the Australopithecines had died out, probably due to morphological overspecialization and robusticity which, if the gorilla is any indication, limits the habitat and food sources. The robust forms of a primate genus seem to be less agile, less mobile, and less adaptable. Whatever the case, *Australopithecus* as a genus had disappeared by one million years ago. It is not known to what extent, if any, he had "competed" with *H. habilis* while sharing the same habitat. Lacking evidence to the contrary, we may assume that each occupied his own niche, co-existing more or less peaceably. What seems reasonably certain is that neither the Australopithecines nor *H. habilis* ever left Africa, at least not in great numbers; none of their fossil remains has been found anywhere outside the continent. This is not merely bad luck. In an interview, Bill Kimbel of the Institute of Human Origins in Berkeley, California, pointed out that there are geological strata in other parts of the world, particularly in Asia, comparable in age and composition to the hominid-rich strata of East Africa. These have been carefully excavated and studied without producing a single hominid of the *Australopithecus* or *Homo habilis* type.[18] It is risky to infer absolutely that the absence of evidence is the same as evidence of absence, particularly in a volatile discipline like paleontology, but thus far the search for early hominids outside Africa has been pursued without success. For now we may assume that these early hominids did not stray outside Africa to any meaningful degree, unlike the earlier apes and the later hominids.

One final note concerning *H. habilis*; though two mya is the customary date given for the appearance of this species, stone tools have been found in Ethiopia which are reliably dated at 2.5 mya. The difficulty lies in the absence of any fossils with these tools, but since stone tools always evince the genus *Homo,* we might reasonable conclude that *H. habilis* appeared some half-million years earlier than is conventionally reckoned.

Just as the Australopithecines were evolving into oblivion, as it were, an entirely new species of hominid was making its appearance out of the habiline line. This was *Homo erectus,* who first appeared about 1.7 mya and was morphologically very close to modern humans, his direct descendants. The main difference between *habilis* and *erectus* would have been in the cranial capacity: the *habilis* skull ranged from 600–800 cc whereas the *erectus* skull ranged from 800–1200 cc's, overlapping the lower limit of the modern cranium. *Erectus* may have ranged up to six feet tall, certainly no more, and he was a skilled tool-maker and fire-builder. Unlike his hominid predecessors, he was an avid wanderer who migrated into Asia and Europe. Peking Man and Java Man, disinterred around the turn of the century, are Asian examples of late *H. erectus.* However, the most numerous *erectus* fossils are to be found in East Africa. *H. erectus,* too, would have been dark of skin but in comparison to modern humans, his skull was lower, flatter, and more heavily ridged around the orbits. The first rudiments of a truly human culture would have been invented by *H. erectus* and he probably was not markedly inferior to modern humans in intelligence. His intellectual level most certainly would have represented a quantum advance over that of *H. habilis.*

H. habilis disappears by 1.6 mya, leaving *erectus* the sole hominid on earth. He may have been the first of the hominids to modify his environment significantly by his tools and "proto-culture." He was the first of the hominids to populate the Old World beyond Africa and therefore the first to adapt to dissimilar ecological niches. However, his migration out of Africa, despite some assertions to the contrary, seems not to have much influenced the further evolution of the human line.[19] These early *erectus* colonizers were small, marginal bands; it has been estimated that no less than 80% remained in Africa.[20] By this time, too, the world-wide Ice Age had set in, cutting off vast sections of Europe and Asia from the hominid advance. The concentration of the bulk of the world-wide hominid population in Africa persisted at least until 50 kya (kilo [1,000] years ago) and probably for a good while longer.

Homo erectus, the sole hominid in possession of the planet after one mya, continued as a distinct species until about 300−200 kya, but then gave rise to a more advanced species that supplanted him: *Homo sapiens sapiens* is the species to which modern human beings belong and represents the culmination of four million years of hominid evolution. Though information about this species fills vast libraries, the circumstances surrounding its appearance and subsequent development appear to be more muddled in the minds of many than is the case with any other hominid. This muddle, unfortunately, has as much to do with ideology as it does science.

It was a profound shock to official anthropology when Dart's Taung Baby shifted the focus of research to Africa, but the Leakey discovery 35 years later of a two million year-old *Homo* genus in Africa doubled the voltage. These two finds proved Charles Darwin a prophet; he had suggested in 1871 that the search for man's origins should be conducted in Africa since that was where man's two closest relatives, the chimpanzee and the gorilla, were to be found. As it ever became plainer that the entire human species originated in that "dark" continent, a small, but influential group of anthropologists taxed their ingenuity to the utmost to come up with explanations to circumvent this painful fact. The most conspicuous of these was Carleton Coon of the University of Pennsylvania, who became the "dean" of American anthropologists. In the 1930's, Franz Weidenreich had formulated a "polycentric" theory of human origins and Coon, a generation later, added certain refinements to it. This theory was the lineal descendant of the rather crude "polygenetic" hypotheses, fashionable at the end of the last century, which proposed that the different races of mankind had arisen from different ape ancestors: the European from the chimpanzee, the Mongolian from the orangutan, and the African from the gorilla. This notion was too preposterous for even the most conservative anthropologists, and it underwent a period of re-tooling until it surfaced in the 30's under Weidenreich as "polycentrism," achieving its final form under Coon in the 1960's.

We can summarize Coon's thesis by saying that, whereas it is true that the earliest and most primitive forms of mankind originated in Africa, these types left Africa early as members of the *Homo erectus* species, and in five different locations independently evolved into modern man! In fact, Coon categorically declared, "If Africa is the birthplace of the human race *it is only the undifferentiated kindergarten* (italics added). Europe and Asia were our principle school."[21] In this argument, Africa is conceded to be the cradle of the earliest pre-human types, but only in Europe did the first "real" human beings appear. There was more: a racial hierarchy was devised based on the skull size and shape where Coon placed the Asiatic and European at the top and the African type at the bottom.[22] Understandably, this kind of reasoning made the entire anthropological community squirm. The Coonian thesis has been categorically rejected by the weight of anthropological opinion, but has by no means died out. It continues to re-incarnate in often subtle ways, as we will have a chance to see. The persistence of the Coonian hypothesis in the face of all evidence to the contrary, testifies to the regrettable tenacity of a way of thinking which distracts science from reasoned, impartial discussion of serious matters. Because of the persistence of the theory, we will devote some space dismantling the tissue-thin foundation upon which it is based.

One of the serious flaws in the Coonian hypothesis is that it violates the Law of Parsimony, enunciated by William of Occam in the 14th century and thereafter known as "Occam's Razor." Occam's Razor simply compels us, if we are confronted with various interpretations of a given body of facts, to prefer the simplest one. Coon's idea that selection pressures in ecologies separated by thousands of miles could be constant or similar enough to push five different representatives of *H. erectus* simultaneously across the species threshold to *H. sapiens* is one almost impossible to accept. The phenomenon of "parallel evolution" cannot be used to substantiate this. One of the most striking examples of parallelism is seen in the evolutionary process of the catarrhine monkeys of the Old World versus the platyrrhine monkeys of the New World; separated by the Atlantic Ocean for more than 30 myr, they still belong in the monkey group. But within that same group, they remain separate species, which is to say that a howler monkey in South America cannot and will not breed with a mandrill of West Africa. Widely separated populations do not converge; they become, genetically speaking, more divergent, not less. Though all monkeys that inhabit the globe descend from a common prosimian ancestor, by inhabiting widely scattered ecological niches, they became reproductively distinct from one another and developed into separate species.[23] Thus even when something like "parallelism" or "convergence" occurs, it never results in the simultaneous emergence of a single species in isolated locations. All human beings inhabitating the earth today belong to the same species, meaning that they all come from one evolutionary line, and one only. Therefore, the creation of *Homo sapiens sapiens* was "monogenetic." To propose, as Coon did, that five widely separate pre-human populations could, over time and in splendid isolation, develop more or less simultaneously and concomitantly into a single species belongs to the realm of fiction rather than fact.

We can bring this issue into sharper relief by considering the people of Tierra de Fuego at the extreme southern tip of Argentina. They inhabit a frigid, windy, almost antarctic environment, but they are so marvelously adapted that they can, without clothing, withstand temperatures and precipitation that would be quickly fatal to any other people. At the time of the first European contact in the 16th century, they were the most isolated people on earth and their peculiar characteristics show that divergence, not convergence, is the rule.

The most telling refutation of Coonian polycentrism lies in the fossil record itself; it does not disclose any European remains of *H. sapiens sapiens* prior to 40,000 kya. It is here, however, that the muddle of *Homo sapiens* origins really starts and it is centered on the three pre-modern hominids found in Europe: Swanscombe Man (England), Steinheim (Germany), and Neandertal Man (Germany). One other fossil find, though less important, has also been thrown into the debate: the Vertesszöllös skull from Hungary. Since Neandertal Man has been at the hub of most of the controversy, we will concentrate our discussion on him.

The type specimen of Neandertal Man was found in 1838 in the Neander Valley in Germany and it generated an instant sensation in European learned circles. Initially, it was deemed a "pathological" human type though within a decade it was recognized as a distinct human variety. An unflattering portrait of Neandertal Man as a beetle-browed, shuffling, slow-witted brute grew up around him and has colored our perceptions down to the present. Since 1960, a reassessment has thrust him back into the limelight of the controversy surrounding the place and time of the appearance of *H. sapiens.*

It can no longer be presumed that Neandertal Man was deficient in intelligence; his skull size ranged from 1500–1700 cc's, well within normal range. He most assuredly possessed a culture and possibly a belief in an afterlife, making him not so different from *Homo sapiens sapiens* as both learned and popular opinion had first thought. Still, Neandertal Man was not *H. sapiens sapiens*; the frontal lobes of his brain were less developed, he had more prominent brow ridges over the eye-sockets, his skull was thicker, and the rest of his body was stockier and more robust. As a species, he was confined almost entirely to Europe and Western Asia and seems to have completely died out 35,000 years ago.[24] What to call him? As Donald Johanson has pointed out, nothing in the field of anthropology contributes more to heated, even vitriolic, professional antagonisms than the business of classifying and naming fossil hominids, and the debate over the exact classification of Neandertal continues without surcease. At first he was called *Homo neandertalensis* implying that he was an altogether different branch than *H. sapiens,* though arising from *H. erectus,* the common ancestor. In the last three decades, there has been an increasing tendency to call him *H. sapiens neandertalensis* to account for his many similarities to modern humans. From this point of view, Neandertal was of the same species as modern humans and both were descended from "archaic" *H. sapiens.* Anthropologists from central and eastern Europe favor this view, even going so far as to say that modern Europeans are direct lineal descendants of Neandertal—the ultimate cachet! Now he is respectable enough to be deemed a European ancestor. Yet this proposal has been far from satisfying because it raises as many difficulties as it purports to solve. If he represents some sort of stage between "archaic" *H. sapiens* and modern *H. sapiens sapiens,* why is the Neandertal virtually absent from Africa?[25] On the other hand, anatomically modern skulls at least 130,000–110,000 years old can be found at four sites in Africa: (1) Omo, Ethiopia; (2) Laetoli, Tanzania; (3) Klasies River Mouth, South Africa; and (4) Border Cave, South Africa.[26] No anatomically modern hominid skulls of this age can be found anywhere else on earth. The Omo skull is the oldest of this group and shows some residual archaic features which suggests that it is a late representative of a transitional type between archaic and modern *H. sapiens.* C.A. Arambourg once said that in Africa alone can be found, in step-wise sequence, all the phases of human evolution from the earliest pre-human hominid ancestors to modern man. This is especially true of the latter phases. This is to say that in Africa alone are to be found first, well-demarcated *erectus* types, then more evolved *erectus* types showing some modern features, followed by early *sapiens* types showing some erectus-like features, and finally modern human beings. Such a progression exists nowhere else, certainly not in Europe, where the first unequivocal *H. sapiens* do not appear until 40,000 years ago.

The idea, popular in Eastern Europe, that European *H. sapiens sapiens* is descended directly from Neandertal is now a distinctly minority view. There are enough discrete anatomical differences between Neandertal and modern humans to classify them as separate species. Moreover, one does not find any unequivocally transitional types between Neandertal and modern humans.[27] Those Neandertal finds in which some claim to see transitional modern characteristics have not been widely accepted as such. Nowhere else in the world is there the slightest evidence demonstrating an ancestral link between Neandertal and modern humans, particularly since Neandertal is no older than anatomically modern humans in Africa and younger than some. That the presumed link between Neandertal and modern man inhabited Europe and nowhere else would be chimerical indeed! Insistence on such a link effectively places Europe outside the mainstream of human evolution elsewhere and while this may appeal to the vanity of Coonians, it has little to do with verifiable facts. As one writer put it:

> The ultimate resolution of whether all, a few, or none of the Neandertals were ancestral to early anatomically modern humans in Europe and Western Asia will be achieved when there is general agreement on how one should interpret the paleontological record and/or there is incontrovertible evidence of local contemporaneity of the two morphological patterns across the northwestern Old World. *Neither of these conditions are currently met, and it is uncertain whether they ever will be* (italics added).[28]

In other words, there is no way to prove that Neandertal is ancestral to modern man in Europe and no likely proof is in the offing. Thus to talk of such a connection is merely idle discussion; it cannot be validated. The crux of this argument has been neatly summed up by C.B. Stringer:

> Regarding the evolution of anatomically modern *H. sapiens,* the fact that Europe appears to record only the evolution of Neandertal-derived characteristics during the Middle and early Late Pleistocene suggests that *modern humans evolved elsewhere* (italics added). In western Europe, the Saint-Cesaire fossil at least provides clear evidence that some Neandertals, at least, were simply too late and too specialized to have contributed to the evolution of modern hominids in the area. *No genuinely transitional fossils displaying combinations of Neandertal and modern derived characters have been found in Europe or southwest Asia* ... (italics added).
>
> It is only in Africa that fossils displaying a clear mosaic of non-modern and modern characteristics exist in the later Middle Pleistocene or early *Late Pleistocene*.... The evidence from Klasies River Mouth, Border Cave, and Omo-

Kibish 1 hominid fossils indicates an anatomically modern presence in southern and northeast *Africa in the early Late Pleistocene.* . . . of modern humans in Africa during the time span of the Middle Stone Age.[29]

The evidence and anthropological opinion, on the whole, run counter to a proposed ancestral relation between Neanderthal and modern humans. We can, therefore, discard it.

We can now consider the group of fossils represented by Vertesszöllös on the one hand and Swanscombe and Steinheim on the other. The Vertesszöllös fossil, which is just the occipital or posterior quarter of a late hominid skull, and the Petralona skull, considered to be broadly in the same class, seem to show mixed erectus-modern features, thus presenting four possible classifications: (1) late *erectus,* (2) an *erectus-sapiens* transition, (3) very early "archaic" *sapiens,* or (4) simply an archaic *sapiens* that is ancestral to both Neandertal and modern humans. The Vertesszöllös and Petralona skulls carry datings of 500,000—400,000 years ago, and the former skull in particular has been designated as a member of *H. sapiens* by Andor Thoma, on the basis of a cranial capacity measurement of 1400 cc's. In *Civilization ou Barbarie,* Cheikh Anta Diop has severely criticized this line of thinking by pointing out that (1) from the Vertesszöllös skull c. 400,000 years ago to the documented presence of *H. sapiens* in Europe c. 40,000 years ago, there are absolutely no intermediate forms, and (2) Thoma has presumed to measure the actual cranial capacity of the Vertesszöllös skull though three-quarters of it is missing.[30] Therefore his measurement must be taken as highly speculative. We can't know the precise cranial capacity of the Vertesszöllös skull, so it is untenable to assign it to the *H. sapiens* species. However much Professor Thoma may wish to believe so, it is not the Vertesszöllös skull that leads to anatomically modern types.

The weight of opinion favors the classification of the Steinheim and Swanscombe skulls, c. 350,000–250,000, as definitively *H. erectus* types antecedent to Neandertal. Is it possible to see in this particular sequence of skulls anything but evidence of the *in situ* evolution of Neandertal in Europe from an *erectus* ancestor between 400,000 and 80,000 years ago? It is only at the latter date that the first unequivocally Neandertal types emerge. We can say for sure, concerning Neandertal, that he is our "phyletic" cousin, similar in many ways to modern man, but definitely not modern man nor ancestral to him. He has disappeared completely by 35,000 years ago, vanishing without leaving a biological trace in the modern humans who survived, multiplied, and prospered.

An underlying question of all such anthropological wrangling is something of a conundrum, namely how much of a difference makes a difference? Humans and chimpanzees are dissimilar in no more than two percent of their genes and yet this minuscule difference in genotype translates into rather dramatic differences in phenotype, that is outward characteristics. This means that chimpanzees and humans, though so close genetically, are, from the point of view of biological interaction, worlds apart. The chimpanzee exerts no more biological or evolutionary impact on humans than a snail. We might speculate that Neandertal was separated from modern humans by less than one percent of his genes but this difference, though vanishingly small, translates into distinct differences of phenotype, certainly enough to create a veritable chasm where it concerns progenitive interaction. Even within our own species, the small variations in phenotype among human sub-groups or races creates a tendency toward a social segregation based on phenotype, never mind that these differences are sub-fractional at the level of genotype. We are therefore driven to the conclusion that as close as Neandertal and *H. sapiens* were, Neandertal ended his span on earth as a side-branch of human evolution. He was "lopped-off" by selection pressures about which we can only speculate and does not figure further in any discussion of how, from whom, or where modern humans evolved.

With the notable exception of Milford Wolpoff and his school, the polycentric idea has largely faded from physical anthropology but has found a home of sorts in the field of population genetics, where it continues to find adherents. The new analytical armamentarium includes DNA polymorphisms, blood groups, gamma globulins, abnormal hemoglobins, and serum proteins, all of which certain population geneticists are utilizing in attempts to prove that (1) phenotypically identical Africans and Australo-Melanesians are unrelated, (2) the center of *H. sapiens* evolution must be sought in Asia rather than Africa, and (3) the "Negro" himself did not originate in Africa. The arguments employed depend on the more or less specific presence of certain biomolecular indices in defined populations. Such indices are used to categorize races (or in some cases "dissolve" them) by serological markers. It is a fact that biomolecular markers can be used to ascertain the relationships of different population groups in time and space and even to track the movements of certain of these groups, but there is a palpable danger of losing perspective when defining races by these markers:

> The racial classifications of the seventeenth century were naturally descriptive... based upon observations of colonial travelers and explorers, and contained much error. Even so, the major races of man were recognized as well by eye in those days as they have since been identified by the complex computer exercises of our time. Biological anthropology, in common with other more matured sciences, passed from a stage of qualitative description to one in which characters were quantified by measurement. Usually such a trend is beneficial; but it created something of a disaster for the students of man.[31]

This aforesaid "disaster" was an attempt to dissolve races by statistical fiat. What was true two centuries ago is true today; a race, such as it is, represents a phenotypic grouping of individuals. As Diop has said, a Bantu at the level of his genes might actually be closed to a Swede than former Premier Botha, but if he is a citizen of South Africa he will live in Soweto and is subject to pass laws. This means that the definition of race is as much socio-cultural as it is phenotypical, but it still allows us to say, as Diop has pointed out, that a person of the Caucasian race will have originated in Europe, of the Mongolian race in the Far East, and of the Negro race in Africa.[32] Merely to say, as many do, that race no longer exists because it has become a concept inconvenient to European science demonstrates the lack of integrity that surrounds discussions of this issue.

This lack of integrity can be shown by the way in which the distribution of sickle cell hemoglobin, HgS, has been interpreted. HgS is one of the most categorical indicators of the African racial type extant and is found over most of the southern two-thirds of the continent. It affects from 20–60 percent of certain populations though it is totally absent in others. It arose originally in Africa as a mutation, and it is very debilitating in the homozygous state, reflecting an inheritance from both parents. The resulting condition, sickle cell anemia, is extremely morbid and incurable. The life expectancy of those affected is severely limited; most die in childhood. A disease imposing such a high biological cost on a population group should have been selected against during the course of evolution except for one important fact: in its virtually harmless heterozygous state, i.e., inheritance from one parent, HgS affords protection against malaria, a disease of high morbidity and mortality. The negative selective impact of the homozygous state of HgS was overcome by its heterozygous advantages. This proved adaptive in the endemic malaria regions of the African rainforests and is termed "balanced polymorphism."[33]

Not surprisingly, the gene is found in people of African descent in the Western Hemisphere, but it is also found in ostensibly non-African populations in Mexico, the Iberian peninsula, Italy, Greece, Turkey, and the Arabian peninsula.[34] This is prima facie evidence that there is a detectable African racial element in these populations derived from historical migrations, or "gene flows," into these countries, forced or otherwise. In point of fact, substantial African in-migrations into northern Mediterranean countries and Western Asia begins at the dawn of history, continues throughout the historical period, and is traceable even in the recent historical past.[35] African migrations into these regions are, therefore, readily documentable but have caused a not inconsiderable amount of discomfiture—so much so that there are those who have attempted to explain away the presence of the HgS gene in these populations by attributing it to "local" selection factors.[36] What this is supposed to mean is that Greeks, Italians, Spaniards, and Turks, et al, experienced *in situ* mutations to HgS also as a response to malarial endemicity.

It has now been reliably demonstrated by "restriction endonuclease analysis" that there exists at least three variants of HgS which have arisen by independent mutation.[37] The oldest of these, called "S-7.6," probably arose sometime between 70–150,000 years ago.[38] The S-7.6 variant of HgS is found predominantly in Gabon, Kenya, Saudi Arabia, and India. It is extraordinarily unlikely that the S-7.6 type arose twice and since there is little doubt about its origin in the region around Kenya, we may reliably infer that it was dispersed from there into Saudi Arabia and India.

The S-13.0 type of HgS is found in populations inhabiting West Africa, the Americas and Southern Europe.[39] It arose as an independent mutation in the region of Burkina Fasso and Ghana and migrated from there into other parts of West Africa and abroad.[40] Thus we can say that all variants of HgS arose in Africa and spread into other parts of the world with African emigrants. The *in situ* mutations of HgS occurred, therefore, *not* in Europe or Asia, but in Africa itself and the presence of any variant HgS in an extra-African population is certain proof of the African origin of part or all of that population.

The African origin of the HgS gene lends an important insight into the Black presence in early India. The Indus Valley civilizations were created by a black-skinned people who originated in Africa, but were pushed to the southern third of the sub-continent with the Aryan invasions of the 2nd millennium B.C.E.[41] Central and southern India are the only regions of the world where the HgS gene is as prevalent as it is in Africa. Up to 30 percent of several populations in these sections of India exhibit the HgS gene, a figure comparable to what is found in the malaria-endemic regions of Africa.[42] South Indian peoples belong mainly to the Dravidian-speaking group, now numbering more than 100 million persons. Numerous subgroups of Dravidians show the typical African phenotype in facial features, skin color, and hair texture.[43] Despite an appearance which makes them nearly indistinguishable from black sub-Saharan Africans, tremendous efforts have been devoted to "proving" that these people, the creators of India's first civilizations, were not originally from Africa. In fact, there are those who have tried to say that black skin evolved *twice* in the course of human evolution, once in Africa and once in Asia.[44] Ancient commentators seem to have been too ingenuous for such contortions: they called Indian Blacks "Eastern Ethiopians," in recognition of their black African phenotype. One of the names given by Greco-Roman writers to Africa, particularly the area now comprising the Sudan, Ethiopia, and Somalia, was "India." Classical scholars, therefore, made no racial distinction between Africans and Indians.[45]

The idea that black skin—or the black African phenotype as a whole, for that matter—evolved separately in Africa and India is improbable enough on the face of it. It becomes ridiculous when the HgS is factored in. It virtually defies statistical likelihood that such an ensemble of macro- and micro-biological characters could have emerged twice—and so quickly—in the evolution of a single species. The manifest absurdity of the idea has not been lost on certain apologists, some of whom have actually tried to propose that, instead, these Blacks arose first in Asia and then later peopled Africa. There is not one shred of fossil evidence that can be adduced to substantiate this claim. For the scientific realists among us, there is only one admissible conclusion: the original inhabitants of India and the founders of its first civilizations were descendants of early black African populations who migrated there sometime in the Late Pleistocene. Any other interpretation is sheerest phantasmagoria.

There are other cases in which molecular biology has been misapplied to obscure and distort the picture of human evolution in Africa, derived from a stubborn tendency to deny that peoples who are phenotypically African in every respect, i.e., black skin, woolly hair, thick lips, broad noses (even steatopygy in the case of the Andaman islanders) and who live in Southeast Asia and the Pacific Islands, are related to the black populations of Africa. This line of thinking is best exemplified by the work of M. Nei and his colleagues.[46] Nei, among others, has developed the concept of "genetic distance" and has worked out a statistical method of determining gene percentages at different chromosomal loci or positions by race. Having done this, Nei then calculated the "net codon differences" by race, thus determining how close or distant the different races are to one another. Even before entering into a critique of the substance of Nei's work, some methodological difficulties command attention. For one thing, the accuracy of individual classifications based solely on serological markers varies tremendously. Moreover, classifying racial groups by serotyping or genotyping still depends on phenotypic correlations:

> When a population is being investigated, an adequate sample of the people is classified *according to phenotypes* (italics added). The gene and genotype frequencies can be computed from the phenotype percentages.[47]

We can illustrate this point by the example of HgS. It is perhaps the best "African" seromarker that we have and we can use it to detect African gene flow into non-African populations in southern Europe and elsewhere. But if we took a random blood sample and looked only at its HgS marker, we would not know intrinsically whether the sample came from a southern European or an African unless we could visually identify that person. We might then rhetorically ask at what point genetically does one cross the threshold from African to Caucasian? Is the question even meaningful? Furthermore, if the HgS marker is absent in any of these random sera, it does not rule out an African origin for the serum donor because not all Africans carry the HgS gene. Again, the only way to tell is by visual identification of the donor. Along with HgS, there are several serological markers that are more or less specific for black African populations, but there are many Africans who carry none of these markers, showing that biomolecular indices, by themselves, do not substitute for phenotypic identification and therefore, by themselves, cannot define a race.

Certain of Nei's own results exemplify these difficulties even further. For example, the differences between sub-groups within a racial population are nearly the same as those between the races themselves. This means that there is considerable genetic overlap between racial populations, and that "mean codon differences" between them, as determined by Nei, appear to be little more than statistical artifacts. Nei has determined that Caucasians and Mongolians are "closer" genetically than either is to Africans, yet is forced to admit that net codon differences are not statistically significant in comparing individuals from these races! Moreover, depending on the data collected, who collects it, and the methods used, contradictory results are often obtained. Nei himself obtained different results from serum proteins than blood groups. The serum protein studies gave him closer affinities between the Caucasian and the African than between either and the Mongolian.

Confronted with such a difficulty, Nei introduced a "fudge-factor" to resolve the contradictory results. In his analysis, he used sera from American Blacks and Whites and since his results showed a closer proximity between African and Caucasian, he chose to "correct" them by "factoring out" the presumed 20 percent Caucasian contribution to the African-American gene pool, while assuming that there is no net African contribution to the Euro-American gene pool. Had he been more conversant with the history and sociology of race relations in this country, he might not have made such an egregious error. Since the beginning of U.S. history, untold thousands of persons classified as Negroes have passed into Caucasian society—clandestinely to be sure—by virtue of their fair skin. An exact accounting of the number choosing this option will remain forever beyond our grasp, but it is certainly enough to account for a significant, if immeasurable, African genetic contribution to the Caucasian gene pool of this country. Thus one of the main premises of Nei's thesis is flatly wrong and therefore the conclusion is invalid because he can't control for the African genes floating in the Caucasian gene pool of the United States.

Nei, and others like him, have simply chosen to ignore the phenotypic likenesses of African and Melanesian populations by inferring that the net codon differences are more reliable measures of racial kinship. Following

FIGURE 1

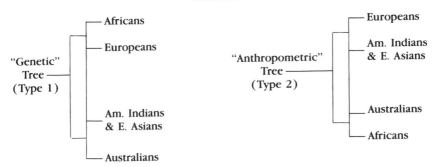

the oddities of Nei's logic, the minuscule codon differences between the kinky-haired, thick-lipped, broad-nosed black Melanesian and the equally kinky-haired, thick-lipped, broad-nosed black African "prove" that there is no historical relationship between them. Instead, it is merely the similarity of selection factors, i.e., two hot, tropical environments, that account for these traits. It is another way of saying that black skin and the ancillary "negroid" phenotypic traits evolved twice.

To understand more clearly the quagmire we are led into by this sort of theorizing, we must examine the thesis of another population geneticist, C.R. Guglielmino-Matessi.[48] His group attempted to reconcile the contradictions posed by two phylogenetic racial trees, one a "genetic tree" and the other an "anthropometric tree" based on cranial measurements. The two trees are compared in Figure 1. The trees quite obviously contradict one another. To reconcile this contradiction, Guglielmino-Matessi introduces his own fudge factor—a standard statistical ploy when the results obtained are unacceptable—and this is a formula devised to control for "climatic regression." Simply, this means that phenotypic characters are attributable to climate and environment, whereas genetic indices are more stable and therefore better suited to defining races. The outcome of this reasoning can be summarized as follows: phenotype, i.e., head shape and skin color for example, can be "removed" from a biomolecular analysis of race by attributing them solely to "climatic" factors, so that, as we've seen before, Africans and Australo-Melanesians are phenotypically the same because their environments are the same. Thus, the environmental influence can be "factored out," the two trees can be more nearly superimposed upon one another, and the apparent contradictions between them can be resolved. A diagram can then be constructed to account for all of the relationships between the different groups (see Figure 2).

A number of conclusions naturally follow from this diagrammatic argument: (1) modern man did not originate in Africa but in Asia, (2) the

FIGURE 2

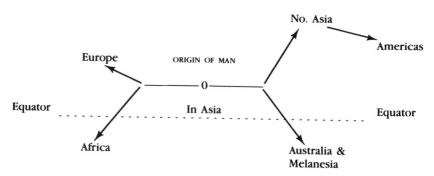

Negro came into Africa from outside it, (3) there is a close African-Caucasian genetic relationship, and (4) there is a close Mongolian/Australo-Melanesian genetic relationship. However, the analysis appears to depend, among other things, on a very recent date for the appearance of *H. sapiens sapiens*:

> There are very few fossil H. sapiens known to be older than 35,000–40,000 years, but shortly after that time H.s.s. is found all over the world. It is of course possible that many more early fossils will be found and push way back the origin of H.s.s.[49]

It is indeed possible. We have already mentioned the *H. sapiens* fossil finds at Omo, Border Cave, Klasies River Mouth, and Laetoli, all of whom are African and all older than 100,000 years. The fossil evidence breathes not a word of the origins of *H. sapiens* in Asia.

In point of fact, Guglielmino-Matessi and his group are not unaware of the precariousness of the ledge upon which they stand:

> The major weakness of interpretations of phylogenetic history like the present one is . . . lack of fossil evidence. Hopefully such evidence will be forthcoming and prove or disprove the geographical-historical speculations just made.[50]

They may be considered disproved; the fossil evidence has been very forthcoming!

> Among other weaknesses is the present scarcity of data on correlations between gene frequencies and climate, at a world-wide level. . . . Also unsatisfactory is the fact that the correction for climate did not result always and unequivocally in the genetic "tree;" and that it did not improve on the poor treeness of the anthropomorphic trees. Of course it is likely that our climatic data and our techniques of correction are incompletely adequate.[51]

An apologia such as this raises the question of why such an article was ever submitted for publication. The authors are their own worst critics and rebut their own argument. Moreover, it is of no little interest that the published work of Nei in the same field is not cited at all. The close Caucasian-Mongolian relationship that Nei posits fits nowhere in the scheme of Guglielmino-Matessi nor does Nei's assertion that the Caucasian-Mongolian branch diverged from the African one at 110,000 B.P. How then are we to interpret the validity of the work of two groups of population geneticists, presumably with access to the same data, arriving at diametrically opposite conclusions? In and of itself, this is not uncommon in science, but it does mean that a modicum of caution would be in order when attempting to define race solely by the tools of molecular biology.

We can summarize our criticisms of the methods and conclusions of these two schools of population geneticists as follows: (1) there is no good reason to suppose that the nearly identical phenotypes of the African and Australo-Melanesian are mere artifacts of climate, (2) there is absolutely no reason to suppose that H. sapiens sapiens originated anywhere but in Africa, and (3) there is no reason to suppose that the races can be defined solely by biomolecular markers independent of phenotype.

We are left with saying, bringing us full circle to the first scientific classification of the human species 200 years ago, that a race is a phenotypic grouping of human beings, no more and no less. It has no particular genetic significance. Since all H. sapiens sapiens, living or dead, belong to the same species, genetic differences among them are infinitessimal, making racial classifications based on these differences extraordinarily problematic. What is more, phenotypic expressions, such as black skin, are themselves genetically-determined, so they cannot be explained away by artifices and fudge-factors like "climatic regression." We can say, parenthetically, that minute differences in genotype between the races have translated into substantial differences on the phenotypic level, and it is these easily perceived differences that create socio-cultural diversity and racial conflict; such diversity and conflict are not biologically determined. But the concept of race is valid insofar as race is a mark of the phenotypic variation within the human species.

With respect to molecular biology, we do not wish to fall into the trap of "throwing out the baby with the bath water." Our critique, therefore, should not be construed as attacking the validity of molecular biology in anthropological research. In fact, recent developments in the field have done much to clarify some of the confusion surrounding H. sapiens evolution. In February, 1986, Wainscot and his associates published a study of DNA poly-morphisms in Nature demonstrating a bifurcation between African and Eurasian populations consistent with a scheme "in which a founder population migrated from Africa and subsequently gave rise to all non-African populations."[52] This conclusion is based on a dominant DNA "haplotype" which is absent in all non-African populations and which means, in Wainscot's opinion, that the founder population(s) must have been small. But the real fillip in anthropological circles came from Rebecca Cann and her associates in an article entitled "Mitochondrial DNA and Human Evolution," appearing in *Nature* on January 1, 1987. The article has already had a radical impact on thinking about human origins and it is, therefore, important for us to explore it in more depth.

One of the many virtues of Cann's research is that her results are "cleaner," and therefore simpler, than what has come before. This is due to her work with mitochondrial DNA (mtDNA) instead of nuclear DNA (nDNA). The mitochondrion is the energy plant of the cell with its own individual single-stranded DNA inherited from the mother alone,[53] as contrasted to double-stranded nDNA derived from both parents. Since nDNA is doubly-inherited, it is subject to recombination, genetic drift, selection, migration, etc., making it hard to trace the history and provenance of particular segments of it. On the other hand, mtDNA, inherited from the mother alone, does not recombine and provides a handy way of determining the genetic relationships between individuals. Moreover, mtDNA mutates much faster than nDNA which means it contains more mutational "prints" to show us the progress of evolution over a relatively short time span. The mtDNA mutational rate, thought to be fairly constant over long periods of time, is two-to-four percent per million years, allowing us to look at mutational events in time segments of tens of thousands of years.

From purified placentas of 145 persons and samples of two cell lines representing the Bushmen (San) of southern Africa and Black Americans, Cann was able to obtain purified mtDNA from five different geographical locations: sub-Saharan Africa, Asia, Europe—which for study purposes included North America and the Middle East—Australia (aborigines), and New Guinea. The results showed that mean interpopulation differences were very small, confirming the findings of older studies that used sero-markers. Cann was able to construct several trees, working on the assumption that if there is no recombination and if the mutational rates are more or less constant at two-to-four percent per million years, the most variable mtDNA would of necessity be the oldest. She and her group narrowed down the trees that best fit her data to two: (1) a "population-specific" tree consisting of five primary branches with each branch leading exclusively to one of five populations and (2) a "minimum length" tree that makes Africa the "likely source of the mitochondrial gene pool." The population-specific tree represents pure Coonian polycentrism, meaning that the human races evolved separately in five different locations and therefore do not share a common *H. sapiens* ancestor. To have adopted this tree would have required 51 more point mutations than the minimum-length tree. Adhering strictly to the Law of Parsimony, the Cann group rejected the population-specific tree in favor of the minimum-length tree.

Cann's preferred minimum-length tree is rooted squarely in Africa, meaning that it is an African *Homo sapiens* ancestor who generates all later African and non-African human types. The African mtDNA's diverge from each other by an average of .057 percent, making them by far the most varied, and therefore the oldest, mtDNA's in the world. With a mutation rate of two-to-four percent per million years, Cann postulates that the common ancestor of all surviving mtDNA's, hence of all surviving human beings, lived between 140,000–290,000 years ago in eastern or southern Africa.[54] In published interviews, Cann gives a mean date of 200,000 B.P. for our first common human ancestor who was female and whom Cann has nicknamed "Eve."[55] Since the oldest mtDNA in Cann's sample came from a Bushman or San individual from the Kalahari Desert, we can say that these people are representatives of the oldest living branch of the human race. Says Allan C. Wilson, "Basically we are all! Kung."[56] Remnants of them, and other "Negrito" or "Pygmoid" peoples, can be found as aborigines in India, southeast Asia, Australia, and the South Pacific.

The fossil record is very supportive of Cann's thesis for it shows anatomically modern man living in eastern and southern Africa at least as early as 130,000 years ago. In addition, Cann has tackled the issue of polycentrism head on:

> An alternative view of human evolution rests on evidence that Homo has been present in Asia as well as Africa for at least one million years and holds that the transformation of archaic to anatomically modern humans occurred in parallel in different parts of the Old World. This hypothesis leads us to expect genetic differences of great antiquity within widely separated parts of the modern pool of mtDNA's. It is hard to reconcile the mtDNA results with this hypothesis. The greatest divergences within clusters specific to non-African parts of the Old World correspond to times of only 90,000–180,000 years. This might imply that Asian Homo . . . contributed no surviving mtDNA lineages to the gene pool of our species.[57]

One of the unlooked-for, but salutary, effects of Cann's study is that it drives another stake through the heart of polycentrism. Every day and in every way, the monogenetic theory of our origins in Africa becomes an incontrovertible fact.

We have now established with the greatest degree of certainty the anthropological record allows that humankind, from its earliest hominid ancestors four million years ago to its latest and most modern form as *H. sapiens sapiens* 200,000 years ago, evolved entirely in Africa. This monogenetic evolution means that all other peoples in the world are more or less direct descendants of small founder populations which left Africa, probably in waves, between 100,000–50,000 years ago. As C.L. Stringer has said, "We are all Africans under the skin."[58] The remnants of these original human beings, who emerged in Africa between 200,000–130,000 years ago, are seen today in the pygmies or Twa of the Congo forests and the Bushmen or San of the Kalahari Desert. This is reflected in their cultural organization, mode of life, language (the San clicks), and subsistence technology which is very archaic. It is virtually confirmed by the results of mtDNA analysis, which shows theirs to be the most varied and hence the oldest of all.

The development of racial variations out of the original African type takes place between 50,000–30,000 years ago, leading to the three great contemporary sub-divisions or races of humanity: (1) the original African, (2) the Caucasian, and (3) the Mongolian, corresponding to Africa, Europe, and Asia, respectively. None of these races at present is "pure;" not only are there tremendous variations within each, but there are numerous sub-races which represent confluences between the three major groupings. The genetic differences between the races are vanishingly small and the only significant differences appear at the level of phenotype. Such hierarchies as exist among the races have been forcibly imposed, are subject to the fluxes of history, and bear no relationship whatever to "innate" capacities of intellect or character. The African race, once inhabiting the cultural pinnacle of the world, now seems to occupy the "lowest" rung among the world's communities. Such are the forces of history and the workings of fate which, however, have little to do with biological evolution. Nature cares nothing for races per se. In fact, gene pools act in such a way as to ensure their own survival; some prevail, others pass away. Thus all of the races that exist today are contingent upon proven adaptability; nothing more, nothing less.

The appearance of the Caucasian presents a compelling model of racial evolution. Though a complex of ecological factors figured in the process, the transition from black skin to white was the most decisive single event. The change of skin color, more than any other feature, put its stamp on the various races. Our analysis of the Caucasian is based on the following premises: (1) the process occurred in an ice age environment near the southern limit of the great line of European glaciers along the 51st parallel of southwestern Russia; (2) white skin was more favorably adapted to the ecological conditions of this region during the critical period; and(3) the proto-Caucasian population experienced a more or less prolonged period of isolation enabling it to develop into a distinct race.

From 1.75 million to 12,000 years ago, the earth experienced an extended period of cooling—an Ice Age—divided into four glacial interspersed with four interglacial periods. During glacial periods, the mean temperature of the earth dropped, whereupon great sheets of ice formed and gradually flowed down over vast land masses of North America, northern Europe, and Siberia. Smaller glaciers formed in the mountainous regions of tropical Africa, southern Europe, and southern Asia. During interglacial periods, the earth re-warmed and the glacier retreated. The most recent ice-over in Europe was the Wurm glacial, occurring between 75,000–12,000 years ago. During this period, a vast sheet of ice more than a mile thick extended down from the Arctic Circle to a line roughly defined by the 51st parallel, stretching across southern England, northern Germany, Poland, and southern Russia. Within the Wurm period occurred two sub-periods called "stadials" interspersed with two "interstadials." The stadials represented the maximum extent to which the glacier line penetrated southward, while the interstadials represented a partial retreat. The most important sub-periods for our investigation are the Wurm I Interstadial, 50–40,000 years ago, and the Wurm II Stadial, 40–20,000 years ago. We propose that Caucasian evolution was decisively impacted by permutations in the ice age ecology of the mid-Wurm period, 50–20,000 years ago.

We know that *H. sapiens sapiens* had appeared in Africa no later than 130,000 years ago, but it is uncertain when this primordial *H. sapiens* began to migrate out. The emergence of *H. sapiens* in Africa more or less coincided with the Riss glacial period in Europe which ended about 120,000 years ago, so if they had migrated into Europe across the Gibraltar land bridge prior to 120,000 years ago, they would not have penetrated very far because of the glacier barrier. It is extremely unlikely that they did migrate into Europe during this period because no anatomically modern human fossils can be found there older than 40,000 years ago, when the African Grimaldi Man first makes his appearance. Even Neandertal is not seen in Europe earlier than about 80,000 years ago. Before that, the last hominid in Europe was the late *erectus* type represented by Swanscombe and Steinheim Men at around 250,000 years ago, leaving a gap of 170,000 years.

The Riss-Wurm interglacial between 120,000–75,000 years ago was a period of significant warming which caused the glaciers to retreat, leaving the southern two-thirds of Europe habitable. This is the age of Neandertal who, as we have seen, presents many conundra in the scheme of *H. sapiens* evolution and who may have evolved *in situ* in Europe from the late *erectus* types found there. Others think he is a branch of "archaic" *H. sapiens,* but difficulties abound with any interpretation.

Around 75,000 years ago, the Wurm glacial re-introduced the Ice Age to Europe and for the next 25,000 years, Europe below the 51st parallel was inhabited exclusively by Neandertals who disappeared completely by 35,000 years ago. Evidence of *H. sapiens sapiens* occupation of Europe does not turn up until after 50,000 years ago, during the temporary glacier retreat in the Wurm I Interstadial. These first European *H. sapiens sapiens* were immigrants from Africa coming by way of the Gibraltar isthmus or Western Asia.[59] Theirs would have been a typical early African phenotype: peppercorn hair, brown-to-black skin color, small stature, prognathous jaw, dolichocephaly ("long-headedness"), and feminine steatopygy.[60] They would have looked very much like the Khoisan, i.e.,

Left: **Khoisan female of southern Africa with typical steatopygy of the buttocks.** *Right:* **The "Venus of Lespugue" (France); Aurignacian figurine from 25–30,000 years ago, also with steatopygy.**

Bushman-Hottentot type of South Africa today. The famous "Venus" figurines found at Aurignacian sites all over Europe and the skeletal remains of the Grimaldi Man of southern France confirm this. The Aurignacian period dates from 40,000 years ago. and the *H. sapiens* present in Europe at this time would have shared the habitat with Neandertal for 5–10,000 years. A small group of this early African type of *H. sapiens* would have settled in southwestern Eurasia, modern Russia, sometime before 40,000 years ago and would have remained there even after the onset of the more frigid Wurm II Stadial at 40,000 years ago. In this place and time, the climate would have been cold, icy, overcast for long periods, and that meant drastically reduced sunlight.

What did all this have to do with the emergence of the Caucasian? In order to arrive at a plausible explanation, we must look at Vitamin D metabolism. One of the most vital functions of human skin is to produce

Unknown Black from Anatolia: 100 B.C.-100 A.D. (Photo: Chandler)

Vitamin D from a substance called 7-dehydrocholesterol by interacting with the sun's ultraviolet light. Vitamin D is absolutely essential for proper bone mineralization and, if deficient, results in a softening of the bones, producing rickets in children and osteomalachia in adults. This leads to serious bone deformities in the skeleton, causing the deformation and fracture of bones unable to bear the weight of the body. It would be especially devastating for reproduction because the deformation of the pelvis of an affected woman would compromise her ability to push a baby through the birth canal during parturition. Then, as now, almost all of the Vitamin D in the body would have been produced in the skin through its reaction with ultraviolet light. In modern times, dietary Vitamin D supplements have practically eliminated rickets in the industrialized world. In the tropics, even without exogenous supplementation, rickets is rare because of constant and direct sunlight. Natural dietary sources of vitamin D are to be found mostly in northern salt-water fish, so that in the tropics natural dietary Vitamin D is of little consequence. We have already seen that melanin protects skin from the cancerous effects of ultraviolet light in the tropics; the difficulty is that it screens out ultraviolet light necessary for Vitamin D production. However, in the tropics, there is so much sunlight available so much of the time that enough ultraviolet light penetrates the melanin barrier to produce sufficient Vitamin D for the body's needs—hence the rarity of tropical rickets.

The situation changes radically, however, in a frigid, northern clime with many sunless days, shorter hours of daylight through much of the year, and a more oblique angle of sun irradiation which weakens its effect. Under these conditions of drastically reduced sunlight, the melanized dermis, i.e., black skin, becomes a liability. In northern latitudes, the protection melanin affords against skin cancer becomes nearly superfluous while it screens out sunlight, already severely reduced, which is necessary to produce Vitamin D in the skin. Simply put, black skin in a northern ice-age environment becomes an adaptive liability. We see this today in the two-to-threefold higher susceptibility of Blacks to rickets in northern latitudes compared to Whites. White skin, lacking the melanin barrier, can more efficiently utilize the limited northern sunlight to produce Vitamin D than can black skin.[61] What is more, white skin has been shown to be more cold-resistant than black skin. This was observed in the two world wars and the Korean War, wherein Black soldiers were five times more likely than White soldiers to develop frostbite. Laboratory tests have confirmed that melanized skin is much more susceptible to cold injury than is unmelanized skin.[62] White skin therefore has two adaptive advantages in an ice-age northern clime: more efficient Vitamin D production and greater cold resistance.

We are entitled to assume that, under the intense selection pressure of the Mid-Wurmian Ice Age in southwestern Russia, the dark skin of the African *H. sapiens sapiens,* who had migrated there during the Wurm I Interstadial between 50–40,000 years ago, would have permuted to white skin. This is consistent with the tendency to experience rapid phenotypic change with the abrupt onset of extreme environmental conditions. In this cold, isolated environment, three adaptive choices would have presented themselves: (1) out-migration, which must have occurred to a greater or lesser degree; (2) exploitation of dietary sources of Vitamin D which, coming from northern ocean fish, would have been unavailable in landlocked southern Russia; or (3) loss of skin pigmentation. This last event is what we surmised occurred in this surviving *H. sapiens* population in southwestern Eurasia. Pale-skinned people would gradually have replaced dark-skinned people, though pockets of dark-skinned African types survived well into the historical period. Indeed, there are Celtic and Viking reports of "little Blacks" still living in northern Europe as late as 1000 A.D.[63] These little Blacks could survive here because they had access to Vitamin D-laden northern salt-water fish and therefore escaped the kind of selection pressure seen farther inland. There are those who

Africoid type from southern Russia: 100 B.C.-100 A.D. (Photo: Chandler)

think that northern European tales of elves, wee folk, and leprechauns might have come from the presence of these little Blacks in pre-Medieval Europe.[64] Some Celtic tales present leprechauns as deeply swarthy in color.

It remains for us to propose a plausible *modus operandus* explaining the emergence of pale skin under the pressure of Vitamin D deficiency. On the scale of evolutionary time, this development occurred in a re markably brief period, 10–20,000 years, and such rapid change is almost always mediated through pre-extant genetic mutations. The one genetic mutation that can account for the depigmentation necessary to produce white skin is albinism. Other causes of depigmentation, such as leprosy or vitiligo, are non-genetic, non-transferrable to daughter populations, and therefore provide no model to explain the rapid whitening of an entire population. Genetic mutations are relatively rare and usually deleterious to the organism because they often stem from the deletion of an nDNA fragment.[65] This is how the HgS gene came into being, involving the loss of a single base pair, and it also accounts for albinism, a well-documented disorder in Africa. It is, in fact, more prevalent there than anywhere else in the world.[66] In this disorder, the melanocytes of the dermis lose the ability to produce melanin, leaving the skin white and the hair white or straw-colored. The outlook for African albinos is grim: if they are not shunned altogether, which often happens, they are invariably stricken by grostesque, devastating skin cancers by the end of the second decade of

Black female from Odessa, southern Russia: 300 B.C. (Photo: Chandler)

life, rapidly bringing an uncomfortable and distressing life to a close. In Africa, albinism is a high-morbidity, low-survival condition.

The situation is altogether different in a northern environment where the whitened albino skin becomes a decided asset. In modern times, albinos live out normal life spans in Europe and are not markedly different in color from the general population. Thus, a mutation, deleterious in one environment, confers a distinct advantage in another and swiftly propagates for that reason. There are three distinct classes of albinos of which only two are important for our discussion: (1) tyrosinase-positive [tyr (+)] albinism and (2) tyrosinase-negative [tyr (-)] albinism. In the tyr (+) type, the tyrosinase enzyme is still present and some residual ability to produce melanin is retained. In the tyr (-) type, the inability to produce melanin is absolute. Both types of albinism are determined by autosomally recessive genes at two separate gene loci. To produce an albino child, both parents must carry the same class of albino gene, though neither has to be an albino. If one parent carries the tyr (+) gene and the other the tyr (-) gene, they will not produce albino children. Because the albinism gene of either class is recessive, a high prevalence of albinism will only be found in populations with long-standing consanguinity.[67]

In tyr (+) albinism, the infant will begin life with white hair and skin, and gradually the hair may darken to a blond or even light-brown color and the skin will show the capacity to tan when exposed to sunlight. Moreover, eye color will vary from blue to hazel. In the tyr (-) type, the skin and hair will always remain stark white and the skin will never tan. This type of albinism generates more morbid features than the tyr (+) type. In Africa, the tyr (+) type is two-to-three times more frequent than the tyr (-) type. A sub-class of the tyr (+) albinism, called "albinoidism," is incomplete and exhibits a fair degree of coloration of the skin, hair, and irises.[68] The integument of African albinoids ranges over a color spectrum very similar to what is seen in Europeans and European albinoids are virtually indistinguishable from the general population.

We propose that the *H. sapiens sapiens* population that survived the last glaciation in southwestern Eurasia was largely a group of albinoids who were better adapted to the ecology than their darker relatives who had originally colonized the area. These latter were gradually replaced by albinoids, though small groups of African aboriginal types long persisted on the North Atlantic seaboard because of the availability of Vitamin D-rich salt-water fish. This "goodness of fit" of the albinoids in this northern environment was due to the more efficient Vitamin D production and utilization in the whitened skin in these sunlight-deficient latitudes and better cold resistance. The Ice Age had the practical effect of isolating this marginal group from other populations for a prolonged period, promoting a consanquinity that would have allowed the recessive albinoid genes to express and propagate themselves. Creation of a new race via depigmentation is consistent with the tendency in nature of new species and subspecies to form out of marginal groups that have become isolated from their "parent" populations and subjected more or less abruptly to extreme environmental conditions, which generate intense selection pressure. Genetic drift, the tendency of small populations to lose certain genes of the population of origin, would have exerted an effect as well. Color variations in the hair, skin, and irises of Caucasians are manifestations of the "incomplete penetrance" and variation of expression of the (4) genes characterizing albinoidism. We have already pointed out that nature reflects the survival and perpetuation in different niches of variant gene pools otherwise characteristic of the species as a whole. The evolution of the albinoid Caucasian meant that a branch of *H. sapiens sapiens* could occupy a niche theretofore closed to it. Human beings could then expand their range of habitats into colder climes and enhance the ability of the species to survive. As far as nature is concerned, the race is only as important as the species.

What of other Caucasian traits? Early on we noted that much of early hominid evolution was driven by a need to promote ventilation of body heat in a hot environment. Eighty-five percent of the heat loss from the human body comes from the head and face. In equatorial Africa, the kinky, and particularly the peppercorn, hair of the early human types would expose more of the scalp to the atmosphere and so promote heat loss. The typical Negroid broad nose and flaring nostrils would enhance the loss of moisture, and therefore heat, during respiration. The thick Negroid lips would increase the surface area of the face and further facilitate heat loss. Bodily leanness, so characteristic of the East African Nilotic types, would also promote heat loss. Among Caucasians of the frigid north, by contrast, body heat would have to be conserved. The characteristic Caucasian narrow nose and thin lips, by reducing surface area, would help preserve heat. The narrowed nostrils would also aid in warming inspired air. Caucasian straight hair, falling down on the back of the neck, would help preserve heat in the head and neck region. The tendency in the male Caucasian to more profuse body hair may have also been an aid to heat preservation on the hunt and away from his campfires. We have already noted that hominids, like other warm-blooded animals, are regulated by the effects of Gloger's Law, which states that the closer an animal is to the equator, the darker his coat; the closer to the Arctic Circle, the whiter his coat. The polar bear, the arctic fox, and the snowshoe rabbit are all examples of winterized white-coated Arctic animals who illustrate Gloger's Law. The Caucasian phenotype among *H. sapiens sapiens* also follows it. Intensity of sunlight and temperature had originally driven human evolution in Africa and the sharp diminution of these two climatic factors in a northern setting was the driving force behind Caucasian evolution. The new Caucasoid race was, in effect, cold-adapted. In this scenario, Vitamin D regulation was the stimulus; albinoidism was the response.

The earliest European Caucasian was Cro-Magnon, who appeared between 30–25,000 years ago.[69] Cheikh Anta Diop asserts that Cro-Magnon represents the *in situ* evolution of the African Grimaldi Man, Europe's original *H. sapiens sapiens*.[70] In southern France, Grimaldi and Cro-Magnon Man were found together in certain caves; Grimaldi is situated in the deeper, hence older, strata and Cro-Magnon in the higher, hence later, strata. These Cro-Magnon were dolichocephalic, a skull type they inherited from the Grimaldis, showing them to have been a more archaic Caucasian than the brachycephalic modern type that emerges around 10,000 B.C. Some Eastern European anthropologists have suggested that Cro-Magnon was the earliest of the *H. sapiens sapiens*, who originated in Europe and then migrated to Africa where he was "negroidized" under the pressure of warm climatic conditions.[71] We might as well say that it is the son that begets the father. Such a scheme defies all known hominid chronology and there is no plausible genetic model that explains how a white-skinned population can be turned black. There is no "blackening" mutation analogous to albinism that would permit it.

Our general theory is buttressed by certain archeological finds: three Aurignacian sites, representing the African Grimaldi culture, have been found in southwestern Russia between the 51st and 52nd parallels on a more or less horizontal line extending from west to east.[72] The Aurignacian period dates from 40,000 years ago, so we know that an African type of man was present in southwestern Eurasia at the beginning of the Wurm II Stadial along the southern glacier boundary, therefore satisfying an important premise of our theory. Within 10–15,000 years, the Aurignacian culture had given way to the Solutrean culture in Europe, representing a different type of *H. sapiens sapiens*. This was Cro-Magnon, the earliest Caucasian prototype.

C.A. Diop proposed another area of Europe as the site of Caucasian evolution—the mountainous southern borderlands of France.[73] This area was certainly glaciated in the critical period and we have already alluded to finds in the mountain caves of Monaco where Grimaldi Man is found in the deeper layers, circa 39,000 years ago, whereas Cro-Magnon is found "super-imposed" upon Grimaldi in the upper layers of the same caves dated at 25,000 years ago. For Diop, this was prima facie evidence of the evolution of the Caucasian from the African in southern France and he proposed that Europe was peopled from west to east. His case is most compelling, but only additional research will tell whether southwestern France or southwestern Russia represents the true cradle of the Caucasian.

Left: Twa female from Uganda. *Right:* Andaman female from island off the western coast of Indochina.

We must account for the evolution of the third great branch of the human species, the Mongolian race. According to Diop, the Mongolian is the last of the major races to appear and represents a cross between the African and Caucasian types. An alternative scheme, which incorporates Diop's theory, suggests that proto-Mongolians, whom Diop calls "Paleosiberians," were originally Bushmanoid or Khoisan types who migrated to the far northeastern steppes of Siberia from southern Asia sometime between 30–20,000 years ago. This is adduced from several facts: (1) the typical Khosian has a yellow-brown skin tint that is evocative of Mongolian skin color, (2) the Khoisan has scant body hair which is typical of the Mongolian type, (3) he is diminutive as Mongolians tend to be, and (4) he has the characteristic epicanthal folds around the eyes which is the most distinctive feature of the Mongolian facial type. The Paleosiberians underwent some special adaptations resulting from an environment which was cold, dry, and windswept. They developed a certain stockiness of body which is conducive to heat retention and which was evident in Slavic Caucasians. The Khoisan epicanthal fold became accentuated to protect the eyes from the winds of the steppes. They probably interbred with Caucasians from the western end of the great Eurasian continent who had migrated east of the Ural Mountains and this admixture could well account for their long, straight hair which would have been adaptive in a cold climate.

One of the many interesting results of Cann's mtDNA-derived phylogenetic tree, i.e., the minimum tree, was to show that several Melanesian mtDNA's are closer to Asiatic mtDNA's than they are to any other, including those within their own group. This powerfully supports the supposition that there is a close genetic tie between the African type of the

Negroid head from Mohenjo Daro, Indus Valley: 3000 B.C. (Photo: Brunson)

southern Far East and the Mongolian type of the more northerly Far East. Moreover, the fossils of the Paleosiberians reveal distinctly dolichocephalic skulls, further suggesting they are derived from the African type of southeast Asia in the same way that Cro-Magnon is derived from the African Grimaldi Man.

Let us now summarize human evolution to take into account all the various facts and interpretations brought to light up to this point. It is a model like any other, attempting to organize and make sense of the data in the most coherent and parsimonious form. However, the nature of anthropology is such that even the most ingenious models are liable to be modified, and sometimes discarded outright, in the light of new fossil discoveries or biomolecular research. Our understanding of human evolution is a palimpsest, revealing itself by degrees. If a definitive picture of human evolution is ever to emerge, it will indubitably represent a composite of many different views. To wit:

For seven million years, hominid evolution, from our pre-Australopithecine ape ancestors to *Homo sapiens sapiens,* unfolded in the eastern half of Africa. All in the hominid line were brown-to-black skinned. In the hundred or so millenia after his emergence on the African continent between 200,000–130,000 years ago, *H. sapiens sapiens* migrated to the far corners of the Old World. The first such migrations moved eastward along tropic latitudes into India, southeast Asia, and finally Australia and the Pacific Islands. During the greater period of this migration, mile-high walls of ice blocked significant penetration into Eu-

Black woman from Khamba, Vietnam: 650 A.D. (Photo: Chandler)

Kuei Woman—Thailand and Cambodia (Photo: Chandler)

rope, channelling the migratory flow eastward along the southerly latitudes. Human occupation of Asia had occurred by at least 75,000 years
ago.[74] Human remains in Australia date from 32,000 years ago and it is
not too much to infer that human beings were there as early as 40,000
years ago. Modern man came to occupy Europe between 50–40,000
years ago, during the Wurm I Interstadial, and his near-relative, Neandertal Man, had preceded him there by at least 30,000 years. These two
closely-related species of late hominids shared the European habitat until
35,000 years ago when Neandertal disappeared completely. A small group
of immigrants from Africa colonized a portion of southwestern Russia, near
the southern edge of the great Wurm glacier along the 51st parallel, and
in this relative isolation underwent adaptations in a frigid, relatively sunless environment which created a new human race characterized by pale
skin, lightened straight hair, varying shades of eye color, and narrowed,
angular facial features. These phenotypic changes were the outcome of
cold adaptation and produced the Caucasian race by 25–20,000 years ago.

From southern Asia, groups of Khoisan types migrated northward after 30,000 years ago into the Siberian steppes. Their adaptations in this new environment produced the Mongolian type—short of stature, yellow-tinted of skin, straight of hair, and with accentuated epicanthal folds around the eyes. The evolution of this race of humans was influenced to a greater or lesser degree by intermixture with Caucasians, probably in the middle of the Eurasian continent. This new race, however, continued to receive intermittent gene infusions from the south for a considerable period.[75] Parenthetically, it might be said that an old Japanese proverb recognizes the connection of the historical population of that island to the aboriginal Melanesian inhabitants: "A samurai, to be brave, must have a little black blood."[76]

"Australomelanesian" type—royal personage in bronze from Shang or Zhou Dynasty, China: 1100 B.C. (Photo: Chandler)

The African type that came to inhabit the Australo-Melanesian world in the Pacific also underwent certain adaptations at the micro level. Unlike the Mongolians who arose from them, they remained phenotypically unmodified because the climate in their new Pacific home was similar to conditions in their ancestral African home.[77] Population geneticists are fond of complicating the discussion about the origins of Australo-Melanesian populations by noting the biomolecular differences or "distances" between them and modern Africans. These "distances" have been invoked to claim that the Australo-Melanesian and the African do not belong to the same race. This notion can be rebutted in a number of ways. W.W. Howells asserts: "Generalized genetic distances can be measured but deductions from them are quite unsafe."[78] Largely, this is due to the phenomenon of genetic drift, which means that a small population isolated from its parent can, in a short time, lose genes it had inherited from its parent. It has happened among the Australian aborigines themselves. Certain groups in the past broke off from the continental population and migrated to offshore islands where their descendants remain to this day. These islanders show marked biomolecular differences from the parent aboriginal populations on mainland Australia, a clear example of genetic drift at work. In fact, these island aborigines show a high prevalence of

Left: **Young African male from Chad.** *Right:* **Masculine face in stone from the Shang Dynasty, China: 11th-century B.C. (Photo: Chandler)**

Kuei boy from present-day China. (Photo: Brunson)

the Rho blood group that is found with equal prevalence only in Africa.[79] Are they therefore genetically "closer" to an African population from which they are separated by 10,000 miles and 40,000 or more years than they are to their own parent population in Australia? We can see why W.W. Howells considered problematical any deductions about racial relationships or historical connections between populations based on genetic distances.

Some population geneticists also convey the misleading impression that the genotype is "stable," that is, relatively resistant to environmental influence. It is hard to understand such reasoning since the evidence is so much against it.[80] The prevalence of the HgS gene in Africa is but one well-known example of the effect of environmental pressures on genotype. Moreover, it has been well-demonstrated that the genes that determine blood types and serum proteins will react to changes in environment. This is especially true regarding challenges posed by new microorganisms:

Africoid warrior from Pasemah, Sumatra: 200 B.C.-100 A.D. (Photo: Chandler)

> That man evolved in Africa and migrated from there around the world is an accepted concept today. In Africa, he had a host of infections, but many of them were left behind when he drifted away. All those needing special vectors or intermediate hosts not found in new homes failed to survive. These would include schistosomes, trypanosomes, tick-transmitted infections, arboviruses, and so on. Temperature variation would affect malaria and yellow fever. Only those that belonged directly to man could go with him. . . .
>
> On arriving at a new location, man would find a host of parasites already established in the animals and some would affect him also. In the Far East, there would be new schistosomes . . . and new arboviruses.[81]

These new challenges to the human immune system would select for modified blood types and serum proteins—modifications mediated through genetic mutations. However, these modifications did not create a new race out of the Australo-Melanesians, only an oriental African varietal.

The model presented above allows the resolution of a number of ostensibly contradictory findings in population genetics: (1) that Africans appear to be closer to Caucasians by some genetic indices, (2) that Caucasians and Mongolians appear to be closer by other indices, (3) that Mongolians and Australo-Melanesians appear closer by yet other indices, and (4) that Africans and Australo-Melanesians appear genetically "dis-

**Anthropomorphized vase from the Shang Dynasty, China: 11th-century
B.C. (Photo: Brunson, with permission from the Freer Gallery)**

tant." The apparent genetic proximity of Caucasians and Africans derives
from the evolution of the Caucasian out of the African some 30–40 millenia ago and by continued genetic interchange in historical times. The
genetic linkage of Caucasians and Mongolians is explained by the inter-
mixing between the two populations in north-central Asia some 20–25
millenia ago. The closeness of the Mongolian and the Australo-Melanesian
reflects Mongolian evolution from the Asiatic African type, ancestral to
the contemporary Melanesian, 25–30 millenia ago. The apparent distance
between the African and the Pacific Black populations is a function of
genetic drift and microevolution within the emigre African populations
that came to inhabit the South Pacific. A diagram of all of these relationships would appear as shown in Figure 3. The model represented by this
figure accounts for the genetic and phenotypic relationships notable
among the races today.

FIGURE 3

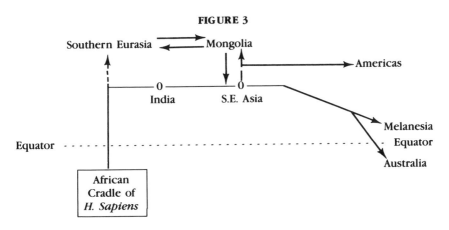

All human beings belong to the same species and their genetic differences are minuscule to the point of insignificance. If we are to classify human beings in any manner, we cannot do so by biomolecular analysis alone; we still depend on the grouping of people by phenotype. It is puerile to insist that individuals or groups of individuals who are near-identical in phenotype are unrelated to one another based on genetic distances on which there is no clear or consistent consensus and which are statistically insignificant anyway. As Diop has put it, someone is always trying to drown a fish. A difference must make a difference, something that genetic distances within the human species do not. Moreover, we are so obsessed with genetic distances proclaiming a difference we fail to recognize that phenotypical features such as skin color, hair texture, and facial morphology that proclaim the racial identity of two populations are *also* genetically determined. Biomolecular definitions of race are red herrings; we will find ourselves in a lot less trouble if we define race as we always have—with our own two eyes!

Over a period of four million years, the hominid line leading to modern man emerged, evolved, and attained its final form in Africa: the weight of the fossil evidence and DNA studies proclaim this. All human races, therefore, are branches off a trunk whose roots lie in African soil. The races are merely variations within the human species that allowed that species to maximize its habitat, and therefore its opportunities, on this planet. But there is only one mother and nurse of humanity—Africa.

Addendum

After this chapter was completed, while cogitating over Bill Kimbel's commentary, this writer began to realize that there were evolutionary scenarios that could be compatible with Milford Wolpoff's fundamentally polycentric model of "multiregional evolution." Our scheme for the emergence and evolution of races is, in fact, such a model. Moreover, the evolution of *H. sapiens sapiens* on the one hand and *H. Neandertalensis* on the other, out of *H. erectus* is probably another example of multiregional evolution. But, in the first instance, multiregional evolution created three variations or races *within* the species; in the second instance, multiregional evolution created two separate species out of a parent species. In each case, multiregional evolution caused a splitting that led to raciation on the one hand and speciation on the other; there was no convergence or reduction leading to a *single* species from multiple separate populations. Thus where we do see multiregional evolution in action, it achieves the exact opposite of what Wolpoff proposes. That Wolpoff's version of

Stone figure of temple guard from Sumatra: 9th-century A.D. (Photo: Brunson)

multiregional evolution flies against the evidence doesn't seem to disturb him or his adherents in the least.

Glossary

Adaptation: A change of behavior or characteristics resulting from natural selection that better suits a population to its environment, thus improving its chances for survival; a characteristic resulting from such a change.

Arboreal: Pertaining to a tree-dwelling style of life.

Biomolecular Markers: Biochemical factors in the serum of the blood that aid in the determination of the genotype of an individual or population group; examples include blood groups, serum proteins, enzymes, and abnormal hemoglobins.

Chromosomes: Threadlike structures that carry the genes in every living thing. There are 46 human chromosomes: two are sex chromosomes that determine gender; the remainder are autosomes. Each parent contributes 23 chromosomes (1 sex chromosome and 22 autosomes) to the individual.

Convergence: The development of similar forms in separate and unrelated evolutionary lines.

Terracotta bust of a Negro woman from Java: 1350 A.D. (Photo: Chandler)

DNA (deoxyribonucleic acid): The long, double-spiral molecule that forms the genetic material. It is the fundamental constituent of the gene.

Codon: The functional unit of heredity that occupies a particular place on a chromosome and controls the coding and transmission of physical traits.

Gene Flow: The hybridization that occurs when the genes from one group are transmitted to another.

Gene Pool: The sum of all the different genes contained within a population.

Genotype: The genetic make-up of a living thing, that is, all the characteristics contained in the organism's genes.

Genus (pl. *Genera*): Taxonomic category composed of a group of species having more in common with each other than with other groups.

Haplotype: A linked group of paired genes (alleles) contributed by either parent.

Hemoglobin: The protein molecule of the red blood cells that transports oxygen to the tissues via the blood stream. The sickle hemoglobin (HgS), which causes sickle cell anemia, results from a genetic defect causing the red blood cell to form a sickle shape, impeding its movement through the capillaries and often leading to a painful crisis.

Hominid: The primate family which includes all of the genus *Homo* and the genus *Australopithecus.* Modern humans are hominids.

Homozygous/Heterozygous: Since all genes and chromosomes are paired, identical genes at paired loci in related chromosomes give homozygosity; different genes at paired loci in related chromosomes give heterozygosity. If one gene is "dominant" over the other at the paired loci, it will be expressed instead of its heterzygous partner; if a gene is "recessive" relative to the other, it will only be expressed when it is paired with an identical partner in the homozygous state. Thus recessive genes will more frequently appear in the offspring of two relatives since, by possessing many of the same genes, two identical ones are more likely to turn up at the same loci in the genotype of the offspring.

Lacustrine: Of, or pertaining to, lakes or lake regions.

Locus (Pl. *Loci*): The place on the chromosome occupied by a gene.

Microevolution: Small-scale evolution involving short time periods.

Mutation: A change in the character of a gene which is perpetuated in the subsequent daughters of that gene. On the evolutionary time scale, such changes are usually abrupt or punctuated rather than gradual and radically affect the phenotypic expression of the gene.

Niche: The environmental habitat of an animal species and its pattern of exploiting that habitat.

Osteomalachia: The softening of adult bones due to Vitamin D deficiency, which may cause serious bony deformities (see Rickets).

Parallel Evolution: The development of similar forms in two separate but related evolutionary lines.

Phenotype: The outward or observable characteristics of an individual as determined by genotype.

Primates: Placental mammals, most of them arboreal, with two suborders, the anthropoids, including (1) monkeys, apes, and hominids, and (2) the prosimians.

Protohominid: A higher primate type which diverged from the chimpanzee on the road toward hominid status. No fossils of this intermediate type have yet been discovered.

Race: A subspecies or regional variation of a species whose members resemble each other more than they do other members of the species.

Rickets: Deformities in children caused by a softening of the bones due to Vitamin D deficiency (see Osteomalachia).

Savannah: A tropical or sub-tropical grassland containing scattered trees and drought-resistant undergrowth.

Selection: The principal mechanism of evolutionary change by which individuals best adapted to the environment contribute more offspring to succeeding generations than the remainder. As more characteristics of such individuals are incorporated into the gene pool, the characteristics of the population change.

Serology: The study of blood serum and its factors.

Species: A population whose male and female members can mate and produce fertile offspring.

Taxonomy: Classification of living things into groups according to their relationships and ordering these groups into hierarchies.

Tree: A diagram or graph that branches from a simple stem; used to illustrate relationships between types or groups.

Vectors: Insects that can carry and transmit pathological microorganisms to or between animals.

Appendix

THE QUESTION OF INFANTICIDE

We know that infanticide has been practiced by various tribal peoples well into this century. In his typically encyclopedic fashion, James George Frazier reported numerous examples in the third section of *The Golden Bough,* published in 1911 (Frazer J.G., "A Dying God," Part III of *The Golden Bough,* London: MacMillan and Co., Ltd., 1911, pp. 160–95). There seem to be three conditions under which infanticide is practiced: (1) Among the !Kung of the Kalahari, an infant born to a mother still nursing is allowed to die because the extreme marginality of life does not allow her to suckle more than one child at a time; (2) some peoples have sacrificed children in observance of mytho-religious rites similar to those made infamous by the ancient worshippers of Moloch; (3) in remote districts of India and China, traditional preference for male children has been so strong that a succession of female births in a household without sons has led to the killing or exposing of the infants. It seems likely that in proto-hominid and early hominid times, any infanticide would have been motivated by factors similar to the first type since the second and third types of infanticide could only have occurred at a much higher cultural level. Thus if the early hominids killed infants, it was only to preserve the lives of living children.

Notes

1. The three ground-dwelling apes include the chimpanzee and gorilla of Africa and the orangutan of the Indonesia archipelago. The orangutan is still primarily a tree-dweller but ambulates when travelling long distances.
2. Cf. Birdsell JS, *Human Evolution*, Boston: Houghton Mifflin Co., 1972, pp. 197–9.
3. Cf. Leakey R, *People of the Lake*, Garden City: Anchor Press/Doubleday, 1978, pp. 200–2.
4. See "Among the Wild Chimpanzees," with Jane Goodall, National Geographic Video, 1984.
5. Inter-species comparisons of DNA polymorphisms indicate a chimpanzee-human split between eight-five million years ago. Some postulate that the split happened as recently as five million years ago, but a few fossil fragments from East Africa indicate that some hominization probably had already occurred by then. For this and other reasons, many anthropologists consider a date of seven million years ago as more reasonable for the split. See Johanson D and Edley C, *Lucy: The Beginning of Humankind*, New York: Simon & Schuster, 1981, p. 316, for a discussion of the five million year-old hominid fossil fragments.
6. Leakey, op. cit., p. 129.
7. When water evaporates, it takes heat with it. Evaporating sweat can remove from the surface of the body up to ten times the normal basal rate of heat production. Guyton AC, *Textbook of Medical Physiology*, Philadelphia: W.B. Saunders Co., 1981, pp. 889–90.
8. See Campbell BC, *Humankind Emerging*, Boston: Little, Brown, & Sons, 1985, 472–3.
9. The association of tools with human evolution is not as clear-cut as once thought since chimpanzees exhibit an elementary form of tool-use. However, tool-construction is generally seen as a human skill.
10. Lovejoy CO, "The Origin of Man," *Science* (1981) 211: 1/21/81, pp. 341–50.
11. Ibid., p. 345.
12. "Human Origins," An interview with Tim White, Bill Kimbel, Berhane Asfaw, and Prosper Ndessokia, KPFA Radio, Berkeley, California, February 21, 1987 (unpublished transcript).
13. Cf. Birdsell, op. cit., pp. 182–3.
14. See Jane Goodall, op. cit.
15. Though apes and other higher primates appear to live in male-dominated troops, true primate society consists of the females and their young. However, chimpanzees are unusual because sexual relations within their troops are promiscuous rather than monopolized by a dominant male.
16. See Note 15.
17. Tim White, op. cit., "Human Origins" interview.
18. Bill Kimbel, ibid.
19. See discussions in this chapter, infra, concerning the polycentric or "multi-regional" hypothesis of human origins.
20. Leakey, op. cit., p. 253.
21. Coon C, *The Origin of the Races*, New York: Alfred A. Knopf, 1962, p. 656.
22. Ibid., Plate XXXII, after p. 370.
23. What defines a species is the ability of the males and females of the group to mate and produce fertile offspring; donkeys and horses can mate but the

mules they produce are infertile. Therefore, donkeys and horses, though closely related, belong to different species.

24. There is controversy here, too. There are those who think that Bkroken Hill man in southeastern Africa, dated at 125–110 mya, exhibits some Neandertaloid characters though most others classify him as *H. sapiens* of an archaic type. But he is the only African hominid fossil with "quasi-Neanderaloid" traits so it seems evident that, fundamentally, there were no Neandertals in Africa.

25. See Note 24. There are only two areas of the world where Neandertals have been found in any significant numbers: Europe and Western Asia. But, not only are there no Neandertal-sapiens intermediate types anywhere, there are several African sapiens fossils *older* than the oldest Neandertal.

26. See Day MH, *Guide to Fossil Man,* Chicago: University of Chicago Press, 1986, pp. 181–94; 240–9; 328–34.

27. Stringer CB, Hublin JJ, Vandermeersch B, "The origins of Anatomically Modern Humans in Europe," in *Origins of Modern Humans,* Smith GH and Spencer F, editors, New York: Alan R. Liss.

28. Trinkhaus E and Smith FH, "Fate of the Neandertals," in *Ancestors: The Hard Evidence,* Delson E, editor, New York: Alan R. Liss, 1985, p. 294.

29. Stringer CB, "Middle Pleistocene Hominids," in Delson, op. cit., p. 294.

30. Diop CA, "Critical Review of the Most Recent Theses on the Origin of Humanity," translated by E. Taylor, in *Great African Thinkers,* edited by Ivan Van Sertima, New Brunswick: Journal of African Civilizations, Ltd., 1986, p. 213.

31. Birdsell JB, "The Problem of Evolution of Human Races: Classification or Clines?" *Social Biology,* 19:2, p. 137.

32. Finch C, "Further Conversations with the Pharaoh: Interview with Cheikh Anta Diop," Van Sertima, op. cit., p. 236.

33. Birdsell, *Human Evolution,* op. cit., p. 358.

34. For Mexico, cf. PiSunyer O, "Historical Background to the Negro in Mexico," *Journal of Negro History* (October 1957) 42:4, pp. 237–46 and Davidson DM, "Negro Slave Control and Resistance in Colonial Mexico, 1519–1650," in *Maroon Societies,* Price R, editor, Garden City: Anchor Press/Doubleday, 1973, pp. 82–100; for Italy and Greece, cf. Rogers JA, *Sex and Race,* Volume I, New York: Helga Rogers, 1967 and Snowden FM, *Blacks in Antiquity,* Cambridge: Harvard University Press, 1970; for the Arabic world, cf. Lane-Pool S, *A History of Egypt in the Middle Ages,* London: Methuen & Co., 1901 and Lewis B, *Arabs in History,* New York: Harper & Row, 1966. These sources amply document the African presence in these nations.

35. Cf. Van Sertima, editor, *African Presence in Early Europe,* New Brunswick: Journal of African Civilizations, Ltd., 1985, 1986.

36. Watson JC, *Recombinant DNA: A Short Course,* New York: W.H. Freeman, 1984, pp. 218–9.

37. Serjeant GR, *Sickle Cell Disease,* New York: Oxford University Press, 1985, pp. 13–24; Wai Kan Y and Dozy AM, "Evolution of the Hemoglobin S and C Genes in World Populations," *Science* (209), 18 July 1980, pp. 388–91.

38. Serjeant, op. cit., p. 15.

39. Wai Kan and Dozy, op. cit., pp. 388–9.

40. Ibid., pp. 389–90.

41. Cf. Van Sertima I and Rashidi R, editors, *African Presence in Early Asia,* New Brunswick: Journal of African Civilizations, Ltd., 1985, 1988.

42. See Lehman H, "Distribution of the Sickle Cell Gene," *Eugenics Review* (1954) 46, pp. 101–21 and Papiha SS, "A Genetic Survey in the Bhil Tribe of

Madhya Pradesh, Central India," *American Journal of Physical Anthropology* (1978) 49, pp. 179–86.

43. Cf. Rashidi R, "Africans in Early Asian Civilizations," in Van Sertima & Rashidi, op. cit., pp. 15–52. The inhabitants of South India have woolly as well as wavy hair.

44. Birdsell, op. cit., *Human Evolution,* p. 364.

45. "... and if we drew one of these Indians with a pencil without color, yet he would be known for a negro, for his flat nose, and his stiff curling locks and prominent jaw, and a certain glean about his eyes, would give a black look to the picture and depict an Indian... " (Philostratus, *The Life of Apollonius of Tyana,* translated by F.C. Conybeare, 2 vols., Cambridge: Harvard University Press, 1912, 1969, p. 179).

46. Nei M and Roychoudbhury AK, "Gene Variation Within and Between the Three Major Races of Man, Caucasoids, Negroids, and Mongoloids," *American Journal of Human Genetics* (1974) 26, pp. 421–3; also Nei M, "Evolution of Races at the Gene Level," *Human Genetics,* New York: Alan R. Liss, 1982, pp. 167–181.

47. Lawler S, "Blood Groups," *Encyclopedia Brittanica* (1984) 2, p. 1148.

48. Guglielmino-Matessi CR, Gluckman P, and Cavalli-Sforza LL, "Climate and Evolution of Skull Metrics in Man," *American Journal of Physical Anthropology* (1979) 50, pp. 549–64.

49. Ibid., p. 562.

50. Ibid.

51. Ibid.

52. Wainscot JS, Hill AVS, et al, "Evolutionary Relationships of Human Populations from an Analysis of DNA Polymorphisms," *Nature* (319), 2/16/86, p. 497.

53. The mtDNA in spermatozooa disintegrates at fertilization which is why there is no paternal contribution to cell mtDNA and why it is single-stranded.

54. Weiss R, "Many Faces of a Gene Mapping Project," *Science News* (13), 10/14/89, p. 254.

55. See "Children of Eve," transcript of NOVA, WGBH, Boston, 1986, p. 24.

56. Cited in Weiss, op. cit.

57. Cann RL, Stoneking M, and Wilson AC, "Mitochondrial DNA and Human Evolution," *Nature* (352), 1/1/87, p. 35. The most prominent of the Coonian-style polycentrists today is M.H. Wolpoff of the University of Michigan. To distance himself from Coon, he calls this latest version of polycentrism "multi-regional evolution," but it is a Coonian model nonetheless. It must also be noted that Chinese anthropologists also favor the model of multi-regional evolution. Cf. Wolpoff MH, Zhi WX, and Thorne AG, "Modern *Homo sapiens* Origins: A General Theory of Hominid Evolution Involving the Fossil Evidence From East Asia," in Smith and Spencer, op. cit., pp. 411–84.

58. See "Mysteries of Mankind," National Geographic Video, 1988.

59. Diop, op. cit., p. 167.

60. Steatopygy represents an abnormal accumulation of fat on the female buttocks. It is a distinctive trait seen only in the Khoisan populations of southern Africa and Andaman Islanders off the western coast of Indo-China. The Upper Paleolithlic Venus figurines of Europe depict striking representations of this trait.

61. There is a three-to-five times greater penetrance of ultraviolet light in white skin compared to that in black skin. Moreover, there is a greater serum concentration of Gc, the Vitamin D carrier, in Caucasians compared to Africans,

indicating greater Vitamin D production in white skin. See Thompson ML, "Relative Efficiency of Pigment and Horny Layer Thickness in Protecting the Skin of Europeans and Africans Against Solar Radiation," *Journal of Physiology* (1955) 127, pp. 236–46; Neer RM, "The Evolutionary Significance of Vitamin D, Skin Pigment and Ultra-Violet Light," *American Journal of Physical Anthropology* 43, pp. 403–16; Mourant AE, et al, "Sunshine and the Geographical Distribution of the Alleles of the Gc System of Plasma Proteins," *Human Genetics* (1976) 33, pp. 307–14.

62. Post PW, et al, "Cold Injury and the Evolution of 'White' Skin," *Human Biology* (1975) 47, 65–80.

63. Luke D, "African Presence in the Early History of the British Isles and Scandinavia," in Van Sertima, op. cit., *African Presence in Early Europe,* pp. 223–44.

64. Ibid.; cf. also Clegg L, "The Mystery of the Arctic Twa," in Van Sertima, ibid., pp. 245–9.

65. "Mutations occurring in the sex cells... can be transmitted to descendants—and so are of evolutionary signficiance. Mutations classed in two broad categories—point mutations and chromosomal rearrangements. Point mutations involve a very limited change in genetic code. They may result from the simple substitution of a single base for another base, or adjoining bases may be reversed in the sequence. Point mutations seem to be the smallest units of mutation, but they often produce considerable phenotypic changes in the individuals affected. We know that over 20 abnormal hemoglobins have each been produced by one change in a single base in the DNA code. Such hemoglobins usually affect the individual's health considerably.

"Mutational changes of the second type involve rearrangements of considerable portions of the DNA molecule. External inputs of energy sometimes produce breaks in the chromosomes, and these breaks may reknit in a variety of new positions. The changes include such things as inversions, translocations, and deletions of sections of the chromosome" (Birdsell, op. cit., p. 60).

66. See Manganyi NC, et al, "Studies on Albinism in the South African Negro," *Journal of Biosocial Science* (1974) 6, pp. 107–12; also Okoro AN, "Albinism in Nigeria," *British Journal of Dermatology* (1957) 92, pp. 485–92.

67. See Alexander GA and Henschke UK, "Advanced Skin Cancer in Tanzanian Albinos," *Journal of the National Medical Association* (1981) 73:11, pp. 1047–54; also Okoro AN, ibid. In Africa, albinism is most frequently encountered in populations with consanguineous marriage customs.

68. See Barnicot NA, "Red Hair in African Peoples," *Annals of Eugenics* (1953) 53, pp. 311–32 and Kromberg JGW, et al, "Prevalence of Albinism in the South African Negro," *South African Medical Journal,* 3/13/82, pp. 383–6.

69. If Cro-Magnon represents the first "whitened" *H. sapiens,* we must at least consider the possibility that European *H. erectus* and Neandertal underwent a similar "whitening" prior to the appearance of *H. sapiens* in Europe.

70. Diop, op. cit., passim.

71. Cited in Diop, ibid., p. 192.

72. These Aurignacian sites are: Mizyn near Chernigov (51° 30' N. by 31° 18' E.), Kostienki near Voronezh (51° 40' N. by 39° 10' E.), and Gagarino near Tambov (51° 45' N. by 41° 10' E.). The sites all lie geographically on an east-to-west line at almost precisely the same latitude, varying by no more than one-fourth of a latitudinal degree from one another. Co-incidence seems unlikely. The southern boundary of the Wurm glacier line (in Europe) was situated between 51 and 52 degrees north and extended at least to the 40th

meridian east. These Aurignacian sites were therefore juxtaposed adjacent to the southern glacier line during the Wurm II Stadial. Cf Boule M and Vallois H, *Fossil Men,* New York: Dryden Press, p. 136.

73. Diop CA, "Prehistory: Race and History, Origin of Mankind and Racial Differentiation," translated by E. Taylor, in Van Sertima, op. cit., *Great African Thinkers,* p. 172.

74. The earliest *H. sapiens sapiens* fossil in Western Asia, discovered in present-day Israel, is dated at 95 mya, and probably is representative of the first leg of the earliest significant human migration out of Africa.

75. Cf. Brunson J, "African Presence in Early China," in Van Sertima and Rashidi, op. cit., *African Presence in Early Asia,* pp. 120–37.

76. Cited by Brunson J, "Unexpected Black Faces in Early Asia: A Photo Essay," in Van Sertima and Rashidi, ibid., p. 206.

77. Certain population geneticists assert that black skin evolved twice because of a hot climate, once in Africa and once in Asia. We categorically reject this notion and affirm instead that the hot climate of southern Asia merely "preserved" the black skin and phenotype of the original African inhabitants who migrated there.

78. Howells WW, "Physical Variation and History in Melanesia and Australia," *American Journal of Physical Anthropology,* 45, p. 644.

79. For a discussion of genetic drift and the Rho blood factor in Australian aborigines, see Birdsell, op. cit., pp. 73; 354–7.

80. One of the most striking examples of the impact of environmental changes on both genotype and phenotype is seen in the experience of the peppered moth of Great Britian. Common throughout the Midlands in the pre-industrial period, it displayed a mottled gray color with speckles of black that served as excellent camouflage against predators. With the onset of the Industrial Revolution in England, the Midlands area became covered with soot and other dark pollutants. In 1840, the first of the peppered moths had turned black in the Midlands. This black color was controlled by a single dominant gene that had arisen by mutation and that, because it gave an overwhelming adaptive advantage as camouglage, replaced the original coloration of the species within two generations. This is an outstanding example of selection operating on the phenotype through genetic modification. It should also be noted as an aside that the example of the peppered moth provides a perfect illustration of the process that would have created a Caucasian White out of an African Black during the Wurm Ice Age in southwestern Russia. In both instances, intense selection pressure from environmental alterations generated rapid change mediated by genetic modification in a specific population. See Birdsell, op. cit., pp. 53–7.

81. Cockburn A, "Where Did Our Infectious Diseases Come From?" in *Health and Disease in Tribal Societies,* Ciba Foundation Symposium, New York: Excerpta Medical (1979), pp. 106–7.

II

The Great Mother and the Origin of Human Culture

It is the prevailing opinion in anthropological circles that humankind originated, evolved, and emerged into final form in Africa. But what of human culture? What of that complex of methods, skills, values, and behaviors that have allowed man to modify and superimpose himself on his environment? Though the issue here is, if anything, even less simple to unravel than the skein of biological evolution, it is still possible to discern that, in this domain as well, Africa was the cradle. It does stand to reason. Modern humanity emerged first in Africa and from there spread to the rest of the world. Therefore, culture, the most distinctive product of the human mind and labor, would also have originated in Africa and been carried to the rest of the world by the initial waves of migration out of that continent. Though this would seem to be self-evident, scholarship has been reluctant to face it. Carleton Coon's pronouncement that Africa was the undifferentiated kindergarten of the Race, while Europe and Asia were the "true schools" of mankind, continues to be reflected in more than a few schools of thought. For many, man may have been born in Africa, but he became acculturated and civilized elsewhere. The truth or falsity of such a proposition should become evident in the chapters ahead.

In the last half of the 19th century, as data on non-Western cultures accumulated in countless studies of their customs, myths, religions, and folkways, it became apparent to some observers that the patriarchal structure of modern civilized societies had not always been in place. Instead, they had grown out of matriarchal systems of social organization. This was first brought to the attention of the scholarly world in definitive form by the publication of J.J. Bachofen's *Motherright* which, by more or less systematically sifting through the remnants and artifacts of ancient cultures, supplied the first coherent proof of the priority of the matriarchy.[1] Bachofen's book became a standard reference for all later writers on the subject, though it was thoroughly criticized by many. The book influenced Friedrich Engels, who used Bachofen's thesis to support the Marxist concept of dialectical materialism operating through the forces of history. Other writers followed Bachofen and amplified his thesis, notably Lewis Morgan in his classic study of the Iroquois; Robert Briffault in his massive three-volume tome, *The Mothers;* and the Jungian Erich Neumann in *The Great Mother: Analysis of an Archetype.*

At the same time, cultural anthropology was bringing to light the pervasiveness of matriliny—tracing descent through the female line—in Africa, India, and the Pacific Islands. In fact, prior to significant Islamic in-roads into sub-Saharan Africa in the 12th and 13th centuries, the matrilineal principle of succession was dominant throughout Africa. Arab writers were profoundly shocked in the 11th century to find that the fabulously wealthy West African empire of Ghana was ruled by the matrilineal principle as were numerous other African kingdoms.[2] The persistence of matriarchal norms on three continents was not easy to reconcile with the assumption that father-right and masculine dominance had always been the cultural norm of mankind. Even Bachofen himself, though he conceded the primacy of the matriarchy in the early stages of cultural evolution, insisted that the patriarchy represented a "higher" stage of development. For him, the quintessential patriarchal culture was Rome, which he idealized. Like all 19th century Europeans, he had an unquestioned faith in "progress" and the Europe of his time to him represented the highest expression of a linear cultural evolution from primitive to civilized. The "primitive" represented the matriarchy, the "civilized" the patriarchy. C.A. Diop was one who forcefully challenged these assumptions.

Diop devoted much of his book, *The Cultural Unity of Black Africa,*[3] to a critique of the Bachofen thesis and its impact on early Marxist thinkers. He saw that Bachofen's interpretation could be used to justify the presumption that ancient Africa, so imbued with matriarchal social and political forms, represented only an elementary level of cultural development whereas Europe, profoundly patriarchal, revealed a higher, and finer, level of culture. In demolishing this idea, Diop only had to point out that civilization itself was born, nurtured, and brought to maturity among the matriarchal African cultures of Cush and Egypt. The primacy of the mother in family life and the royal succession through the female line in ancient Egypt are well-known. The mother controlled the household and often the fields as well; the children took their surnames from the mother. Non-royal pharaohs could ascend to the throne by virtue of marriage to the Great Royal Wife presumptive, the eldest daughter of the preceding Great Royal Wife, from whom the right to the throne descended. One of the motivations behind royal incest, in which a brother or half-brother was married to the Great Royal Wife-presumptive, was to keep political power within the family. Even usurpers observed the rule. When Psammeticus, the first pharaoh of the 26th dynasty, ascended to the throne after the Assyrian expulsion of the Cushite 25th Dynasty, he took care to marry the reigning Cushite Chief Priestess of Amen, the ruler of Upper Egypt, as a way of legitimizing his rule.[4] In Cush, the Queen Mother, or Kendake, actually had the right to choose the next pharaoh. So powerful did these

Kendakes become that they were able eventually to rule in their own right without interference.

The high state of civilization attained by Cush and Egypt is attested to by archaeological remains and the eyewitness testimony of Greek writers. The Greeks, consciously proud of all they had achieved in the cultural domain, referred to all other peoples as "barbarians," except the Ethiopians (Cushites) and the Egyptians upon whom they looked with unabashed admiration.[5] In fact, we can say that in some areas, contemporary man has not achieved the standard set in the ancient Nile Valley. For these reasons, Diop categorically denied the linear progression of culture but rather emphasized cycles of cultural evolution. A culture advances to a high plateau of civilization, but after it reaches maturity, it regresses, usually degenerating into barbarism and often disappearing altogether. Diop emphatically rejected the idea that patriarchal culture in any sense represented an "advance" over matriarchal culture.

Diop proposed a counter-argument, the "two cradle" theory of cultural origins, to account for the division of the world into matriarchies and patriarchies.[6] According to this thesis, the world was partitioned more or less along geographical lines into two zones, the "southern cradle," i.e., Africa and southern Asia, and the "northern cradle," i.e., Eurasia. An intermediate "zone of confluence," represented most conspicuously by the Mediterranean basin and the northern parts of Western Asia, was situated between the two cradles and exhibited a blend of influences. From Diop's perspective, the southern cradle was distinguished by agrarian societies in which the female/maternal role was dominant because of the woman's primary role in cultivation. A focus on intra-group harmony, an intimate relationship with nature, and the central place of the mother in family and social affairs promoted a co-operative, non-competitive social ethic. Because these agricultural societies produced a surplus of food, a certain amount of occupational differentiation and specialization was possible, allowing the elaboration of ever-more complex social systems. The dependence of these southern cradle agriculturalists on the periodicity of the seasons stimulated the invention of accurate time-keeping systems; and the need to predict and regulate the floods in these largely river-valley cultures, particularly the Nile, stimulated science. With such a high value placed on social co-operation, natural harmony, and the "feminine mystique," intra-group aggression would have been considerably attenuated.

This is all contrasted to the northern cradle, a cold, harsh, forbidding environment hostile to crops but supporting a nomadic life-style with a premium on herding, fighting, and raiding skills as small nomadic bands competed with one another for water, forage, and livestock. Therefore, masculine attributes would have been highly prized in this setting and women, poorly-suited to these pursuits, would to a large extent have been reduced to procreative vessels, concerned exclusively with domestic chores. Male status would have been paramount because the life-way would have put a premium on combativeness, competitiveness, and individuality, leaving little room for the development of broader, more co-operative social structures. The northern cradle, in the Diop scheme, would have given rise to the patriarchy.

We can epitomize this analysis by saying that in the protohistorical epoch, there would have existed two opposite and hostile world-views, the matriarchy and the patriarchy, each conditioned by its own geographic and climatic conditions. The zone of confluence, the Mediterranean and the northern parts of Western Asia, would serve as the first "battle-ground" of these opposing world views. In the northern Mediterranean, for example, it is possible to dislimn the early dominance of matriarchal societies, but they gradually became permeated, then subsumed, under patriarchal cultures. This process here and farther east has been described by several writers. Robert Graves, in his analysis of Greek myths, tells of the tremendous struggle in the Peloponnese between the matriarchal autochthones the Pelasgasians and the later patriarchal invaders, of whom the Dorians are merely the most notorious.[7] Godfrey Higgins in *Anacalypsis* writes of the conflicts that convulsed India wherein the "yonic" or female principle was locked in mortal struggle with the eventually triumphant "lingam" or male principle.[8] Whether in the Aegean or in the Indus Valley, the phenomenon seemed to have issued from the great Aryan migrations across Central Asia around 1700 B.C., sending shock waves against the established matriarchal cultures and civilizations to the east, west, and south.

Summarizing Diop's viewpoint, we can say that the matriarchy of the southern cradle and the patriarchy of the northern cradle sprang up more or less independently, but became ineluctable antagonists. The matriarchal south, which first attained civilization, succumbed to the politico-military onslaughts of the patriarchal north occurring in waves for more than 3500 years after 1700 B.C. The outcome of this repeated onslaught over thousands of years is seen in the contemporary military, political, and economic pre-eminence of the Western world.

Diop's two-cradle theory has proved quite valuable as a conceptual and analytical tool but is susceptible to further clarification. A somewhat different approach follows Bachofen up to the point of proposing a generalized or universal matriarchy for all early humanity. In the Diop model, the establishment of the matriarchy is closely tied to the invention of agriculture, which may have occurred as early as 15,000 B.C.E., and the patriarchy to the domestication of animals. The two-cradle theory follows logically enough from these premises. But there seem to be good reasons to believe that matriarchal customs actually preceded the invention of agriculture. Farming was almost certainly a female invention; it strengthened and amplified the matriarchy while materially and symbolically enriching it. Though archeological remains are scarce, twenty surviving statuettes from the Aurignacian period (40–20,000 B.C.E.), fifteen female and five male, shed light here. The female statuettes are the famous "Venuses," beautifully sculptured figurines of obese, steatopygous women with peppercorn hair.[9] These figurines are almost certainly mother figures modeled on the African Grimaldi women, the standard-bearers of Aurignacian culture in Europe. In non-Western traditional cultures, particularly in Africa, obesity is often a mark of beauty and whenever an obese female is figuratively represented, she is invariably a mother figure. The five male figurines are of youths, imperfectly rendered. Clearly, these are "son" types, part and parcel of the matriarchal ethos that the collection as a whole epitomizes. We will elaborate on the special position of the "sonship" in the matriarchy later on, but consider the meaning of 40–20,000-year-old representations of human females well before the advent of agriculture. This seems to be prima facie evidence of a pre-agricultural matriarchy, or proto-matriarchy, extending, as Aurignacian culture did, from the Pyrenees to Siberia. Thus, these figurines lie well within the geographic domain of Diop's northern cradle. If we are correct, then at a time in fairly recent pre-history, the north was itself matriarchal, or at least proto-matriarchal. When we remember that the first *Homo sapiens sapiens* inhabitants of the north, the Grimaldis, were immigrants from the south, where humanity itself began, this is easily understandable. Inasmuch as Caucasians evolved from African Grimaldis *in situ* in southwestern Eurasia (or southern France), it must be presumed that early in their existence, at least during the Cro-Magnon era, they were more or less matriarchal. Elements of this ancient northern matriarchy persisted in certain Norse myths as well as in material artifacts.

At the far eastern end of the northern cradle, the dominant cultures were matriarchal right up to 1700 B.C.E. when the Duke of Chou founded the first Chinese kingdom. Matriarchal societies persisted in Japan until 600 A.D. Caucasians and the eastern inhabitants of the northern crescent seemed to have shifted more rapidly to the patriarchal phase by virtue of their special environmental circumstances. However, it is not as if patriarchal societies were totally absent in the far south. Contemporary pastoral societies in Africa tend to be patriarchal and there is no reason not to assume that this was the case in the late prehistoric and proto-historic periods. Pastoralism in and of itself, regardless of its geographic situation, seems to lend itself to a patriarchal social structure. It is agriculture, a cultural invention of the southern cradle, that established the dominance of the matriarchy there. All this said, it is still possible to delineate an *in situ* evolution from matriarchal to patriarchal values in certain southern agrarian civilizations, Egypt being the most outstanding example. But in Egypt, the process never overreached itself, ending in a kind of equilibrium between matriarchal and patriarchal values not seen elsewhere, contributing mightily to the 4,000-year stability of dynastic Egyptian civilization. Despite an apparent patriarchal "gloss" on pharaoonic civilization, its foundation was solidly matriarchal and the mother principle maintained a firm grasp on Egyptian psyche and sensibility down to its last days.

To summarize: all human cultures began as, at the very least, "proto-matriarchies" (40,000 to 15,000 B.C.E.), including cultures of the northern cradle, which, however, underwent a transition to patriarchy more rapidly than elsewhere due to a pastoral or nomadic way of life dictated by environment. This way of life put a higher premium on masculine skills and values. By the end of the proto-historical period, circa 5,000 B.C., most of the peoples of the northern cradle had virtually completed a trend that turned them into patriarchates. On the other hand, the invention of agriculture in the southern cradle, possible as early as 15,000 B.C.E, strengthened and intensified matriarchal social structures, which were more conducive to development of the technical skills required for the creation of civilized life. When history proper begins, between 5,000 and 4,000 B.C., the world was divided roughly into southern matriarchal and northern patriarchal zones, with an intermediate zone of confluence in between.

Is it possible to probe into the evolution of human consciousness in the same fashion as we do human biological evolution, particularly during the period we call the Upper Paleolithic, c. 40–10,000 B.C., when African *Homo sapiens sapiens* was sowing the seeds of modern culture? To the extent we are able to trace the history of the human mind, we must rely on material ordinarily considered "non-historical," i.e., folk customs, myths, religious symbols, and language. Most historians shun the use of such materials because it is difficult to impose rigor upon them and they are usually impossible to date precisely. Still, such material has provided a wealth of valuable information. Gerald Massey is the outstanding example in the last century and in our own time, C.A. Diop has greatly enlarged the horizons of cultural history by recourse to such materials. The peerless Diop was one of the first to state clearly that history is more than a chronological account of events and/or a description of the deeds of great personalities. In Diop's view, it is the study of culture as a whole that has best contributed to our understanding of the human experience in time and space. Diop, the first modern African humanist, outlined three factors necessary for the proper study of culture: (1) the historic factor, (2) the linguistic factor, and (3) the psychic factor. Diop applied himself primarily to a study of the first two but unequivocally recognized the legitimacy of the third. We propose to include this third factor, the psychic factor, in what we call a "psycho-mytho-historical" approach to the study of the evolution of human culture, at least during the Upper Paleolithic period.

Little in the human experience is totally lost; its deposits are left in language, myth, history, religion, architecture, literature, art, and the psyche itself. Concerning Africa, Ivan Van Sertima has put it vividly when he compares African history and culture to a "shattered diamond" whose "shards" have been deposited all over the globe. Thus if we are to recover African history and the African experience in time and space, we cannot look merely at the continent itself or purely at one kind of artifact. Historical facts are often camouflaged in a wide range of material and we have to mine it all if we are to obtain more than a one-dimensional vision of things. There is a common cloth of history, psychology, myth, and language and it is this that we propose to explore and interpret.

Through the work of Gerald Massey, the 19th-century English socialist, poet, and antiquarian, we can track the common psycho-mytho-historical thread of African culture in global society.[10] Massey was a confirmed evolutionist and believer in the scientific method. He was an empiricist of the most rigorous kind whose patient research had convinced him that early humanity had emerged and evolved in Africa, both biologically and culturally. An admirer of Darwin, and personal friend of Alfred Russel Wallace, it may have been the former's *Descent of Man,* published in 1871, which first put Massey on the track of human evolution in Africa. But he reached an unshakable conviction that humans, biologically and culturally, originated in Africa through his exhaustive "typological" studies of myth and symbol. Massey reasoned that in its embryonic stage, the human mind was something of a *tabula rasa* (clean slate). The first human beings did possess instincts inherited from their pre-human forbears, but instincts function more on a neural rather than psychic plane. Under these circumstances, nature would have been man's first teacher. Alone in the living kingdom of nature, the human brain possessed sufficient powers of memory, reflection and discrimination to draw from nature the models to fashion the symbols that came to populate the human mental universe. In Massey's words, "thoughts were things": ideas were concrete and symbolic at the same time and derived from man's intimate experience with nature. These ideational "things" were the "types" around which Massey's analysis was constructed and foreshadowed by 50 years the Jungian concept of "archetypes."

In the concrete mental world described above, early humans had no knowledge of procreation as such. Though intimately acquainted with the sex act, they knew nothing of the connection between sex and procreation. On the face of it, there was no reason why they should. Certainly none of the higher primates can be said to "know" that the sex act begets offspring: that would presuppose a reflective consciousness which, as we have seen, does not appear until the emergence of *Homo sapiens sapiens* 200,000 years ago. Even this consciousness, the thing that separates modern humans from the rest of the animal kingdom, was, at this time, a nascent, slowly-evolving phenomenon. It is only as articulate language evolves that the kind of "ratiocination" necessary for the empirical discovery of causation through time can come into play. As the Jungians might say, the conscious mind was still overwhelmed by the unconscious. The process was entirely analogous to the progression of human life-stages where, from infancy through childhood to maturity, the individual gradually and sequentially learns language, expands his self-awareness, and gains the powers of judgement and insight. As in early childhood, the thoughts of early man were both symbolic and concrete—and the thought merged with the thing.

Massey reasoned that the first language was an inarticulate sign-language; in order to communicate, humans "became" the object or action they wished to convey. They did this with gestures and bodily movements, so that what we may think of as dance, theatre and panto-mime were forms of communication ages before they became "art." If early man wished to describe an animal to be hunted, he became that animal in order to communicate his message. To express a state of hunger or thirst, he would make signs of eating or drinking with his hands and mouth. We do the same when trying to communicate with someone who does not understand our language; at a time when there was no symbolic verbal communication, this sign-language would have been far more important. The evidence for the existence of primitive "gesture-language" abounds and the number of peoples who still preserve it are legion. American Indians used to communicate with persons from other tribes through a universally understood sign language. The !Kung possess a vigorous gesture-language; numerous commentators have noted their remarkable gift for mimicry and pantomime, still used to describe a successful hunt. Articulate vocal language would begin at the point when early man substituted the sound of things, rather than the mimes of the thing itself, to communicate. A bird call might be used as a signal, an animal call might be used to attract it while hunting. These and hundreds of other sounds could be used abstractly to describe things to others: the "thinging" of thought that Massey describes. He states, furthermore, that the clicks of the present-day Khoisan (!Kung) peoples are remnants of an incredibly old language patterned after the clicking sounds made by cynocephalic apes or baboons.[11] The connection is evident in the figure of the Egyptian god Thoth who took the form of a baboon as the herald of the sun-god and master of speech. This form of Thoth was drawn from the propensity of baboons to chatter at dawn, right before the rising of the sun.

All this goes to show that the original vocal language would have been imitative and onomatopeic, that is to say, similar in sound to the thing represented. All African languages, including the ancient Egyptian, reflect this venerable pattern. The god Shu, whose name sounds like a sneeze, was said to have been created when Atum, the creator-god, sneezed. Shu became the personification of the airspace between earth and heaven. His sister Tefnut incorporated the principle of moisture and was created by being spat out of the mouth of Atum. The root of her name, TEF, means "to spit," and in fact is not dissimilar to the sound made by spitting. Such examples from old Egyptian could be multiplied indefinitely.

Returning to sex and procreation, there are paleolithic peoples today who as yet do not acknowledge the male role. One outstanding example is the Trobriand Islanders of Melanesia who, when Bronislav Malinowski studied them in the 1920's, emphatically denied the existence of physiologic paternity.[12] Certain groups of Australian aborigines also hold this view, and the pre-classical Greeks attributed impregnation to the action of the north wind.[13] The Trobriand Islanders and the Australian aborigines are remnants of a cultural stage that is at least 30,000 years old. Therefore, we probably are entitled to conclude that this view of conception was universal in the world at that time.

This fundamental fact of primitive sociology meant that all new life was seen as created from the female, the mother, alone. Such a perception would have impressed itself very powerfully upon the emerging consciousness of early human beings. All around them in nature they would perceive life emerging from the female without any ostensible contribution from the male. In the menarchal human female, the time would come when menstruation would cease and she would swell in a manner both mysterious and awe-inspiring. In the space of 10 moons, new life would come gushing forth in an inundation of blood and water. Modern science has taken the mystery and awe out of the process, reducing it to a rather prosaic physiologic event, but to the embryonic human mind the feminine creation of new life would have been a matter of overwhelming fascination. Thus when the human mind began to grapple with what the Jungians call the "superordinate idea," i.e., "God," the female in her life-producing capacity would have served as the first model of prime causation. Still close to his animal beginnings and still closely bound to nature, man would use the models that nature provided to give shape and form to his slowly expanding mental universe.

The mental world of the earliest human beings would have been radically different from that of their modern descendants, who see nature as something apart from themselves. The super-human and extra-human

Figurines of the (pregnant) Egyptian mother-goddess, Ta-Urt, the hippopotamus deity who is the oldest in the Egyptian pantheon.

guises of nature would have provided early human beings with their first concrete ideas of that which was greater than themselves. The human female, therefore, would not constitute the first image of the divine; more powerful creatures would more readily supply these images. The female hippopotamus, because of her size and corpulence, would be one of the earliest images of the deity as pregnant Mother. Floating in the waters of inner Africa, she would evoke the maternal amniotic image. Indeed, this image would have made the lakes and rivers themselves female and maternal. The tree, with its overarching branches providing protection and nourishment, would have been maternal. Caves, evocative of the womb, would have been maternal. The great female python, slithering through arboreal branches and coiling around her eggs to incubate them, would have been another natural symbol of the "super-human" mother. Early humanity evolved manifold ways to symbolize the feminine/maternal principle in all its aspects. The Mother was the producer, the nourisher, and the protector of life, echoed in the vast natural panorama of the Great Lakes region of East Africa, the cradle of the Race.

The woman was intimately connected to blood, revealing itself in the four blood "mysteries." The first of these was the female menses, whose onset in the 11th–14th year "magically" transformed girls into life-giving, life-bearing adult women. Menstruation was therefore not the "curse" it

The Manes (soul) kneeling beside a pool in Amenta receiving water from Hathor, goddess of the sycamore tree.

came to be in the later patriarchal period when strict taboos surrounded the female and her period. Instead, it was a momentous celebrated occasion because it meant that a new life-bringer was being added to the community. Gerald Massey affirms that the periodic menses of the female were early man's first time-keeper, before he began to look to the heavenly bodies for temporal-reckoning.[14] Eventually, the moon, with its changing phases over a 29½-day period, became a celestial calendar linked to the menstrual cycle because of their seeming co-incidence. So the moon, like so much else, was originally feminine, and in Egypt, was first identified with Hathor and Isis. But the woman, on account of her natural periodicity, is, as Newmann calls her, "a type of time": she creates time and is the first guardian of time.[15]

The night especially belongs to the feminine sphere and in this epoch was not the source of dread and fear that characterizes it at a later stage of consciousness. The sun, on its part, was not the beneficent Power that it was in the later patriarchal era, for in equatorial Africa, the burning solar heat brings thirst, dessication, and death. The sun was seen thus as anti-human. This ancient attitude persists; the Nuer of the southern Sudan declare that the Devil resides in the sun.[16] Among the dynastic Egyptians, the god Set, the Archenemy, personified the power of drought, the desert, and the scorching heat of the sun. The Egyptian term SET could mean "burning," "fire," or "rays of the sun."[17] In this primeval time, the power of the sun was not venerated, and the tree figured so powerfully in early symbolism because its leaves and branches, in addition to providing fruit, protected against the deathly rays of the sun.

The passage of time was first measured in nights rather than days, a habit of time-reckoning that persists in our "fortnight" of 15 days. It is also reflected in our "equinox," the mid-point of the sun's ecliptic path, which actually means "equal night," in reference to the equality of day-light and dark at this juncture. Our 24-hour "day" actually begins at the deepest, darkest hour of the night, 12 o'clock midnight. These are all remnants of the matriarchal epoch, where the night was the unit of time measurement.

The supremacy of the feminine principle is also seen in the pre-eminence of the left side, almost unquestionably due to the position of the heart on the left-side of the body. The heart, being the source of blood, and therefore of life itself, would naturally be feminine and maternal.[18] In ancient Egyptian iconography, since the left side was the "life" side, living figures were always depicted striding with the left foot

Hathor in the Heaven-Tree providing the deceased with food and drink.

forward. On the other hand, anthropologists feel that human beings have been predominantly right-handed for many millenia, based on the traumatic evidence of certain fossil skulls showing fractures preponderantly on the left side of the head. This would indicate that those delivering the blows were mostly right-handed. If this is the case, it means that in early times the relative symbolic pre-eminence of the left side was not ordained by actual handedness.

A "feminine mystique" even seemed to dominate what would ordinarily be considered masculine pursuits, i.e., hunting and war. We infer this from the powerful position of the goddesses of hunting and war in Egypt, Western Asia, and Greece. Erich Neumann attributes this to the power of the archetypal figure, the "Lady of the Beasts," who ruled over animals.[19] Indeed, female animals represented the super-human feminine archetypes who take the concrete shape of "totems." This perceived feminine power over animals would account for a special feminine archetype in the guise of a patronness of hunting. Because certain forms of the Mother were identified with carnivorous, predatory animals, she presided over death as well; it was this terrifying face of the Mother which made her a patronness of war.

Predynastic Upper Egyptian female figurines with the characteristic accentuation of the buttocks and thighs.

Such society as did exist among early humans coalesced around the mother and her children, that is, those who sprang from her and were of her blood. Primatologists have identified several types of ape and monkey societies described respectively as "dominant male," "age-graded male," and "multi-male" troops.[20] Though these troops are described in terms of the role and status of the males in the troops, what really stands out is that the true social core is always the females and their children. They are the real community, and though the males in various ways incorporate themselves and superficially dominate, the community is not really centered around them. A very similar arrangement must have characterized early hominid social groupings which, by the time *H. sapiens sapiens* appeared on the scene, would have evolved more or less completely into female-centered and female-dominated societies. Communal membership became determined by ties of blood, and since the blood relationship to the mother was the only demonstrable fact, these communities were necessarily mother-centered and mother-dominated.[21] The super-female types of nature, the lionness, the pythonness, the tree, etc., each became symbolic of the Motherhood of a particular bloodline or lineage. The mem-

Cow-eared Hathor, mother-consort of Horus and goddess of the sky; patron deity of love, marriage, and childbirth.

bers of the hippopotamus clan, the snake clan, or the tortoise clan would claim descent from totemistic animals who, in their female forms, were symbols of Motherhood. The human mother provided the blood, the totem animal the type, for the organization of early society. The emergence of totems brought forth the first taboos, which centered around food. The taboo could be of two types: (1) most commonly, a prohibition against eating the totem animal or (2) less commonly, a prohibition against eating any animal except the totem. As we will have occasion to see, this totemism was directly related to the primitive "eucharist."

We have already alluded to the four blood-mysteries of the woman. The first is the menstrual inundation transforming the pre-pubescent girl into the life-producing woman. The second is the binding up and cessation of menstrual flood in the pregnant state so that the "retained" blood can "nourish" the life germinating within the womb. The third mystery is the renewal of the inundation with the release of blood and water during childbirth. The fourth mystery is the final binding up and preservation of the blood through matrophagy. When the mother of old passed child-bearing age, she would often voluntarily give herself up to death to preserve herself from the ravages of old age, which would pose a tacit "ontological" threat to the bloodline. In death, she would be solemnly eaten by members of the lineage and thus re-united with it, so that the group as a whole could be fortified by the preserving of her blood within it. This was the original eucharist: the mother surrendering her body and blood in a "sacred" meal that her lineage might be renewed and preserved by her sacrifice. That this actually happened seems to be indicated by scenes from the so-called "Cannibal Hymns" from the Egyptian Pyramid Texts in which Unas is said to feast off the bodies of his mothers.[22] This is not to say that the dynastic Egyptians indulged in such a practice, but that they preserved as a religious metaphor actual events of a much earlier time. Right up to this century, anthropologists recorded customs among paleolithic peoples of ritual parricide. Taboos and myths are never rooted in anything imaginary, are never merely psychic emanations; they arise out of memories and concrete human experiences. The ancient Egyptians were not merely confabulating when they listed as one of the great achievements of Osiris his successful eradication of cannibalism in the parts of the world where he established his rule.[23]

In those cases where totem animals come to represent motherhood, they would be sacramentally eaten in place of the human mother. But the organization of human groups into totems was also the genesis of a primitive trading economy. Groups would exchange totem animals with each other for food purposes. Members of the Antelope Clan, for example, could exchange antelope, which they could not eat for hare from the Hare Clan which they could. The totem age persisted into historical and even modern times. All 42 Egyptian nomes (administrative units) maintained and venerated their totem animals long after Egypt had moved into the mainstream of history. Even modern nations proudly identify with a "totem" animal: the British Lion, the Russian Bear, the Chinese Dragon and the American Eagle to name but a few examples.

As we have already said, human societies crystallized around the figure of the mother and in this way were quite similar to the communal patterns already well-established among the higher primates. Communal living requires a certain ability to subordinate private needs and wants to the good of the collective. This "bioaltruism" is most highly developed among the females of nearly every mammalian species. The bearing, nurturing, protecting, and raising of offspring conditions the female to look after the wants and needs of those other than herself.[24] The evolution of the higher primates, in particular the hominids, has been characterized by an ever-longer period of infantile and childhood dependence. In humans, the process lasts at least 10 years, necessitated by the evolution of a more elaborate and complex nervous system. The altruism inherent in the maternal instinct would, through the demands of evolutionary adaptation, have to become highly developed in hominids as a survival mechanism, and would therefore have been bred into the female of the species. The long period of child nurturing would also put a high premium on female

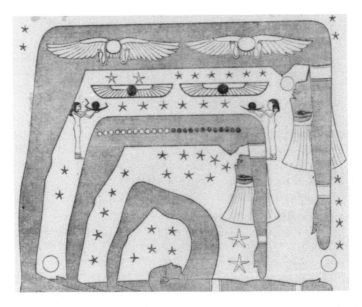

The sky-goddess Nut—the womb and tomb of the sun—overshadowing Geb, the earth-god.

co-operation, showing itself in food-sharing, baby-sitting and grooming, all social behaviors well-developed among the higher primates. Thus prima-tology strongly supports the presumption that it was the interaction of females and their young within the group, instead of male-female bonding, that formed the primary basis of the human community. It is, therefore, not too much to say that human society emerged first as a matriarchate out of the imperatives of biological evolution.

As we have seen, early human societies came to be defined by their boundaries along maternal blood lines through a system of totems. The blood relation as defined by the totem was the first means through which one lineage was discreted from another out of the primal "promiscuous horde," in Massey's phrase.[25] There was no fatherhood at this time be-cause the relationship between sex and procreation was not recognized. The children were born of the mother alone; they were, in Massey's phrase, "born but not begotten." Here is the first and primitive type of the "virgin" mother, the source of the concept found throughout all later pre-classical religions, culminating in Christianity. Here again, a "mythical" concept such as the virgin motherhood comes out of a real, primeval hu-man experience. Even after physiologic paternity became an established fact, the virgin mother concept persisted, though at another level of meaning. Nothing is ever lost, only forgotten.

The mother archetype dominates this primeval age; she is the archetype of humanity itself. As Thomas Huxley said, "For Paleolithic Man, every day was mother's day." This is a chthonic, concrete world, a world where all is contained in the Mother, a world without opposites or polarities. Abstrac-tions like Good and Evil do not exist. In psychoanalytic terms, it is a time when the unconscious still rules over the conscious, a time when instinct and archetype condition all that man does. The nascent light of "mascu-line" consciousness is enfolded like a babe in the arms of the dark, mater-nal unconscious. However, the Mother archetype does experience certain changes, for it undergoes a kind of mitosis by creating separate manifesta-tions of itself. Massey calls this the typology of the "the two mothers" which is virtually the same as the Jungian archetype of "the two sisters." If, as we think, early human societies followed the primate pattern of female-centered communities, the two-mothers/two-sisters archetypology may have been the natural expression of a society in which children al-ways had "multiple" mothers. This is seen in traditional African commu-nities today where all the women of a particular clan are referred to by the children as "mother," and this even allows young children to go to women not their biological mothers to suckle. The archetypology in this schema would be of two kinds: (1) mother and aunt or (2) mother and eldest daughter. The first is seen explicitly in Egyptian mythology in the persons of Isis and Nepthys, the former the mother of Horus and the latter his aunt, who nurture, protect and raise him safe from the depredations of Set, the Archenemy. In Greek mythology, the archetypology is depicted in Demeter and Persephone who are mother and daughter. The eldest daughter becomes a proxy for the mother as the "second" mother or "little" mother. In African villages, young children, after weaning, are turned over to their older sisters who keep them, watch over them, and feed them. These young children are often so attached to their elder sisters that they turn to them first when hungry or upset. The author himself witnessed this in a small village in Senegal.

Neumann points out that the dominance of the feminine/maternal archetype is equipotent in men and women, just as the later dominance of the father archetype equally influenced both sexes. Some of the staunchest defenders of matriarchal privilege during the periods of conflict with the militant patriarchate were, in fact, men.[26] Though we will examine the patriarchate more fully in the next chapter, we can devote some attention here to the role and position of the male in the matriarchate. Fundamental to understanding this is that, in the early matriarchate, there was no incest taboo. This is not hard to understand. If there is no realized connection between sex and procreation, there is no reason for there to be an incest taboo. Higher primates do not have any aversion to mating with close relatives and it is unlikely that any of the hominids, including the early humans, did either. Sex was a powerful, though inchoate, drive with as much impact on human behavior as hunger and thirst. Another way of saying this is that the human female does not have an estrus cycle. We can therefore infer that there must have been a time in human communities when sex was essentially promiscuous, indicative of the Masseyan "promiscuous horde." Sexual activity would have largely been determined by proximity. In the primate world, it is interesting to note that chimpanzees, our nearest non-human relatives, are the only apes living in multi-male troops in which sexual relations are promiscuous.[27] It has been suggested that this type of arrangement does not present a valid prototype for human sexual relations in light of male-dominant and male age-graded groups among the apes.[28] But since we are closer to the chimpanzee than any other ape, theirs might reasonably be the model for sexual relations in early human groups.

It would have been the mother and older sister(s) who initiated the males of the group into sex. The first consort pair, therefore, would have been the mother and the son, before there ever was a notion of fatherhood.[29] The myths of all lands support this assertion for they are very explicit in depicting in one form or another a primal mother-son consort pair. Ancient Egyptian religion offers a most instructive example. All of the important male deities in the Egyptian pantheon have the epithet KAMUTEF attached to their names. The word KAMUTEF means literally "bull of his mother." Each one of them is also styled "he who is his own father." This concept is echoed also in the religion of the Dogon of Mali, where "Original Sin" is committed by the jackal (or fox), the first Son of the World Mother, through his sexual congress with her, which brings discord into the world.[30] Now this Dogon jackal, Ogo, is one and the same as the Egyptian jackal-god Anubis, an early form of Set, one of the earliest of the Kamitic* male deities. Osiris is another case in point. According to Plutarch, Osiris is the husband of his sister Isis and the father of Horus.[31] He also has the title Kamutef, the full implication of which is revealed through an analysis of his name: in Egyptian Osiris is ASAR or USIR. Broken down into its component parts, we have AS(US) AND AR(IR). AS is the diminutive form of AST, the Egyptian name of Isis, and AR or IR means "created" or "beget."[32] Thus the name ASAR literally means "begotten of Isis," making Osiris a type of the son of Isis while also being her consort. What makes this even more interesting is that Set, the great archenemy of Osiris, is an even more ancient type of son-consort to Isis than is Osiris. His name in Egyptian is ST which also derives from the Egyptian name of Isis, AST.[33] Isis is sometimes rendered simply as ST, which is identical to the Egyptian form of Set's name. We will have cause to deal further with this ancient Kamitic "menage-a-trois." Myriad other examples of this primordial mother-son consortship could be adduced from the mythologies of the world. In Greek mythology, Uranus is the consort of the World-Mother.[34] By the time world-mythologies were absorbed into various religions, mother-son incest had long since been tabooed, but the fact of its early existence was preserved in these otherwise incomprehensible tales.

After the incest taboo between mother and son had been established—and it is now the most powerful universal taboo in the world—the brother-sister dyad took its place. This evolved more or less naturally from the mother-daughter archetypology of the Two Mothers and derives from the role of the eldest daughter as an extension or proxy of the mother. Like the mother-son consortship, examples of divine or mythic brother-sister marriages abound throughout the world and the consortship of Isis and Osiris is the known prototype. As we have seen, in an earlier phase Isis had been the mother, but in the historical period, she assumes the role of the divine sister who is married to her equally divine brother, Osiris. In Greek mythology, Kronos is married to his sister Rhea and Zeus to his sister Hera. In the Old Testament, Abram is married to his half-sister Sarai.

---

* "Kamitic," derived from the Egyptian word meaning "Black Land," is descriptive of the entire northeast African, and even African Great Lakes, culture complex, which, of course, includes Egypt.

On the sociological plane, the typology of the brother-sister consort pair was represented in a widespread pattern of rulership. The outstanding example is the Nile pharaonocracy wherein the male pharaoh routinely married his sister, the Great Royal Wife, through whom the royal succession passed. Even the Macedonian Ptolemies overcame their repugnance to incest to adopt this form of pharaonic marriage. The brother-sister marriages among the ancient kings of the Incas and old Hawaii are two other examples of a common practice dating from proto-historical times. The Dogon of Mali say that the brother-sister marriage is ideal since it represents the form of marriage of the eight celestial ancestors.[35] The Dogon themselves do not actually practice brother-sister marriage, but prospective marriage partners do undergo certain ceremonies that establish a symbolic brother-sister relation. This mythically ideal marriage is the reason why the Dogon favor cross-cousin marriages where a man marries a woman from his mother's lineage. Since the bride comes from his natal lineage, she is automatically considered his "sister."[36]

The oldest and most powerful sexual taboo is that of mother-son incest; the prohibition against brother-sister marriages came later. For a long

The cow-headed Isis pouring a libation to the soul of Osiris rising as a man-headed hawk from plants growing in a sacred lake.

time royal houses were exempt from this latter prohibition because of their "divine" status. This meant, particularly where ritual obligations were concerned, that they were not subject to ordinary human constraints. Again, taboos did not arise from imaginary fears or a nameless dread, in classic Freudian fashion, but out of a need to control and regulate certain kinds of behaviors for the good of the group. Intrafamilial conjugal relations were assuredly practiced without shame in early human pre-history. The idea of incest, with the rules and regulations that grew up around it, came into being only as man's expanding awareness taught him the physiologic facts of nature.

It seems likely that the essential elements of advanced human culture were discovered or invented under the matriarchate. It was the Motherhood that surely first instituted taboos and laws to govern human behavior. Largely this involved a long-term project of taming, acculturating, and civilizing the male. As mistress of the hearth, it was she who controlled the fire and its uses. As food-gatherer, the woman would have discovered the utility of woven baskets as containers and later, of fire-baked clay pots to collect, store, and preserve food and water. She would have been the clan's first maker of animal skin cloaks and then fabrics of bark, felt and flax. Thus the important handicrafts that ultimately led to industry and civilization would have originally resided in the feminine domain. Everything in the ancient iconography proclaims this. In Africa, hand-made pottery was, and is, the exclusive province of women and whenever pottery remains are found in human shape, they are invariably female. Only when the potter's wheel is invented do men take a hand in ceramics, finally turning it into an industry.[37] Basket-weaving, too, was and is almost exclusively a feminine craft. We know that cloth-weaving was a feminine task both from surviving ancient scenes as well as representations of the Egyptian goddess Neith, the patronness of weaving. Her Egyptian name NET means "to weave." The word NET also means "that which is" or "being" so that Neith as NET is quite literally "the fabric of existence."[38] There was a famous inscription over the door of the Temple of Neith at Sais that said, "I am all that is, has been, and shall be. No mortal shall lift my veil." This inscription confirms the supposition that Neith, as NET, is the "veil of existence," a meaning inherent in her very name. Athene, the Greek goddess of weaving, was identified with her.

The greatest single invention in the history of civilization and the very thing that made it possible was agriculture. The ability to cultivate grains at seasonal intervals was probably the most decisive step in freeing mankind from the absolute, immediate grip of nature. It made possible settled communities, food surpluses, population expansion, occupational diversification, and acquisition of specialized knowledge to boost productivity. Agriculture had to have been a female invention. It was the woman who collected most of the grains, seeds, roots, berries, and plants for the group's nutritional consumption and millenia of observing how seeds sprout when they spill onto the ground would have gradually led to purposeful cultivation. This may have occurred as early as 15,000 B.C.E. in northeast Africa.[39] In Africa, the fields still belong to and are cultivated by the women. In ancient Egypt, fields were passed down from mother to daughter and were the source of their considerable social and economic independence. Mythology, as usual, is instructive, for the earliest grain or corn deities are invariably female, of whom the Egyptian Isis and the Greek Demeter are outstanding examples.

If the figure of the Egyptian goddess Sesheta is any indication, women may have even presided over the beginnings of writing. The attributes of this patron deity of writing powerfully suggest a female provenance for this profoundly important skill. Originally pictographic, writing would have arisen out of the function of art as language. The marvelous examples of Paleolithic cave art found in Africa and Europe demonstrate the tendency of early man to identify the thing with its representation, thus extending human "control" over the environment. Diop described the process by which the paleolithic hunter would pantomine the hunt in ritualistic dances to symbolically and spiritually "kill" the animal prior to the hunt itself.[40] Art arose as a technique to maximize hunting success and minimize danger. Early dance, music, sculpture, and painting arose out of a need to recreate life in order to better understand and control it, making art, in its various forms, a language. It was not a long step from there to using conventionalized artistic forms as glyphs. We do not know when writing per se appeared, though a formal system of pictographic writing was already in place in Egypt by 4200 B.C. and in Nubia 300 years before that.[41] Remarkably, Egyptian hieroglyphics retained their pictographic character down to the end of Egyptian history, a period of 4,000 years. Though other writing forms developed in Egypt, the cursive hieratic and demotic, hieroglyphs were reserved for all ceremonial and sacred inscriptions. They are the surest keys to Egypt's psycho-mytho-historical ethos and we may presume that they, too, were legacies of the matriarchate. Pictographic writing was another of the cornerstones of civilization laid down when the matriarchate governed the southern cradle.

In the previously-considered totemic phase of culture, the totem animal became the proxy for the human mother as a species of eucharistic sacrifice. This did not mean the end of human sacrifice, however. The advent of agriculture seems to have had the effect of intensifying the dominance of the matriarchy and bringing another type of human sacrifice into prominence. As we have seen, the overwhelming dominance of the female and the mother in the early agrarian age probably arose from two circumstances: (1) agriculture as a female invention and (2) the feminine character of the earth and its vegetation. Thus, the feminine maternal domination of early human culture seemed to have derived from the perceived female character of nature and its secret, awesome, and terrifying forces. Thus we re-iterate that birth, life, death, and re-birth, all mediated through the female, were tied to blood and its attendant mysteries. In this configuration, death was never an annihilation but a prefigurement of new life, and therefore the indispensible element connecting life and death in a perpetual cycle. This was the reason for the ancient end-of-life self-sacrifice of the mother; with the advent of the agricultural revolution, the blood mysteries would be transferred to a new life mode. But the new sacrificial victim was to be none other than the mother's son-consort.

It is not known when the role of the male in procreation was finally discovered, but as in all other things, nature would have been the first teacher. Gradually, the connection between copulation, impregnation, and parturition was recognized. In the beginning, this did little or nothing to enhance the status of the male because it was overshadowed by the profound changes wrought by agriculture, totally under the dominance of the woman which ensured by her control of "earth magic." Possibly, the fact of physiologic procreation was not discovered until after the agricultural revolution was in full swing in the southern cradle, but one consequence of this new factor in human affairs was the gradual insinuation of masculine symbolism into the myths and religions of early agricultural societies. Thus the principle of fecundation and growth would come to have a specifically masculine character. However, from the male point of view, there was a terrible consequence: selected males from within the society would be impelled into a role not at all unlike those of male insects whose sole purpose is to fertilize the queen-mother of the hive and then, the purely phallic role fulfilled, die or be killed. Thus, at regular intervals, a carefully-selected son-consort from within the clan would fecundate the clan mother, then be killed and torn to pieces so that his flesh and blood could be strewn over the fields in a rite of fertilization. This, then, was the primitive "sacred king" whose duty it was to fecundate the mother, then voluntarily submit to death and dismemberment so that his body and blood could ensure the growth of the crops upon which the entire community depended. This would also involve castration because, symbolically, the phallus of the sacred king "belonged" to the Mother as the necessary instrument of her fecundation. Thus, at this stage, the sacred king, or son-consort, had little existence apart from his role as the "bearer" of the phallus, in reality the Mother's "possession."

As Neumann relates, the sacred king, was a simulacrum of the wheat that grew to ripeness, ejected its seed, was mowed down, ploughed under, and then reborn as the new wheat of Spring.[42] His sacrifice was the prefigurement of his own resurrection, tangibly experienced in the new sprouts of Spring. His "body" was eaten as the bread made out of grain from the field that his flesh and blood had fertilized. So his sacrifice brought the sustenance of life to the entire community. The primordial eucharist had originally required the body and blood of the mother; here it is taken a step further by demanding a sacrifice of the youthful sacred king who is the "bread of life." This transformation is an arresting example of what Gerald Massey calls the "natural genesis," a tangible human practice, belief, or custom emanating from the experience of nature and being preserved in the highly refined doctrines of the later "revealed" religions.[43]

We have seen that in the matriarchal phase, the Mother is creator, nurturer, and preserver; but she is also the destroyer of the sacred king. Life issues from her and returns to her at burial by re-entering the original earth-womb out of which all things came. The Mother is at once the source of awe, adoration, and terror. She gives life, nourishment, protection, and pleasure so all that makes life worth living comes from her. But life also returns to her and she is Death incarnate. Life is hers to take as necessary for the good and well-being of the group, which she embodies completely. The Mother is the one thing that seems permanent and un-

Isis in her "negative" aspect as the scorpion-goddess Serqet.

changing through all the permutations of life so she is often figured as the rock or mount, the image of permanence. But in her deathly aspect, she destroys, dismembers, and devours: the maw of death to which all things return. Her womb is the tomb. Since the phallus belongs to her, she appropriates it for her own fertilization which is indispensible for the fertility and growth of the community. Thus she is also the "castrator." In the guise of the "terrible Mother," she takes on the hideous aspect of such zootypes as the crocodile, the snake, the lionness, and other carnivorous female animals. Or, she will be a composite of several such animals. In the Bible, the devouring Mother is preserved as Leviathan, the whale that swallowed Jonah.

All of these facets of the primordial Mother and her relationship with the sacred king, her Son-Consort, are preserved in Egyptian mythology, most prominently in the Osiris cycle.[44] We have already seen that Osiris is the son of Isis to whom he is also the consort. Plutarch relates that it was he who taught men agriculture; he is identified with grain and all vegetable matter in its growing aspect. He is also the full moon, the celestial image of the sacred king in all of his youthful splendor before he submits to death. He is killed by Set, who is merely the negative masculine image of Isis (Aset), and cut up into fourteen pieces, a reference to the fourteen waning phases of the moon.

In a subtext of the myth, he is placed in a coffin and floated out upon the river, but when it lands in Byblos, a tree grows up around the coffin, symbolic of the resurrection of Osiris in new plant life whether as the grain or the tree. It is Isis who looks for the dismembered parts of Osiris, gathers them together, and then reconstitutes his body except for the phallus, which is never found because it has been swallowed by a fish. Instead, Isis fashions an artificial phallus which she re-invigorates. She fans the breath of life back into his body and after reviving him, impregnates herself with the phallus, eventually giving birth to Horus, who is but Osiris re-born. In this mythos, we can readily discern the mother-son consortship, the sacrifice and dismemberment of the son-consort (sacred king) in the prime of life, his resurrection in growing plant life (tree), the reconstitution of the dead body of the sacred king by the Mother who presides over his rebirth, and the appropriation of the phallus by the Mother herself.

Egyptian inconography corroborates everything related in Plutarch's narrative. One scene shows stalks of grain emerging out of the inert body of Osiris, emblematic of his identification with the grain and his resurrection through its renewed growth. Numerous other scenes show Isis fashioning and impregnating herself with the phallus of Osiris. That Osiris is linked with lunar imagery is also demonstrated by various iconographic forms depicting him with the lunar crescent carrying the full moon upon his head. The Tet cross, called the "backbone of Osiris," is but the conventionalized image of the tree which, as Plutarch relates, grew up around his coffin. Then, of course, the epithet that applies to him, KAMUTEF, i.e., "Bull of his Mother," confirms his consortship with his mother.

Though in dynastic times, Isis seemed to display a completely benign character, traces of her "terrible" aspect persisted. This aspect is manifested indirectly through Set, the negative masculine image of Isis and the actual murderer and dismemberer of Osiris. In essence, Set, in the historical period, functions as a kind of proxy for the Mother, i.e., Isis. That she is not altogether ill-disposed to Set is clear when she sets him free after Horus, her son by Osiris, has defeated and bound him.[45] Isis is also manifested as the scorpion goddess Serqet and it is a scorpion which stings and kills the child Horus, the re-incarnated Osiris, whom Isis then revives with her magic powers. We might also note, in this connection, that the death of Osiris occurs in the season of harvest, under the sign of Scorpio. This fatal element in the character of Isis is further revealed in the Ra cycle when, seeking the secret name of Ra, Isis causes a viper to sting him, bringing him close to death, in order to extract the secret and impose her power over him. In historical times, the terrible and beneficent aspects of the Mother Goddess became incarnated in separate forms, so that instead of one great Mother figure embodying all the forces of life, several goddesses emerged, each manifesting one of her various aspects.

The Terrible Mother can be found in many guises in Egyptian myth. The composite female monster Ammit, literally "Devourer of the Dead," consumed the unjustifed souls in the Judgement Scene in the *Book of the Dead.* The lion-headed goddess Sekhmet, also depicted as Hathor, ravened through the impious human race at the command of Ra and became so intoxciated with the blood of the slaughtered, that humanity was on the verge of annihiliation until Ra assuaged her thirst with beer. She is the deified feminine aspect of the dry heat of the desert as well as the sexual fire, therefore exhibiting an erotic component. Ta-Urt, one of the very oldest of Egyptian deities, was a hippopotamus goddess having a mixed character, sometimes beneficent, sometimes dreaded. Her son and consort is invariably Set who, among his many other types, is also the male hippopotamus deity. Finally, there is the Archenemy of all, the most dreaded of all evil powers, Apep, the dragon of darkness, originally female and later male.

Many practices, customs, and beliefs exemplifying the matriarchal phase of human history are, to say the least, disconcerting to modern sensibilities. We inevitably recoil from anything we deem incestuous or inhumane. But these elements of culture constitute a phase in the struggle of human beings to cope with the world: to understand it, to give it coherence, and to exercise some control over it. The matriarchate was a time when the moral polarization that we take for granted did not exist; all things intermingled in a monistic maternal totality. It was a world still closely connected to nature and the instincts; ritual human sacrifice and cannibalism would not have been perceived as reprehensible, but *de rigueur.* However horrible such customs may seem to us, they grew out of and helped define the rhythm of life. The only good was survival and perpetuation, the only evil was unfitness.

In our own age, we have witnessed men by the millions willingly sacrificing themselves on the battlegrounds and killing fields of ideology. The periodic ritual killings of sacred kings of old seem rather paltry by comparison. Natural symbolism ruled the mental universe of archaic humanity, just as ideology rules ours today, and there was a rigorous *internal* logic behind the primitive eucharistic sacrifice. Indeed, many modern religions are built around just this same principle of sacrifice, however much we have substituted the abstract symbol for the naturalistic one. If we are to understand the natural, psychic, cultural, and historical forces that shaped humanity, we must to a certain extent rethink some of our modern preconceptions. We like to think that we have morally evolved beyond the sanguinary rites of the past, but perhaps we have just substituted more sanguinary ones.

The matriarchal dominance in the millenia leading to the historical period was all-encompassing, but within it lay seeds of an evolution that led by degrees to the emergence of a triumphant patriarchy. With the patriarchy came the inevitable reaction. We must not lose sight of the fact that the Great Mother prepared the way for modern civilization which, in fact, emerges first in the matriarchates of the southern cradle. By the dawn of history, these matriarchates, in northeast Africa at least, had tamed and sublimated certain of man's rawest instincts and had surmounted its own excesses. That this did not happen sufficiently elsewhere would lead, by degrees, to the overthrow of the matriarchy around the world.

Glossary

Archetypes: A Jungian term describing forms extant in the psychic unconscious that serve as templates of universal human symbols. These are manifest in dreams, visions, and myths.

Archetypology: A term coined here to denote the fusion of the Jungian "archetype" with the Masseyan "typology." They are but the inner and outer expressions, respectively, of the same idea.

Aurignacian: A pre-historic cultural period extending roughly from 40–25,000 B.C.E. The Grimaldi (Khoisan/Twa) African racial type dominates this period.

Autochthones: The original inhabitants of a place.

Cro-Magnon: A proto-Caucasoid race that evolved either in south-western Russia or southern France out of the earlier Grimaldis. The name is derived from the French town near the locus of the original fossil specimen.

Eucharist: As used here, it refers to the ingestion of the body of a sacrificial victim, whether human or animal, to absorb its life force and "divine" potency, thereby experiencing renewal.

Feminine Mystique: As used here, this phrase applies to the power and fascination of everything connected with the female.

Grimaldi: A group of early human inhabitants of Europe derived from the Khoisan stock, now limited to marginal habitats in southern Africa. The original fossil specimens of this stock were unearthed in what is now Monaco, the principate in the Grimaldi family.

Khoisan: The correct name for a group of southern African peoples otherwise known as the "Bushmen-Hottentot" peoples. Today, they are most characteristically represented by the !Kung of the Kalahari whose phenotype evinces a yellow-brown complexion, peppercorn hair, diminutive stature, dolichocephalic skulls, and steatopygy in the women. They and the Twa ("Pygmies") are the remnants of the oldest *Homo sapiens* on earth.

Matriarchy/Matriarchate: A socio-cultural system characterized by the pre-eminence of the mother (and women) in familial, social, political, and religious affairs.

Patriarchy/Patriarchate: A socio-cultural system defined by the dominance of the father (and men) in familial, social, political, and religious affairs.

Proto-history: The transitional period from pre-history to history proper—recorded history—between 8,000–4,500 B.C.E.

Sacred King: The human personification of the divine masculine principle whose original role was to be sacrificed at harvest time, then be reborn in the rites attending the new crop, thus signalling the rebirth of the community.

Taboo: Any act forbidden because of fear of divine or spiritual retribution capable of affecting both clan and individual.

Totem: A natural entity—plant or animal—that is emblematic of a family or clan and is mythically a figuration of the clan's original ancestor.

Typology: Gerald Massey's term for the plants, animals, and other phenomena of nature that in human prehistory came to be the visible expressions of certain cosmic powers and attributes. In Massey's view, these constituted man's first symbols.

Notes

1. Bachofen JJ, *Myth, Religion, and Mother-right*, translated by Ralph Mannheim, Princeton: Princeton University Press, 1973.
2. See Trimingham JS, *A History of Islam in West Africa*, New York: Oxford University Press, 1962, p. 52, for a quotation from the Arab traveler al-Bakri, describing the matrilineal royal succession in 11th-century Ghana.
3. Diop CA, *The Cultural Unity of Black Africa*, Chicago: Third World Press, 1978.
4. Williams L and Finch CS, "The Great Queens of Ethiopia," in *Black Women in Antiquity*, edited by Ivan Van Sertima, New Brunswick: Journal of African Civilizations, Ltd., 1948, p. 24.

5. Hansberry WL, *Africa and Africans as Seen by Classical Writers*, edited by Joseph E. Harris, Washington, D.C.: Howard University Press, 1977, passim. Thales, Pythagoras, Anaximander, Solon, Plato, Appolonius of Tyana, and Galen are just a few of the Greeks who studied among the sages of Egypt.

6. Diop, op. cit., pp. 55–112.

7. Graves R, *Greek Myths*, Volume I, New York: Penguin Books, 1955, 1970, pp. 11–20. In his Introduction, Graves provides a succinct and edifying account of the matriarchy in early Greece.

8. See Higgins G, *Anacalypsis*, Volume I, New Hyde Park: University Press, 1965, pp. 342–3.

9. See Note 49 in Chapter I, supra. That these female statuettes represent the Khoisan type is indicated by the characteristic peppercorn hair and the steatopygy depicted. Because it evokes maternal abundance and fecundity, feminine obesity is invariably indicative of a mother type in Paleolithic art.

10. Massey G, *Book of Beginnings*, London: Williams and Norgate, 1881; *Natural Genesis*, London: Williams and Norgate, 1883; *Ancient Egypt*, New York: Samuel Weiser, 1970.

11. Massey, *Ancient Egypt*, op. cit., p. 39.

12. Malinowski B, *The Sexual Life of Savages in Northwestern Melanesia*, London: Routledge & Kegan Paul, 1929, pp. 2–7.

13. Graves, op. cit., p. 27.

14. Massey, *Natural Genesis*, Volume II, op. cit., pp. 269–74.

15. Neumann E, *The Great Mother: An Analysis of an Archetype*, translated by Ralph Mannheim, Princeton: Princeton University Press, 1955, 1974, pp. 226–7.

16. An attitude of avoidance and even antagonism toward the sun among Nilotic peoples is strongly suggested in Nuer and Shilluk tradition. Cf. Evans-Pritchard EE, *Nuer Religion*, New York: Oxford University Press, 1956, 1974, p. 81; also, Lienhardt G, "The Shilluk of the Upper Nile," in *African Worlds*, edited by D. Forde, London: Oxford University Press, 1956, 1974, pp. 148–9.

17. See Budge EAW, *An Egyptian Hieroglyphic Dictionary*, Volume II, New York: Dover Publications, Inc., 1920, 1978, pp. 628; 653.

18. In Chapter 30 of the funerary ritual, Osiris says, "My heart, my mother; my heart, my mother. My heart of my existence on earth." Budge EAW, *The Book of the Dead*, New York: E.P. Dutton & Co., 1928, p. 146.

19. Neumann, op. cit., pp. 268–80.

20. Birdsell JB, *Human Evolution*, Boston: Houghton Mifflin Co., 1972, 1981, pp. 183–5.

21. Massey, *Ancient Egypt*, op. cit., pp. 61; 69.

22. Cited in Budge EAW, *From Fetish to God in Ancient Egypt*, London: Oxford University Press, 1934, p. 323.

23. See quote from Diodorus cited in Budge EAW, *Osiris: The Egyptian Religion of Resurrection*, New Hyde Park: University Books, 1961, p. 9.

24. Cf. Bachofen, op. cit., p. xxxi and Briffault R, *The Mothers*, New York: The MacMillan Co., 1927, p. 145.

25. See Massey, op. cit., pp. 47–109, passim. Bachofen was the first among antiquarians to postulate a generalized promiscuity among early human groups.

26. The conflicts that arose between the traditional matrilineal succession, favoring the maternal nephew, and the new Islamic patrilineal succession, favoring the biological son, are eloquently explored in Senegalese history by the film maker Ousmane Sembene in "Ceddo."

27. See Birdsell, op. cit., p. 185.

28. Ibid.

29. Massey, op. cit., p. 59.

30. Griaule M, *Conversations With Ogotemmeli*, New York: Oxford University Press, 1965, 1975, pp. 21–2.

31. See Plutarch's "Of Osiris and Isis," reprinted in Mead GRS, *Thrice Greatest Hermes*, London: John Watkins, 1949, pp. 255–368.

32. Budge, ... *Hieroglyphic Dictionary*, op. cit., pp. 68; 83. The Egyptian name for Osiris is given hieroglyphically as:

The upper glyph is the "seat" or "throne" whose literal meaning is AST, the Egyptian name of Isis. The bottom glyph is the "eye" which translates as AR or IR, meaning "create" or "beget." Thus Osiris' name in Egyptian is ASAR, meaning "begotten of Isis."

33. Ibid., Volume II, pp. 633; 707.

34. Graves, op. cit., Volume I, p. 37.

35. Griaule M and Dieterlen G, "The Dogon," in Forde, *African Worlds*, op. cit., p. 90.

36. Ibid., pp. 91–3. A similar system of cross-cousin marriages designed to foster a "brother-sister" linkage exists among the Trobriand Islanders. Cf. Malinowski, op. cit., pp. 80–4.

37. The divine creator-figures in ancient Egypt, Ptah and Khnum, employed the potter's wheel to fashion, respectively, the World Egg and individual human beings. See Budge EAW, *Gods of the Egyptians*, New York: Dover Publications, Inc., 1904, 1969, Volume I, p. 499 and Volume II, p. 50.

38. Capra F, *The Tao of Physics*, Berkeley: Shambhala, 1975, pp. 138–9; 203. The author gives a clear-sighted description of how the idea of a cosmic "fabric" or "web" has entered into quantum physics.

39. Fred Wendorf was the first to propose a 17,000 B.C.E. date for the invention of agriculture in Africa. Wendorf first found grinding stones older than 10,000 B.C.E. and then cultivated grains originally dated at 15–16,000 B.C.E. Further testing failed to support dates that old for Nile Valley cultigens. Wendorf still believes in a date older than 10,000 B.C.E. for the beginning of Nile Valley agriculture but this rests now on the existence of grinding stones of that age rather than actual cultigens. See Wendorf F, "An Ancient Harvest on the Nile," reprinted in *Blacks in Science*, edited by Ivan Van Sertima, New Brunswick: Journal of African Civilizations, Ltd., 1983, pp. 58–64; also, Desruisseaux P, "The Archaeological Revolution That Wasn't," *The Chronicle of Higher Education*, Nov. 16, 1983.

40. Diop CA, *Civilization ou Barbarie*, Paris: Presence Africaine, 1981, p. 10.

41. See Williams B, "Lost Pharaohs of Nubia," reprinted in *Nile Valley Civilizations*, edited by Ivan Van Sertima, New Brunswick: Journal of African Civilizations, Ltd., 1985, pp. 29–43. In this watershed article, which rocked conventional Egyptology, the author describes recently-discovered artifacts that prove the existence of a pharaonic Nubian dynasty 300 years before the first Egyptian dynasty.

42. Neumann E, *The Origins and History of Consciousness*, translated by Ralph Mannheim, Princeton: Princeton University Press, 1954, 1973, p. 49.

43. Gerald Massey devotes both volumes of *Natural Genesis* to an explanation of how the first natural types generated the more rarified religious symbols of later ages.
44. Cf. Plutarch's version of the Osiris myth (Note 31). Though Plutarch was a Greek, writing in the first century A.C.E., his version is almost entirely corroborated by monumental inscriptions.
45. Budge, *From Fetish to God...* , op. cit., pp. 450–1.

III

The Emergence of the Patriarchy: Paradigm of "Becoming"

The material that we have brought forward from anthropology, mythology, and archaeology points to the primacy of the matriarchy, hence the woman, in early human affairs. There is a certain poetic logic in the finding that the oldest hominid fossil yet discovered, Donald Johanson's "Lucy," is that of a female. But the logic of the mitochondrial DNA studies of Rebecca Cann, pointing to a single female living in East Africa 200–140,000 years ago as the first identifiable *Homo sapiens sapiens* ancestor, is a higher poetry yet. The Aurignacian Venus figurines, depicting Khoisan mother-types, demonstrate the pre-eminent position of women even in the northern cradle in the latter half of the Upper Paleolithic period, one maintained in most of the world down into historical times.[1] All bias aside, the evidence available points conclusively to the matriarchy as the first mode of human culture, society, government, and religion; of necessity, the patriarchate would have arisen out of it. In the realm of religious cosmogony, this all-encompassing matriarchate is figured as the primeval uterine darkness from which all things emerged and to which even a staunchly patriarchal deity such as Zeus was bound to pay deference.[2] The Jungian analyst, Erich Neumann, has clarified the links between this mother-cosmos and the expansion of consciousness that took place with the emergence of solar symbolism in religion and the rise of the patriarchate.[3] In all the world's creation myths, light is said to be born from and out of the primal dark and this is the archetype and allegory of the process that Neumann describes.

As we have shown, the realization that the male contributed to procreation through sexual congress at first did little to enhance his position. It may have actually given some impetus for a time to incestuous marriage as a mode of promoting the blood "purity" of the clan. The phallus had to be appropriated by the Mother because she controlled all fertility, all gestation, all birth, all life, all death. At periodic intervals, now, the son-consort/sacred king submitted to sacrifice and dismemberment in the process of giving up his life-force and his phallus, the instrument of that life-force, so that the fertility and survival of both crops and clan could be assured.[4] Though this was a willing sacrifice, it must be said that at this stage, the son-consort hardly had any existence apart from his phallus, whose sole purpose was to fertilize the clan Mother. Mythology, history and archaeology abound with example. The Osiris cycle is the prototype of this early phenomenology and finds its echo in many lands. In the myth of Cybele from Asia Minor, Attis serves as the sacrificial sacred king who unsexes himself, dies, and then is dismembered as a mode of giving up his flesh, especially the phallus, and blood to the Mother. Reborn as a pine tree, he shows himself to be the same type as Osiris, who was, in effect, reborn in the tree that grows up around his coffin.[5] In actual fact, the male priests of Cybele did emasculate themselves to re-enact the sacrifice of Attis and assimilate themselves to him. In old Mexico, Aztec priests also emasculated themselves as a sacrifice to their terrible Mother-Goddess who, to be placated, demanded an almost unending stream of bloody human sacrifices. There are references in the Old Testament to Hebrew men who, forsaking Yahweh, became priests of the Great Goddess

The Kendake, Shenakdakhete, ruler of Meroe (Cush), with her son and heir.

and castrated themselves as part of their initiation.[6] In archaic sites in southern Europe, Western Asia, Africa, and India, sacred phallic images abound. It was initially assumed that they represented merely an exaltation of the masculine principle but deeper investigation has shown instead that they belong to the matriarchal cycle of worship. They are images of the phallus that fertilizes the Mother and so belong to her.

The various stages in the evolution of the matriarchate and its eventual transition into the patriarchate do not correspond to discrete chronological eras. In Egypt, for example, there is preserved a record of the transition, but an equilibrium was reached that makes Egypt almost unique in antiquity. On the other hand, some later cultures like Crete, show distinctly archaic matriarchal features with few compromises. Crete, the transitional culture between Africa and Europe, remained stoutly matriarchal down to the Mycenaean invasions of the 12th century B.C., long after its mentor, Egypt, had undergone a modicum of patriarchal transformation. Cush, the parent culture of the Nile Valley, was like Crete in maintaining a markedly matriarchal cast down to the end of its history in 300 C.E. The Aztecs, even to the time of Cortez, had retained distinctly matriarchal elements as is seen in their notorious obeisance to the Terrible Goddess. Among the Indians of North America as well as in Africa, India, and the Pacific Islands, matriarchal and patriarchal societies existed side-by-side into the 20th century. Contrariwise, the Indo-European tribes of Central Asia were already mostly patriarchal when they first enter history around 1800 B.C.E. as barbarian hordes who swept down in waves on settled matriarchal cultures and civilizations in Asia and southern Europe.

The Indo-Europeans became patriarchal relatively early because their ecological circumstances were conducive to a comparatively rapid development of male-centered life-ways at the expense of matristic patterns. The ambience of the steppes fostered nomadic and pastoral life-styles, which favored the ascendancy of the aggressive masculine virtues over the feminine. It is worth pointing out that pastoral societies in Africa also show pronounced patriarchal traits, much more so than in settled agrarian communities.[7] The pastoral Masai of East Africa have been patriarchal for as long as can be remembered, in a culture that also puts an emphasis on hunting, herding, and raiding. The Masai, therefore, most admire the masculine qualities of physical bravery, strength, and fighting skill. Indeed, the pastoral mode of living seems to favor masculine values in either cradle. But in the southern cradle intensive agriculture firmly entrenched the matriarchate and the sustained onslaught of the patriarchates of historical times could never entirely dislodge it.

The social history of the early Hebrews illustrates these dynamics very clearly. When they passed from a nomadic, pastoral style to a settled, agrarian life, there commenced a long struggle between patriarchal and matriarchal modes of life. The settled Hebrews gravitated repeatedly toward the matriarchal lifeways of their Canaanite neighbors and the role of the prophets must be appreciated in that light. Over the centuries they kept urging the Israelites to hold fast to the canon of their "received" patriarchal, Yahwistic religion. This conflict and its perils are brought into sharp relief by the Hebrew women's response to Jeremiah's lugubrious diatribes—they coolly inform him that the Queen of Heaven, i.e., Astarte, had done more for them than Yahweh ever had.[8] The issue hung in the balance for nearly 600 years. Only the profound trauma of the Temple's destruction and the Babylonian Captivity decided it in favor of the exclusive fatherhood of Yahweh.

In the matriarchate, the male, though clearly the secondary sex, was not exactly a drone. He was, of course, essential for military security, hunting, and all manner of heavy labor. As the fecundator, he was indispensable. However, he was under the absolute sway of the Mother and unquestionably followed her dictates. He was too cowed by the forces of nature she seemed to control; by the magic and ritual she commanded. She was, after all, Life itself, and Death. But under the impulse of evolving human consciousness, this state of affairs could not last. Though the discovery of physiologic procreation did not immediately produce an enhancement of male status, it was still a turning point. The male could no longer be construed as peripheral to the central concerns of the community. Like it or not, the community could not exist without him.[9] Gradually, masculine symbols began to be integrated into the core of community life. A time would come when the continuing enhancement of male status, coupled with the leverage conferred by his physical prowess, would enlarge the male's perquisites in an other-wise female-dominated society. One of the earliest marks of these new prospects is the emergence of kingship by martial contest. This meant that the sacred king, instead of more or less passively submitting to a sacrificial death, could, at prescribed intervals, defend his position by combat or athletic contest against a rival. This was a mortal duel in which the loser, be he king or challenger, would become the sacrificial victim. If the king was victorious in this encounter, his rule was safe until he had to face another challenger at the end of the prescribed period.[10] This process put a premium on martial and athletic skills and the early kings would have been the most vigorous warriors in the community. Into recent historical times, rulers were expected to be warriors; many 20th century heads of state were soldiers first. This martial posture was so imbued in the Egyptian idea of kingship that some dynastic pharaohs were not above manufacturing battlefield exploits where none existed. Even female pharaohs, such as the Candaces or Kendakes of Cush, had themselves represented as warrior-queens.

The pervasiveness of kingship by combat and contest throughout pre-classical Greece has been explored by Robert Graves in his study of the Greek myths.[11] Hercules, Theseus, Jason, Perseus, Oedipus, and Odysseus are merely the best known of the Greek heroes who, as challengers or defenders, fought the fight or ran the race of the sacred king. The practice continued in the medieval custom of jousting. Even the gladiatorial contests of Rome were manifestations of this ancient ritual and, again, the prototype is found in the Osiris cycle with Set's murder of Osiris followed by the titanic battle between Set and Horus for the throne. As with the Great Mother before him, the sacred king's magical force, personifying the strength and vitality of the entire community, had to be preserved at all costs. Old age, disease, disability, or blemish in the king threatened the very existence of the community, so under these circumstances he had to be put to death. Naturally, an aging monarch would sooner or later succumb to the superior strength of a younger challenger. Even when kingship by combat had fallen into disuse, the magical character of the royal person still abided and he was expected to allow himself to be put to death when old age or infirmity supervened. Among the Yoruba, the secret, all-powerful Ogboni Society was in the habit of sending parrots' eggs to a king whom they felt had ruled long enough. The message of the parrots' eggs was: "You have ruled a long time and you must be tired. It's time for you to go to your rest." Upon receiving this message, the king had no choice but to opt for a graceful suicide.[12] This custom so constrained the kingship in Nigeria that, as C.A. Diop pointed out, there never was an abundance of candidates for the throne.[13] As recently as 1970, a hereditary Nigerian prince needed round-the-clock police protection against his subjects who felt that his life had lasted long enough for the good of the community.[14] In ancient Egypt, the pharaohs had managed to transcend the custom of ritual death, though they had undoubtedly yielded to it in earlier times, but they did submit to the Sed ritual every 30 years to restore the magical potency of their bodies, in which resided the strength of the nation.[15] The Zulu king Chaka's fear of gray hairs and other signs of aging was legendary, for this reason, and he periodically underwent rejuvenation rites similar to the Sed festivals.[16] The ancient kings of Cush were also known to go voluntarily to their deaths when requested by the priesthood and Diop has wryly observed that the despotism of Wolof kings dates from the beginning of the conversion to Islam, in which the ritual death of kings was outlawed. While such a practice is completely incompatible with modern sensibilities, it had the rather salutary effect of reigning in royal absolutism and its manifold abuses.

The next phase in the archetypal evolution of masculine consciousness was the emergence of a male twinship. The original twinship had been that of the Two Sisters, followed by the brother-sister consort pair person-

ified in Egypt first by Shu and Tefnut, created from Atum,and later by
Osiris and Isis. As we have seen, the brother-sister connubium became
important after the proscription of mother-son incest and therefore established as the mythical ideal of marriage. The next twinship type was that
of the Two Brothers and Neumann sees its emergence as a psychological
defense by which the male distinguished himself from the Mother.[17]
Graves calls this twin the "tanist," who is the alter ego of the sacred king
and succeeds him after his ritual sacrifice.[18] Massey sees the twinship as a
mode of "mapping" the divided halves of nature: dark and light, heaven
and earth, Upper Egypt and Lower Egypt. According to Massey, the twinning phenomenon began in man's primeval East African Great Lakes
home, at the headwaters of the Nile, where he first mapped the heavens.[19]
In this equatorial region, the seasons are perpetually equinoctal—day and
night are 12 hours long throughout the year. Moreover, the pole-stars are
not "above," but low on the northern and southern horizons. This means
that there is no one pole above but two "pegs," one in the north and one
in the South. This is early cosmic typology of twinship. Since the poles are
low on the horizons, heaven is said to be "close " to earth and this is
ideographed in Egypt as the skygoddess Nut locked in a tight embrace
with the earth-god Geb. The Dogon of Mali also speak of a time when
heaven was close to earth which also refers to the time when the first
ideographers were living in the equatorial regions of East Africa. Heaven is
"raised," so to speak, when these early ideographers migrated northward,
toward the lands from which the cooling breezes blew, all the while observing the northern pole star slowly rising upward. In Kamitic ideogra-
phy, the elevating of heaven is depicted as Shu lifting the heavenly Nut
up from the reclining earth-consort Geb. But the twinship appeared before this raising occurred, before the Afro-Kamitic ideographers migrated
northward from the Great Lakes. The twinship represented by the north
and south pillars is a typology which continued in Egypt where the
constellation Gemini, the Twins, was depicted as two shoots or reeds.[20]
In historical times, the twinship was anthropomorphized as Set-Horus in
Egypt and as the Dioscuri, Castor and Pollux, in Greece.

We have coined a word, "archetypology," to express the integration of
Jungian archetypal psychology with Massey's natural typology. The Jungian method is invaluable in delineating the archetypal psychologic pro-
cesses behind symbols, ideographs, and myths but it suffers from a
tendency to overdraw the analysis, of psychologizing too much. The Jungian Erich Neumann, for example, sees all myth and symbols as arising
from the archetypes of the collective unconscious and seems unwilling to
consider their derivation from concrete natural phenomena. We fully accept the paradigm of analytical psychology demonstrating a fundamental
association between external myths and allegories and the content of hu-

man dreams, fantasies, and visions. This is the psychic factor that Diop says is an essential element of culture. But mythographers such as Massey and Graves demonstrate conclusively that these mythic figures originated as expressions of natural, cosmic, and social phenomena: the facts and experiences of the natural human habitat supplied the "templates" for unconscious archetypes. Conscious experience was funnelled into the unconscious reservoir of the human mind and in this crucible, "transpersonal" archetypes were formed. During the infancy of human culture and consciousness, there was a complete interpenetration of subject and object, a unity rediscovered in the realm of quantum physics.[21]

We can summarize the elements of the masculine twinship by saying that it was (1) a product of an expanding masculinizing consciousness struggling to distinguish itself from the all-inclusive Mother, (2) an expression of the relationship of the sacred king and his successor, the tanist, and (3) a mode of mapping the complementary dichotomies of nature. On the plane of sociology, this was to ramify into the creation of male age-sets, an institution very prominent among pastoral cultures, though not limited to them, in Africa. Co-operative hunting and the need for mas-

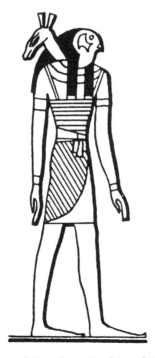

This composit figure exemplifies the twinship of Set and Horus, symbolizing the Age of Gemini, 6538–4378 B.C.

culine co-operation in the military defense of the community would have been the early impetus to the age-set system. This system, wherein all boys of a certain age were organized as a body for the rites of passage, hunting, herding, and fighting, was utterly masculine in character and served to continually reinforce the masculine ethos. The spectacular Zulu army of Shaka was organized around the age-set concept because of the tight personal bonds and esprit-de-corps that the institution engendered. The age-set exerted such a telling influence that its loyalties sometimes overshadowed family ties. A man could always turn to an age-set brother in times of need and never be denied. These peers supported each other during all rites of passage including manhood initiation, marriage, birth of children, and death. Our own culture has created simulacra of age-sets in organizations like the Boy Scouts, fraternities, lodges, etc. The modern military "boot camp" and fraternity "hazing" are parallel versions of the training every African boy was obliged to undergo to attain formal manhood. His personality was broken down and dissolved through painful trials and hardships so that he could be born again as a man. Death and rebirth symbolism were prominent features of these manhood schools just as they are in fraternity initiations. The evolution of masculine bonding, exemplified by the age-set institution, was potentiated by a twinning process that emancipated the male from the Mother principle.

The twins were originally complementary and the first such masculine pair was Set-Anubis. Set was unquestionably the earliest of the masculine types concreted into a deity. He was, therefore, the first typological Son, making him the Mother's Son par excellence, i.e., the Son when there was no Fatherhood. His archaic character is reflected in his numerous zootypes: the male hippopotamus, raven, serpent, jackal, ass, boar, goat, and okapi or antelope. As Massey states, these were the Son-types of the totemic phase before they could have become humanized. This zootypical, totemic Son would have been represented with a tail because of his animal character. Among the several meanings of the word SET in Egyptian is "tail." Many legends of traditional people refer to a time when men were said to possess tails, referring to the Sethian totemic phase when the zootypical Son of neccesity had a tail.[22]

As part of their sacerdotal raiment, the ever-conservative Egyptian priests wore aprons with tails, which effectively linked them to the early Sethian, totemic condition. Set is also the personification of the South and one form of his name, SUT, may be the root of our word "south."[23] The earliest documented Nile Valley civilization was Ta-Seti of Nubia, which may be translated either as "land of the bow" or "Set's land."[24] When dynastic Egypt succeeded as the dominant state of the lower Nile, the southern portion of the new country took on the name Ta-Seti, very likely because of its prestige. To the Egyptians, the South was always and forever the land of beginnings, the origin, the source, the top, the chief.[25] So, imbued with the prestige of the South, Set gives his name to the Egyptian word for "king," SUTEN.[26] He is also the "Sudani Set" in his manifestation as Set Nehsi: NEH is the blackbird or raven and SI is "son," giving "son of the black bird," as early zoo-type of SET. NEHSI was an Egyptian name for the inhabitants of the Sudan, indicating their close ties to Set. Having presided over primeval Golden Age—like the Greek Kronos or Saturn—he is also the Golden Set. His "golden" character may also reflect his early connection to the sun: SET can mean "solar rays" or "burning fire." The word SET is also defined as "earth," identifying him as the earliest type of masculine earth, who later is Geb. Set presides over the stellar mythos because he is the celestial jackal and/or dragon in which are situated, respectively, the magnetic north pole and the north pole of the ecliptic. He is also identified with the Sirius, the Dog Star, the most important star in the Egyptian planisphere outside the solar system. Sirius is the bringer of the flood, the announcer of the sun, and the opener of the New Year and we will explore its central importance in Egyptian history and chronology in Chapter IV.

But what is interesting about Sirius with respect to Set is that Sirius is identified with Isis. In an earlier chapter, we suggested that Set was the

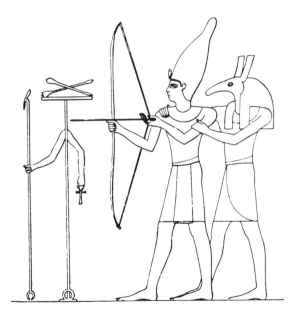

Set, patron deity of the bow, instructing the young pharaoh. The Egyptian word for bow is SETI, a variant of SET; thus Set gives his name to the bow. TA-SETI is either "Land of the Bow" or "Land of Set."

original son/brother-consort of Isis prior to the Fatherhood or to Osiris. We have shown his name, SET, to be derived from hers, ASET, and the mutual identification with Sirius, the Dog Star, is further testament to this relationship. It provides some insight into the mortal antagonism between Set and Osiris which arose from Set's loss of his position to Osiris. The classical mythographers do allude to this interplay by saying that Set was bent on destroying Osiris so that he could marry Isis, by force if necessary.[27]

However, this may be, Set was originally a benevolent deity, represented in the *Book of the Dead* as friend and protector of the deceased, who must pass through the terrors of the underworld. He is also shown in the prow of the boat of Ra fending off the Dragon who tries to swallow the sun. Moreover, the pharaohs of the first dynasty invariably took a Set name as well as a Horus name by way of demonstrating their relationship to each of the Twins. These functions account for the amazing persistence of Set-worship long after he was officially anathemized by Egyptian state religion. His cultus could be found in Western Asia, Egypt, and Cush (Ethiopia) down to the end of the dynastic period, withstanding all assaults by the Osirian-Ammonian priesthoods. The pharaohs of the 19th dynasty were particularly noteworthy for having been Set-worshippers.

Set is frequently depicted ideographically as a jackal-like animal so that he and the pre-dynastic Anubis were clearly identical and therefore the first of the masculine twins from which a patristic religion eventually blossomed. The primary role of Set as the primal Son-type is echoed in Dogon mythology. The jackal Ogo emerges as the first son of the World Mother who commits incest with her and so brings disorder into the world. As related by the Dogon sage Ogotemmeli, this is a pre-paternal schema and shows Set, in his Dogon guise, to have been the Son of the Mother alone.[28] The jackal in Afro-Kamite typology was the seer by night, on account of his nocturnal habits; thus he was the earliest type of the guide through the underworld darkness, before there ever was a Thoth-Hermes. The jackal is also the eater of carrion and could be found frequenting the western desert where Egyptian tombs were placed. Thus, before there ever was an Osiris, the jackal-god, Set-Anubis, was the god of the dead and resurrection. That he was so manifestly a desert animal solidifies our assumption that the jackal is both Set *and* Anubis. As the original lord of the dead, it would stand to reason that the Jackal-god would figure prominently in the *Book of the Dead,* which he does, even though this is largely an Osirian document. The jackal-headed Anubis serves as the guide of the manes, the mummifier, and the weigher of hearts. In his Sethian persona, the Jackal is the author of all disorder but he is also the resurrector of the dead. We can see, therefore, that by the time of the Osirian ascendancy, Set had been fissioned into two characters: negatively, he personified disorder, drought, desert, and death; positively, he was either Anubis or Up-uat (also a jackal), thus the "opener of the way," the guide of souls, the mummifier of the dead, and the "weigher of hearts."

Set/Anubis is the progenitor of all later male deities for they, one by one, come to assume specific aspects of his original nature. One seeming consequence of this parallelism is that Set himself acquires a new role as the Great Antagonist. At a certain point, he is twinned with the Elder Horus, orginally in complementary fashion, but they end by being implacable opposites. Horus is HERU, "the face of heaven," which contrasts him to the terrestial Set. The zootypical Horus is the Golden Hawk, expressive of solar splendor, contrasted to Set Nehsi, i.e., Set the Raven. Horus is the Above and Set is the Below; Horus is the Light and Set the Dark. The opposition between Set and Horus occurs first in the domain of natural typology, which prefigures their "armageddon" in the eschatology of the Osiris cycle.

The Afro-Kamitic cosmic mythos imperceptibly shifted over the millenia from a stellar to lunar to solar orientation. During the ascendancy of the matriarchy, night was pre-eminent over day and therefore the night Lights, the stars and planets, exerted a more telling influence on the human imagination than the daytime sun. Moreover, naked-eye observation of these bodies is only possible before sunrise and after sunset meaning that the heavenly bodies of nighttime were the first to be observed in a systematic way. Set, the Master of Darkness, dominated the astronomical scene; he was the supreme male of the stellar pantheon. He became the male polar dragon or Draco (Ta-Urt, the Hippopotamus goddess, in the Egyptian planisphere) and also the Jackal through which passes the magnetic pole. The north pole of the ecliptic, i.e., true North, runs more or less through the constellation of Draco, the Dragon, the Egyptian Ta-Urt, and thus Set would be the Dragon that guards the Tree (i.e., the pole) that resonates through countless ancient myths. In short, Set is the star-god par excellence, the outstanding type of Cosmic Male at that remote time when the ancestors of the dynastic Egyptians began their migration northward from their equatorial African home. The pole star, of course, rose in the sky as these early ideographers migrated northward, making it the first locale of heaven "above." This polar region was Set's domain and it was the first celestial paradise of Egypt's memory. As the supreme male deity during the time Egyptians mythologized as their Golden Age, he was the Golden Set.

Progressing from the stellar mythos, the early uranographers, i.e., mappers of heaven, in Africa gradually adopted a lunar mythos, whose time was defined by the 29½-day lunation, given contentionally as 28 days for greater ease of division. Like its stellar predecessor, the lunar mythos was originally matriarchal and Set, the Mother's Son, was embodied in it. Before the cults of Thoth, Osiris or Khonsu were fully developed, Set was

the first "lunar" male who waxed through fourteen phases, achieved resplendent youth as the full moon, and was then "dismembered" into 14
pieces (moon's 14 waning phrases). According to Massey, Set's number
was 13, the number of 28-day months in a full year.[29] When Set later fell
from grace, the number 13 became "unlucky" because of its association
with him.[30]

Plutarch's narative relates that Set was hunting boars (a Sethian
zootype) with a pack of dogs by the light of the full moon when he discovered the body of Osiris and hacked it into fourteen pieces. Here, Osiris
is the lunar light and Set is the lunar dark. When the moon wanes over 14
days, it is, figuratively, as Sethian dark half killing and dismembering Osiris
the light half, but Osiris will be reborn as Horus-Khonsu at the new
moon. Thus we see that the warring twin mythos was incorporated into
the lunar cult.

The solar mythos, along with solar time, was the last to emerge as the
pre-eminent celestial allegory. With the ascendancy of the sun as a religious symbol, the patriarchy triumphed. Set is not without his solar aspects, as we know, but he is the blazing solar inferno. But the benevolent,
vivifying sun, the exemplar of Light and Goodness, is now manifested as
Ra and Horus. Whether as Ra or Horus, the solar light is made to triumph
over the Sethian darkness and hence the older matriarchal stellar-lunar
dispensation typlified by Set. Horus, in this guise, is but Osiris reborn as
the rising sun overmastering the Dragon of Darkness, and Ra is Horus in
his full splendor, Lord of Light and Life. On the human plane, this patriarchal triumph expresses itself in the idealization of masculine strength
and potency. The warrior-kings who had started out as sacrificial consorts
to the Mother, were now able, through sheer force of arms, to insist
upon radical changes in the status quo. Their first step in solidifying their
grip on political power was doing away with kingship by contest. This
empowerment of the male kings was guaranteed by standing bodies of
military retainers.

For purposes of ideological control, male deities were promoted to positions of equal or even superior importance to the maternal ones. These
changes in the relative power relationships between male and female did
not occur without a struggle, nor were the battle lines drawn strictly according to gender. As we have already seen the maternal nephews stood
to lose considerably from the "revolution" that was going on, and they
resisted with all the means at their disposal. In many places, especially in
Africa, compromises were worked out in social and economic relationships in order to balance the often competing demands of the entrenched
clan mothers and the rising patriarchate. At the beginning of the dynastic
period in ancient Egypt (c. 4000 B.C.), though the patricarchal principle
was established in major spheres, the matriarchate was by no means sup-

planted. It retained many of its prerogatives and was able to attenuate and modify many claims of paternal precedence. Set and his numerous followers became scapegoats in the new dispensation, but Set's hold on the populace was too deep-seated to be eradicated altogether. A place had to be found for him in the pantheon, and was, though the struggle with the Osirians continued to the end of Egyptian history. The matriarchate in Egypt was accomodated rather than suppressed, permitting a balance of forces *sui generis* and an extraordinary cultural synergism of male and female attributes.

The first task of the newly-ascendant patriarchate was to legitimize the fatherhood. Incest taboos were intensified and broadened and pre-marital chastity was imposed upon the female more generally. The motherhood is a demonstrable fact in nature; the reality of the fatherhood is hidden and invisible. If a man were to be assured of his paternity, and therefore that all-important connection to and control over children, only he could be allowed access to the prospective mother. In the heyday of the matriarchate, no restrictions whatever were placed on female sexuality because the children were perceived to issue from the mother alone. Among the Trobriand Islanders, Malinowski found that unmarried girls suffered no limits of any kind upon their sexual inclinations, for physiologic paternity was not acknowledged.[31] At a later totemic stage, unrestricted intercourse was modified by the practice of organizing males and females into brotherhoods and sisterhoods which would marry each other, all spouses being shared in common.[32] Certain aboriginal peoples in Australia and the South Pacific preserve features of this system. But the individual fatherhood required more stringent controls over female sexuality to ensure the father's connection to the children. The male could never hope to command the same deference as the Mother if he could not stake his claim to the children and the imposition of sexual monogamy upon the female was the only solution. The rule of premarital chastity and female monogamy even came to be observed in societies which remained frankly matriarchal.

With the advent of the divine figure of Atum-Ra, there began an inexorable push toward the exclusive Father-deity that dominated the later "revealed" religions. Atum-Ra is the first of the male deities to bypass the Mother altogether. He creates humanity by two acts, masturbation and sub-incision (and/or circumcision) of his penis, therefore mixing semen and blood to generate life *without* the Mother's participation. The sub-incision of the penis, and the related custom of circumcision is a mode by which the Father deity makes himself "female" by cutting a "womb" into his penis, combining within himself both paternal and maternal elements. The Samburu men of Kenya and the males of certain Australian tribes today undergo penile sub-incision as a manhood rite, so that the feminine, typlified by the "womb-like" opening in the penis, is subsumed within the masculine.[33] Ancient Egyptian texts assert that the people of the Sudan were first created in an act of sub-incision by Atum-Ra, a reference to the inner African provenance of this custom that was preserved by the Kamite ideographers. In the well-known custom of the couvade seen in many parts of the world, the father of an unborn child actually takes to bed and experiences a "phantom" labor as his wife moves closer to the time of delivery. Analogically, the father participates in pregnancy, labor, and delivery and by this mode assimilates to himself the role of bearer as well as begetter of children.

Atum-Ra was also said to have been the first deity to perform circumcision upon himself and this represents a sacrifice of the "female" part of the male, which is considered to be centered in the prepuce that encloses the penis. This is the final ritual act of liberation from the feminine/ mother archetype for it permanently establishes an exclusive masculinity. Throughout Africa, the uncircumcised male is held in sovereign contempt; he is a "non-man" who is not allowed to wear men's clothes, participate in men's councils, or even marry. The typical age of circumcision is 12– 14 years, the time when the boy joins his age-set peers in the manhood training schools. Circumcision is a sacrifice of flesh and blood that reenacts the primitive sacrifice of the sacred king. It is, in fact, the first step on the path toward manhood. In the four-month manhood training school, the boy, in the company of his age-mates, is isolated from all familiarity and comfort, submits to numerous physical and mental rigors, and when he emerges from this ordeal, he is no longer a boy but a man. Until he is thirty, the new man is responsible for the defense of the community and the protection of its economic livelihood. At age 30, having proved his courage, reliability, skill and productivity, he becomes a full-fledged man, is allowed to marry, and takes his place in the council of men. Thus the passage into full manhood is a long trial in which the male is constantly tested. It is directly analogous to the soul's ordeal as described in the *Book of the Dead,* where it undertakes a long, perilous jouney through the underworld of Amenta, its mettle tested at every step, to prove its fitness for salvation and rebirth.

With the rise of the patriarchate, there is a shift in the tone of the myths and symbols. Time is now measured in days instead of nights, because daylight is pre-eminent over night. The right side becomes symbolically dominant over the left side, a new metaphor for all that is correct and true. The symbols of grain and vegetation now accent masculine growth instead of maternal nutrition. Thoth, Khonsu, and Osiris become the dominant lunar deities over Hathor and Isis. Hapi, the personification of the Nile River, comes to embody the fertilizing masculine stream superseding the oceanic womb imagery personified by the heavenly Nut. The sun displaces the moon as the celestial archetype of the Divine Man and the Osirified Soul. The passage of the sun after it sets through the hidden dangers of the Darkland of Amenta is an allegory of the passage of the soul through Amenta after death. The early totemic zootypes take on an increasingly masculine character. For example, the zootypical signs of each segment of the zodiac—Leo the Lion, Khepera (Cancer), Gemini the Twins, Taurus the Bull, Aries the Ram, etc.—are mostly male.

More and more, masculine symbols and archetypes intrude into mysteries and techniques that had been exclusively feminine. In agriculture Osiris is established as the sower of seed and the plougher of furrows, a masculinizing transformation accelerated by the invention of certain implements, such as the plough, which improve crop yields. The god Ptah prefigures even Osiris in agrarian fertility rites—his name Ptah means "to open"—and he is an early type of the "opener" of the female to prepare her for conception.[34] He "opens" the feminine earth by ploughing to prepare it for the planting of the seed. Finally, he is the "opener" of Amenta, carving out a passage-way for the soul through the underworld preparatory to rebirth.[35] Eschatology, with the idea of spiritual rebirth, is the final phase of religious evolution and one of the great achievements of the patriarchate. Ptah is also an important masculine form of the Creator who fashions the world-egg on the potter's wheel. His counterpart, Khnum,

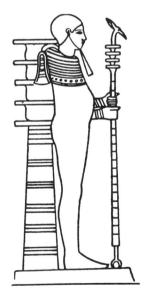

The god Ptah, whose backbone is the Djed (Tet) Cross, the tree conventionalized. Later, the Djed was connected to Osiris.

fashions human beings from clay on the potter's wheel, demonstrating the potter's art as well had slipped into masculine control.

Eventually, these developments in the domains of religion and culture began to have adverse consequences for the matriarchate. When the primal Mother was supreme, she and all that was connected with her inspired awe, adoration, and terror, but as the patriarchate gained ascendancy, everything associated with the matriarchal ways came to be negatively valued. What was once life-enhancing nature magic became witchcraft. The Mother who presided over the killing and dismembering of the sacred king became the monstrous, all devouring Gorgon or Kali who threatens life and light. The left side, the female side, instilled foreboding as seen in our word "sinister" which derives from a Latin word for "left-handed." Darkness became a time of dread, evoking fears of annihilation. The hippopotamus type of the Mother was transmuted into Leviathan, the Biblical Monster. This same Mother, called Rerit by the Egyptians, became, in extra-Biblical Semitic legend, Lilith, the child-eater. The blood mysteries now only brought defilement; menses became a curse requiring women to be sequestered during their periods to avoid contaminating the community. During the performance of the new masculine mysteries, a bull-roarer would warn all females to stay locked up while the male initiates were being summoned to secret rites. A woman indiscreet enough to be found outside when the bull-roarer sounded risked forfeiture of her life.[36]

Khnum, fashioning man from clay on the potter's wheel.

The lore of Judaism, Christianity, and Islam is permeated with this negative valuation of the female. The deity shed its feminine characteristics and became exclusively male. Eve was epiphenomenally seen to be derived from Adam's rib, eventually corrupting him with the "forbidden fruit" and causing the downfall of all mankind. Among Christians, monasticism arose explicitly to emancipate men from the temptations of women so that they could concentrate on achieving "higher" non-carnal and non-feminine spiritual aims. The permanent celibacy of the Catholic priesthood is in the same vein. In a strange twist, some of the early Christian monks emasculated themselves, not as a phallic sacrifice to the Mother, but to liberate themselves from the "tyranny" of sex and hence the power of women.[37] Among Hindus and Moslems, women were relegated to the status of an inferior caste, veiled, and cloistered in the purdah, totally under the domination of men.

This state of affairs is especially disastrous for Set, the archetypal Son of the Mother, who belongs wholly to the matriarchate. In the newly ascendant patriarchate, Set, as her masculine alter ego, becomes the Mother's proxy as an evil-doer. In the Osirian cycle, as we have seen, he is the antagonistic Twin, embodying all negation and destruction. He is the desert that threatens the cultivated lands, the drought that menaces life, the serpentine darkness that swallows light. As the male manifestation of the first blood of the Mother and the personification of the desert, his color is red, the very hue of evil itself. In late dynastic times, the anathema against Set was so pronounced in Egypt that people were in the habit of attacking persons with red hair.[38] All of his zootypes, i.e., the boar, the raven, the ass, the serpent, the hippopotamus, take on a negative character. As the red ass, he is subjected to derision and abuse, as the wild boar he is hated as the destroyer of Osiris, as the scorpion he is reviled as the killer of the Child Horus. In the Egyptian Ritual, Set is the leader of all noxious and demonic powers, called the "Children of Revolt." War and conflict are his special province and throughout dynastic times, the pharaohs are not at all adverse to invoking his name to ensure success in battle. This makes him the god of all things military, of whom the Greek Ares and the Roman Mars are later manifestations. In early dynastic times, he is the god of the bow, which takes its name, STI or SETI, from him. His relationship to the warlike nomads of the northeast African desert is seen in their name, SETIU, "the People of the Nine Bows." [39]

In the place of the Mother, Set becomes the destroyer and dismemberer of Osiris; the one who threatens the life of the infant Horus. Ultimately, Horus, the twin of Set in an earlier manifestation, is raised to manhood and engages Set in a titanic battle. The issue is not resolved either way for a long time. Set tears out the eye of Horus; Horus cuts off the testicles of Set. Finally, Horus is victorious and Set is bound to face judgement. At this critical juncture, Set calls upon his sister Isis to set him free and she, in a moment of weakness, unbinds him. This act provokes the blinding wrath of Horus, who in his fury, cuts off the head of his own mother. Thoth immediately replaces it with a cow's head, her most important zootype.[40] Neumann correctly sees this peculiar episode as a case of the ancient matriarchate reasserting its prerogatives: Set is the uterine brother of Isis, the most ancient tie, and also the consort to Isis prior to Osiris who, with Horus, represents the new triumphant patriarchy. In his most desperate hour, Set appeals to the more ancient loyalties of Isis. The attack of Horus upon his mother Isis is the adumbration of a theme more fully developed in the Orestes cycle of later Greek tragedy. With the connivance of his sister Electra, Orestes kills his faithless mother Clytemnestra, who has murdered their father Agamemnon. At this time, matricide was considered the one inexpiable crime and Orestes is hounded by the Furies, the scourges of the matriarchate, until he is at last exonerated through the intervention of Athena. Though female, Athena is a standard-bearer for the patriarchate, having emerged from the brow of Zeus without the aid of a mother. In fact, the whole Orestes cycle demonstrates that the paternal archetype is not gender-specific; two of its most assiduous proponents and protagonists are female, Electra and Athena. In any event, the myth of Orestes recognizes and confirms the new supremacy of father-right, which has superseded mother-right.

With the ascendancy of the patriarchy, a whole constellation of masculine deities comes to the forefront. In Egypt these include Atum-Ra, who is both the first Man-God and the resplendent Sun; Ptah, the "Opener;" Amen, the "Hidden One;" Osiris, the God of Resurrection; and Horus, the Avenger and Redeemer. In the case of Osiris, and his alter ego Horus, we find the younger Twin superseding the older Set, a phenomenon also met with in the Bible, where so often, the patrimony is passed on to the younger brother at the expense of the older. Frazer calls this "ultimogeniture," and it is a product of the patriarchate.[41] In the new recognition of paternity, Osiris begets a son, Horus, a privilege never accorded to Set. Horus ceases to be solely the son of Isis, his first manifestation, and becomes the son of *both* Isis and Osiris. This double parentage confers upon him a new legitimacy. Moreover, he avenges his father and assumes dominion over his *father's* kingdom. Osiris is now the dying Man-God who is resurrected through his Son, Horus, instead of his Mother, Isis, to reign, not cyclically as in nature, but for eternity as the Judge of the Dead. Osiris is thus the first to transcend time. However, the always-conservative Egyptians never discarded the older mythos but merely grafted the newer one onto it. Egyptian iconography depicts two versions of the reconstitution and resurrection of Osiris: one by his mother-sister-wife Isis and the other, in the later phase, by his son and fulfiller, Horus, who is but a re-manifestation of himself. We must say also that Horus himself has two personae: (1) he is the Elder Horus, often represented as blind or lame because he is the Son of the Mother alone and therefore imperfect, and (2) Horus, King of Glory, who is perfected by virtue of his doubly divine parentage.

Horus, the Avenger of Osiris, is the prototype of the Hero which so abundantly populated later Greek mythology. This is evident in the Afro-Kamite astronomical allegory in which Horus is the youthful solar champion who slays the Dragon of Darkness, representing the sun overcoming the darkness as it rises each morning. Iconographically, this is pictured as Horus strangling serpents, trodding upon crocodiles and spearing the hippopotamus. Similar imagery crops up in the Hercules cycle where the infant Hercules, the Greek Child Horus, strangles two giant snakes sent to devour him and later, in full manhood, kills the nine-headed Hydra. In Egyptian, Horus is HERU, a name that comes to us through Greek as HERO—every one of the heroes of Greek myth are slayers of serpents, dragons, and monsters, all emblematic of the devouring darkness.

Set, the matriarchal protagonist, does not sit idly by while he is being deprived of his position. When he cannot defeat Horus in combat, he takes him to court to charge Isis with harlotry and Horus with bastardy, claiming that without an identifiable father, Horus has no right to the kingdom of Osiris. Through the timely intervention of Thoth, Geb, the Great Magistrate of the Gods, rules in favor of Horus's legitimate paternity and makes him the rightful heir of Osiris.[42] The triumph of the patriarchal succession is assured.

We have already noted that the polarization between the old matriarchate and the new patriarchate was never allowed to become too deep or divisive in ancient Egypt. A key illustration of this moderation is the role of Thoth in war between Horus and Set. Though Thoth aided Horus in his battle to secure the kingship of his father, it was he who intervened in Set's behalf when it seemed as if Horus would achieve total victory. Thoth called an end to the hostilities and restored Set to his place in the pantheon. Isis had in effect done the same thing by releasing Set from his bonds. The matriarchate held too firm a grip on the ancient Egyptians, as it does in Africa to this day, to be utterly suppressed. The old matriarchal cults were simply too powerful, forcing a kind of *modus vivendi* to be established. In dynastic times, the old types of the Mother, Isis, Apt, Ta-Urt, Neith, Nut, Hathor, Mut, and Sekh-met, preserved an honored place in the pantheon. Though new paternal deities took over some matriarchal cult centers, they did not dispossess the original cult figures. Thebes, or Waset, became the cult center of the Ram-god Amen, but this role was merely superimposed upon the much older worship of the hippopotamus goddess Apt in that locale. The Greek name THEBES for the City of Amen is but a corruption of TA-APT meaning "Land of Apt." The fabulous Temple of Karnak in Thebes, the most important religious center of the ancient world, was APIT-ASUT, the "Throne of Apt."

As further testament to the residual power of the goddesses, we find that the one cult that survives the demise of Egypt itself is that of Isis. Her worship crossed over into the Roman empire, where it flourished until the middle of the fourth century. The patriarchal Roman state religion could not compete with Isis among the common people and the forcible proscription by pope and emperor succeeded only by assimilating much of the theology and practice of this persistent faith. The worship was not suppressed totally until 540 C.E. But it is perhaps the unassailable principle of the pharaonic matrilineal succession that testifies most to the continuing power of the matriarchate. Egyptian dynasts had to formalize royal sibling incest to resolve the competing imperatives of succession, matrilineal and patrilineal. Only through such brother-sister marriages could the immovable principle of matrilineal succession be reconciled with the new "Horus" factor of patriliny. To reiterate: Egypt was the most successful culture in its creative reconciliation of matriarchal and patriarchal requisites, quite possibly the single most important social factor in the amazing resilience of this 4,000-year old civilization.

The dynamics of transition did not achieve such an effective result elsewhere. In Western Asia and the southern Mediterranean, the end result of the eruption of militant patriarchates amounted to an "all or nothing" conquest. In Hellas (Greece), the largely matriarchal Mycenaeans were overpowered by invading Dorian barbarians from the northeast about 1200 B.C., ushering in a Dark Age of 500 years. The Greece that emerges out of this Dark Age has almost completely suppressed the matriarchy, at least in social and political relations, as Robert Graves has detailed. In his study of Greek myth, an extreme exaltation of the masculine spirit grew up which, among other things, led to an idealization and institutionalization of homosexuality. This practice would have been considered a grievous offense against the Mother in the earlier matriarchate and so must have been a rare occurrence. The phallus existed for the purpose of fecundating the Mother and so "belonged" to her and her alone. In Athens, love between worldly older men and callow youths became the stuff of panegyrics; homosexual liasons became part of the normal education of upper-class youths. In hypermilitaristic Sparta, the encouragement of homosexuality was a way of promoting bonds between comrades-in-arms. Throughout history, militaristic societies, with their celebration of masculine relationships, have often fostered this practice. Whatever the case, it demanded an utter rejection of the Mother and the female. According to Neumann, the unconscious motivation behind this extremity is a fear of being "devoured" or "castrated" by the overwhelming Mother.[43] The anti-

maternal, anti-female posture is represented in Greek myth by the opposition between Dionysus and Apollo; this posture also crops up in the
cycle of Hercules. Dionysus is another type of the Son of the Mother
whose wild, orgiastic celebrations recall the primeval, promiscuous fertility rites of the old matriarchate. In the Dionysian revels, normal psychic
boundaries dissolve as the exclusively female bacchantes are caught up in
the participation mystique. Men in these rites are the sacrificial victims,
essential to fertility and renewal, and any man caught by the Maenads of
Dionysus is torn to pieces in a frenzy of sex and blood. Apollo, by contrast, is the sublimely ordered, intellectual, and spiritual masculine type
who is the soul of rational thought, philosophic discourse, and ideal artistic creation. He is the "higher" masculine type who liberates men from
the wild, chaotic disorder of the Dionysian, hence maternal, rites of fertility and renewal. According to Graves, he is the first homosexual god who
glories in his exclusive masculinity.[44] He is the implacable enemy of the
matriarchate. So, too, is Hercules, who conducts a lifelong struggle against
the supreme Greek Mother goddess, Hera.

In Western Asia, the matriarchate held fast for a long time; the struggle
of the Hebrews against the centrifugal pull of the matriarchate is chroni-
cled in the Old Testament. But in Western Asia, the matriarchate degenerated into savagery, at last repelling and alienating its devotees to such
an extent that patriarchal religion was able to sweep it away in late antiquity. Moloch and Dagon, for example, seem to have been originally goddesses who, in historical times, became Sethian types, demanding and
receiving the annual sacrifice by fire of hundreds of children. The prophets tirelessly thundered against and execrated this practice which many of
their co-religionists had adopted.[45] Here, as with the Aztecs, the demonic
character of the Great Mother seemed to overshadow all else, so that she
literally washed her hands in the blood of children. As Astarte, she was
the fecund and abundant Mother fertilized by the yearly succession of
son-lovers, true to ancient typology. Thus, the priestesses serving her also
accepted the sexual favors of numerous men in "sacred" prostitution. To
the Hebrews, naturally, this made Astarte the Great Harlot. Time after
time, Hebrew men succumbed to her and Hebrew women joined her
priestesses which incited the incurable wrath of the prophets.[46] The extreme penalties against women for adultery in Judaism and Islam can at
last be understood in this light.

Lastly, there is the example of Cybele and like goddesses of Western
Asia whose male devotees unsexed themselves and then, in the fashion of
priestesses, offered themselves up for prostitution. This ritual homosexuality, instead of being an expression of masculine exaltation, was an aberrant form of the worship of the promiscuous Mother. Here was a real,
gruesome enactment of the scenario Neumann said was at the root of

homosexuality: the killing, castrating, and devouring of the male by the all-consuming Mother. The misogyny evident in Judaism, Christianity, and Islam are undoubtedly reactions to the abuses and excesses of the late matriarchal Canaanites. This profound decadence ended by rendering the feminine archetype and its concomitants odious, thereby fueling a patriarchal religious revolution that in turn generated its own evils.

Neumann has asserted that the male role during the ascendancy of the matriarchate was to be dominated and violated, and this certainly seems to have been the case in Western Asia as elsewhere.[47] The logic of the "revealed" religions of the patriarchate grew out of a kind of intrinsic evolution in consciousness and culture but they also represented a kind of reaction formation against the matriarchate. As we have said, the rise of the masculine/paternal archetype affected both genders but ultimately, the patriarchal reaction had the effect of pushing these religions into a consciously anti-feminine, anti-sexual attitude. But though the severe anti-female proscriptions have been disastrous for women all over the world, they have been detrimental to men as well. The hypertrophy of masculine consciousness and the deliberate exaltation of masculine values have resulted in a world that is unduly competitive, mechanical, extroverted, deracinated, yet emotionally constricted. Mind is exalted over matter, reason over emotion, empiricism over intuition, technology over craft, competition over co-operation, individual over community, rights over obligations. The enmity toward the Mother extends to nature, which is seen as an antagonistic force to be conquered and exploited. Her secrets are turned against her by a rampant technology and the foundations of life crumble before our eyes. Science constitutes the new "state of grace"; what is deemed "scientific" and "technical" defines reality, what is outside of or unexplainable by techno-science is dismissed or ignored. Yet the new-dominant Father seems to demand the blood of nations on a scale undreamed of in the most sanguinary of the old matriarchal rites of sacrifice. This is the outcome of the mass wars characteristic of an age dominated by masculine archetypes, each war stepping up the scale of destruction a notch higher than the previous one. Finally, the attempt to dominate nature has bred a weapons technology that threatens to annihilate all history, all humanity at a single stroke. It is the masculine archetype run riot, threatening to rend all that exists asunder.

The long-standing domination of the old matriarchy had spent itself, creating its own contradiction in the process. An excess of the Female/Mother archetype had become oppressive, destructive and degenerate, requiring a radical adjustment. The evolution of the patristic ideas in culture and religion was a necessary and inevitable phase of human development; the rise of the Male/Father archetype could have served to balance an otherwise overweening matriarchy. The lower cultures of the Nile seemed to have achieved this equilibrium. However, a patriarchal over-compensation occurred in other areas of the world with the consequent excess of the masculine archetype threatening human existence itself. A fundamental re-balancing is in order.

Glossary

Astarte: A Canaanitic goddess styled as the "Queen of Heaven"; equivalent to Isis and Hathor in the Egyptian pantheon.

Attis: The Son-Lover of the goddess Cybele who unsexes himself, dies, and is re-born as a pine tree.

Cybele: The Great Mother goddess of Asia Minor (modern Turkey).

Dioscuri: The Twins, Castor and Pollux, in Greek myth.

The Egyptian Ritual: The Egyptian funerary ritual embodied in the *Book of the Dead.*

Eschatology: The doctrine of "last things." In Kamite religion, eschatology was cyclical and recurring, not lineal and final.

Mycenae: Pre-classic Greek civilization—c. 1400–1100 B.C.E.—largely derived from Crete and reflected in the Homeric epics.

Kendake: The title of the queen-mother of Cush called "Candace" by the Romans. In the centuries before the common era, Kendakes frequently ruled Cush in their own right.

Pastoral: Relating to a way of life dominated by herding.

Sed: The "Festival of the Tail," celebrating a pharaoh's 30-year jubilee. It was a regenerative ritual for the pharaoh who was obliged to run seven times around the temple enclosure to demonstrate his vigor.

Sirius: Called Sepdet by the Egyptians, it is the brightest first magnitude star seen from earth. It is called the "Dog Star" because it is found in the constellation Canis Major. It ranked with the sun and moon in importance in the astronomies of the Egyptians and the Dogon of Mali.

Sub-incision: A longitudinal slit cut into the inferior surface of the penis as a manhood rite among certain peoples of Africa and the Pacific Islands.

Tanist: Robert Graves' term for the twin and successor of the sacred king, taken from a Celtic word meaning "twin."

Trobriand Islanders: A Melanesian people inhabiting a group of islands off the coast of New Guinea. When Malinowski lived among them in the 1920's, theirs was a paleolithic culture that had not changed substantially in 30,000 years.

Notes

1. Briffault R, *The Mothers*, Volume I, New York: The MacMillan Company, 1927, pp. 345–432, passim.
2. Graves R, *The Greek Myths*, Volume I, New York: Penguin Books, 1955, 1977, p. 30.
3. Neumann E, *The Origins and History of Consciousness*, translated by R.F.C. Hull, Princeton: Princeton University Press, 1954, 1973.

4. See Frazer JG, *The Dying God*, London: Macmillan and Co., Ltd., 1911, passim.

5. See Frazer JG, *Adonis, Attis, and Osiris*, Volume I, New Hyde Park: University Books, 1961, pp. 263–80; also Graves, op. cit., passim, for a description of the rites involving the death, dismemberment, and eating of male sacrificial victims in early Greece.

6. I Kings 14:23–24.

7. Cf. Evans-Pritchard EE, *Nuer Religion*, New York: Oxford University Press, 1956, 1974, p. 132, note. An exception to the rule of patriarchal pastoral peoples is the nomadic, non-Arab Tuareg of the Western Sahara who, though Islamic, retain the matrilineal principle of succession.

8. Jeremiah 44:15–20.

9. There are well-known traditions in Greek myth concerning all-female Amazon societies, at least some of which were situated in North Africa. Graves sees this tradition as stemming from the actual existence of pre-historic castes of female warriors. Cf. Graves, op. cit., volume I, p. 135. It is also noteworthy that the Dahomean kings of the 18th and 19th centuries maintained all female corps of soldiers.

10. Frazer, *A Dying God*, op. cit., pp. 46–58.

11. Graves, op. cit., Volume II, pp. 347–8; Volume I, pp. 102–3.

12. Ellis AB, *The Yoruba-Speaking Peoples of the Slave Coast of West Africa*, The Netherlands: Anthropological Publications, 1984, 1970, p. 164.

13. Diop CA, *Civilization ou Barbarie*, Paris: Presence Africaine, 1981, pp. 209–10.

14. Ibid., cf. also Note 3.

15. Reliefs show the pharaoh racing around the shrine to demonstrate his continuing vigor.

16. See Omer-Cooper JD, *The Zulu Aftermath*, Evanston: Northwestern University Press, 1969, p. 135; also, Rogers JA, *World's Great Men of Color*, Volume I, New York: Collier Books, 1946, 1972, p. 274.

17. Neumann, op. cit., p. 96.

18. Graves, Volume I, op. cit., p. 14.

19. Massey G, *Ancient Egypt*, New York: Samuel Weiser, 1970, pp. 324–5.

20. Allen RH, *Star Names: Their Lore and Meaning*, New York: Dover Publications, Inc., 1899, 1963, p. 224.

21. Capra F, *The Tao of Physics*, Berkeley: Shambhala, 1975, pp. 130–43.

22. Massey, op. cit., Volume I, p. 68; also, Budge EAW, *An Egyptian Hieroglyphic Dictionary*, two volumes, New York: Dover Publications, Inc., 1920, 1978, pp. 475; 706.

23. The Germanic word for SOUTH is SUD and is found in many European languages including French, Italian, and Spanish. SUD is almost identical to SUT, a form of Set's name.

24. Set was the patron deity of the bow. Cf. Budge, ibid., Volume II, p. 709.

25. The term encompassing all these meanings in Egyptian is KHENTI; ibid., Volume I, p. 554.

26. Ibid., Volume II, p. 653.

27. See citation by Julius Firmicus Maternus in Budge EAW, *From Fetish to God in Ancient Egypt*, London: Oxford University Press, 1934, p. 182.

28. Griaule M, *Conversations with Ogotemmeli*, New York: Oxford University Press, 1965, 1970, pp. 21–2.

29. Massey G, *Natural Genesis*, Volume II, London: Williams and Norgate, 1883, pp. 302–18.

30. Ibid.
31. Malinowski B, *The Sexual Life of Savages in Northwestern Melanesia*, London: Routledge and Kegan Paul, 1929, 1982, pp. 58–64.
32. Jackson J, *Man, God, and Civilization*, New Hyde Park: University Books, 1972, pp. 164–70.
33. See Margetts EL, "Sub-incision of the Urethra in the Samburu of Kenya," *East African Medical Journal* (37): 2, February 1960, pp. 105–8. This practice is also widespread in Australia, Fiji, and Tonga.
34. See Malinowski, op. cit., pp. 154–5, for a discussion of the male's phallic role in "opening" the female.
35. Massey, *Ancient Egypt*, op. cit., pp. 344–5.
36. Spencer B and Gillen FJ, *The Native Tribes of Central Australia*, New York: Dover Publications, Inc., 1899, 1968, p. 246; also, Briffault, op. cit., Volume II, p. 546.
37. Origen, one of the most influential of the 3rd century Christian Fathers, reputedly emasculated himself so that he could teach female catechists without distraction.
38. Diodorus Siculus, *On Egypt*, translated by Edwin Murphy, London: McFarland & Co., Inc., 1985, p. 114.
39. These Sudani Sethiu were called by the Egyptians PEDJETIW PESEDEJ, meaning literally "the Nine Bows."
40. Budge, *From Fetish to God . . .* , op. cit., pp. 450–1.
41. Frazer JG, *Folklore in the Old Testament*, New York: Tudor Publishing co., 1923, pp. 172–204.
42. Budge, op. cit., p. 180.
43. Neumann E, *The Great Mother: Analysis of an Archetype*, translated by Ralph Mannheim, Princeton: Princeton University Press, 1955, 1974, p. 304.
44. Graves, op. cit., Volume I, p. 78.
45. I Kings 17:16–17; Psalms 106:35–38.
46. II Kings 23:4–7; Jeremiah 2:23–24; Ezekiel 23:27.
47. Neumann, op. cit., p. 304.

IV

Chronology, the Calendar, and the Kamite Great Year

No proper investigation of Afro-Kamitic thought, arising out of what Gerald Massey calls a "natural genesis" in inner Africa, evolving into its mature form in ancient Egypt, and re-manifesting itself in Judaism and Christianity, can proceed without a careful consideration of Kamitic/ Egyptian chronology and the world's Great Year. To us moderns, history has nothing to do with stars and planets. The mechanistic view of the universe ushered in by Isaac Newton leaves no room for "astral influences"* and even to suggest such a thing is to invite the anathema of "pseudoscience" from learned circles.[1] The case was very different in antiquity. Among learned men of that time, including those vaunted "rationalists" the Greeks, the relationship between earth and the empyrean was so palpably self-evident as to require no demonstration. However much we may insist that heavenly bodies and their movements do not affect human affairs, we cannot possibly understand the psychic and cultural worlds of the ancients unless we deign to consider this vital nexus between humanity and the heavens they took for granted.

Even Otto Neugebauer, who affected a studied contempt for the scientific achievements of the ancient Egyptians, was compelled to admit that there never was a more perfect calendar than the one they devised.[2] Our time reckoning is tied to a more less arbitrary moment in history; that of the ancient Egyptians was guided entirely by natural and cosmic cycles, providing the nearest thing we have to an absolute calendar valid for all times and places on earth. Our calendar, with minor modifications the same one the Egyptians devised, is such a commonplace that we have no inkling of the amazing intellectual labor that produced it. The creation of any serviceable calendar requires such detailed knowledge of astronomical movements that it presupposes a long prior period of precise observation and meticulous recording of the results. Plato insisted that the Egyptians had been charting the stars and planets for at least 10,000 years and he does not seem to have been exaggerating.[3] Egypt, being a dry country, lay under clear nighttime skies for months on end, ideal for

---

* Newton is usually credited with introducing the modern concept of a mechanical universe even though he himself practiced astrology.

naked-eye observations of the heavenly bodies. Consequently, they had devised three calendars, stellar, lunar, and solar. The Venusian calendar of the latter-day Dogon makes us wonder if perhaps the Egyptians possessed this one as well.[4] They knew of the lunar year of 354 days, which still determines the Muslim calendar, but at a time long anterior to the dynastic period, they had discovered the solar year of 360 days plus five intercalated or "epagomenal" days. Many think they had originally measured the year mistakenly at 360 days and then added five more when they realized their error. It is hard to justify such a view. Once they had discovered the solar year, they measured it at 365 days from the very first, but being an eminently practical people, they used 360 days for the conventional year because it provided convenient, whole number multiples by which to sub-divide the year—twelve 30-day months, ten 36-day decans, thirty-six 10-day weeks, etc. It is no coincidence that the 360 days of the conventional solar year is the same as the number of degrees in a geometric circle. Egyptian astronomers knew that the world was spherical and described an elliptical path around the sun.[5] There probably have never been more exacting astrometricians than the ancient Kamites and in some domains of physical science, their precision has not been excelled even by modern instrumentation.[6]

The measurement of the solar year at 365 days was close but not exact. However, two more precise measurements for the year were derived: the solar year, measured from solstice to solstice, of 365.24219 days and the Sothic or sidereal year of 365.25636 days.[7] This latter measurement for the year was obtained from a startling celestial event known as the heliacal rising of Sirius, called Sothis among the Greeks and Sepdet among the Egyptians. For most of the year at the latitude of Thebes in Upper Egypt, Sirius, a star in the southern heaven, is invisible, but it appears suddenly on the eastern horizon just before dawn at the summer solstice. This is known as its "heliacal" rising. Within 20 days after this solstitial rising, the Nile flood begins. The coincidence of all these events left a profound impression on the minds of the early Kamite astronomers, who made Sirius the herald of the sun, the announcer of the flood, and the harbinger of the New Year. The ancient Kamites rounded off the length of the "tropical" year to 365¼ years, an almost exact mean between the solstitial and Sothic years.[8]

This discrepancy meant that the civil calendar used by the Egyptians retrograded from the true year by ¼-day per year, reconverging with the true or sidereal year, determined by the heliacal rising of Sirius, every 1,460 years. This is known as the Sothic cycle and its discovery was an amazing feat of astronomical observation, allowing the Egyptians to regulate their calendars according to objective and measurable celestial movements.

But the true significance of the Sothis calendar lies in its role in reconstructing Egyptian dynastic chronology because certain regnal years of several reigns through the course of Egyptian history were recorded by reference to the Sothic cycle.[9] A famous inscription by Censorinus tells us that the Egyptian New Year and the heliacal rising of Sirius coincided in 139 A.D., which means they did in 1321 B.C.E., 2781 B.C.E., and 4241 B.C.E. as well. There are two inscriptions in the records of the 18th dynasty that refer to the regnal years of the reigning pharaoh and their positions in the Sothic cycle, allowing us, by knowing the lengths of all the reigns of the 18th dynasty pharaohs, to fix an almost certain date of 1580 B.C.E. for the beginning of the 18th dynasty. Earlier than that, however, the view of chronology becomes decidedly clouded; though we have the names and regnal lengths of most pharaohs, with the possible exception of Senusert III, it is difficult to relate these reigns to any fixed point in time.[10]

The single most important documentary evidence we have bearing on Egyptian chronology is preserved extracts from the mostly lost history of Manetho, an Egyptian priest commissioned by Ptolemy Philadelphius to write a complete history of Egypt.[11] Manetho, though he wrote in Greek, had access to all the historical archives of Egypt and was the first to arrange the sequence of pharaonic reigns into dynasties, a scheme that has proved so useful to historiography that it remains in force today. According to Manetho, there were 30 dynasties representing 330 kings.

Modern Egyptology, though completely dependent on Manetho's framework, has had difficulty accepting it unmodified, for it would push the beginning of Egyptian dynastic history back to 5500 B.C.E. So much of Manetho's history is lost that long sequences of reigns cannot be connected to established temporal reference points. Consequently, modern Egyptology has subjected Manetho to deep revision. Several Egyptian records—the Turin Papyrus, the Abydos Papyrus, and the Palermo Stone—represent authentic Egyptian king lists and though they seem to corroborate Manetho in many particulars, discrepancies in the lengths of certain dynasties and individual reigns are apparent. Following the lead of Meyer and Breasted in the early part of this century, specialists have sought to reconcile the chronology of Manetho with a presumed date of 3400–3100 B.C.E. for the beginning of Egyptian dynastic history. They have focused most of their attention on the 1st and 2nd Intermediate Periods in Manetho's system which represent more or less prolonged periods of political and social upheaval punctuated by many ephemeral reigns. Chronologists have sought to conflate the reigns in these two periods by presuming that many kings actually ruled simultaneously over different parts of the country. The effect of this approach is to compress the time span of Egyptian dynastic chronology by more than 2,000 years.

Meyer postulated a first dynasty date of 3400 B.C.E., which Breasted adopted, but since his time this date has inched downward, so that chronologists now routinely speak of the beginning of the first dynasty at 3000 B.C.E. This dating has encouraged the supposition that Egyptian civilization "erupted" almost overnight. The well-documented pre-dynastic Egyptian culture and the recently discovered pre-Egyptian Nubian pharaonic civilization at Ta-Seti seem not to have influenced this perception at all. John G. Jackson, in a private conversation, once offered the opinion that the real reason behind this strenuous down-dating was to allow antiquarians to place the beginning of Egyptian civilization after that of Sumer, whose earliest archaeological remains are said to date from 4000 B.C.E., about 1000 years earlier than the received date for the first Egyptian dynasty. It is here, however, that the Egyptian calendar creates a problem. The Sothic Cycle compels us to conclude that the earliest calendar date in Egypt is *no later* than 4241 B.C.E. Such a calendar, due to the high level of astronomical sophistication required to create it, means that civilization flourished in Egypt *at least* 6200 years ago, before there ever was a Sumer. The reasons for wanting to give Sumer pride of place are not hard to determine: Sumer is outside of Africa and if it can be proved to be the world's first high culture, then one need not admit that civilization was born in Africa.

Egyptologists have tried to maneuver around this Sothic date of 4241 B.C.E. for the beginning the calendar by suggesting instead that it was not invented until the later Sothic date of 2781 B.C.E. Whatever chronology is used, this 2781 B.C.E. date comes *after* the beginning of the 1st dynasty.[12] The pre-dynastic specialist Michael Hoffman has argued that once the Sothic cycle was discovered, the Egyptians could start their calendar arbitrarily at any date by calculation, so we need not assume that the first calendar date in history is 4241 B.C.E.[13] This seems to be Hoffman's way of circumventing the incongruity that Egyptian civilization had already been in full-bloom for 400 years (short chronology) before inventing the calendar. It is equally incongruous to suppose that the Egyptians would have installed any time-reckoning system by interpolation, inasmuch as these celestial cycles were sacred, the very movements of the gods themselves, upon which human fate depended. More to the point, there exists an ivory tablet from the first dynasty that describes the coincidence of the heliacal rising of Sirius, the annual Nile flood, and the New Year showing beyond all contradiction that the ancient Egyptians knew of the Sothic cycle and its relationship to the flood and civil calendar well *before* 2781 B.C.E. Thus they would had to have known of the cycle beginning at least at 4241 B.C.E. and it is therefore absurd to think they would have introduced a Sothic calendar any later than that. This latter is as certain a date as we have for any event in antiquity and Egyptian civilization must have been in full flower at that time. Thus the idea that Egyptian civilization sprang suddenly onto the stage of world history circa 3100 B.C.E. is simply inadmissible, nor can Sumer be given precedence over Egypt.

A factor that looms even larger in the debate over chronology is that of the cycle of the Great Year, another discovered by the ancient Kamites. Even the Sothic controversy pales before the rigid attitudes against the idea that the Great Year, or Precession of the Equinoxes, was known and utilized in ancient Kam. It is possible to peruse every available text written by an established Egyptologist without finding a single reference to the Great Year. According to received opinion, the Precession was first discovered by the Greek astronomer Hipparchus in 127 B.C.E.[14] But we should remember that Hipparchus, like most of the reputable Greeks savants of antiquity, conducted his studies in the library of Alexandria. The conclusion should be obvious: Hipparchus learned of the Precession through his research among Egyptian scientific archives in Alexandria.[15] The Ptolemies had systematically collected all of the learned papyri of Egypt that they could lay their hands on and housed them in the library built for that purpose in Alexandria. This collection, containing manuscripts from all over the world, eventually comprised over 700,000 vol-

The ivory tablet of Zer, 2nd pharaoh of the 1st Dynasty, that reads: "Sirius, Opener of the Year, Inundation, 1." Zer ruled between 4300 and 4200 B.C.

umes. But it was the concentration of Egyptian scientific literature in one place that served as the catalyst for the Greek scientific renaissance of late antiquity. The indubitable achievements of Greek science during this period—including the discoveries of Hipparchus—were nothing but refurbished Egyptian science.

The astronomer Biot in 1823 was the first in modern times to realize that the Egyptians had discovered the Precession, i.e., the Great Year.[16] This conclusion was eventually corroborated by major authorities. Chief among these was Norman Lockyer, a renowned astronomer in his day who owed his considerable reputation to his discovery of helium and his pioneering studies of sun spots. In 1894, after spending considerable time in Egypt exploring its temples, he demonstrated that (1) all the important Egyptian temples were precisely oriented to the major northern and southern stars and star groups and that (2) the Egyptians had to have known of the Precession.[17] Among antiquarians, only Gerald Massey in the last century and R.A. Schwaller de Lubicz in this endorsed the findings of Biot and Lockyer.[18] In more recent decades, however, two other scientific authorities, Giorgio de Santillana and Livio Stecchini have confirmed the opinions of their two 19th-century predecessors.[19] Nevertheless, Egyptology as a discipline has evinced a remarkable aloofness from the opinions of those most qualified to investigate these matters.

Hard evidence concerning Egyptian knowledge of the Precession is to be found in the zodiac of the Temple of Hathor at Denderah. This late temple was built in 100 B.C.E., during the Hellenic domination, leading Egyptologists to the simplistic conclusion that the Egyptian zodiac was derived from the Greeks. A closer examination, however, shows that the present edifice, erected upon the foundations of a temple dated at 1600 B.C.E., actually represents just a re-building of the antecedent temple, complete with its original zodiac. The proof is in the zodiac itself, originally inscribed on the ceiling of a second-story chapel within the temple, but now ensconced in the Louvre:

> The mythological figures representing the constellations are entwined in two circles—one around the north pole and one around the pole of the ecliptic. Where these two circles intersect marks the point of the equinox, or due east. The zodiac thus becomes a calendar going back to remote antiquity.
>
> A line due east, which runs between the end of the Ram and the beginning of Pisces, indicates the time when the temple was rebuilt, about 100 B.C. An earlier line runs right through the Ram, indicating a date about 1600 B.C. at the height of Amonian domination, during the Twelfth Dynasty.[20]

In light of this evidence, it is impossible to insist that Egyptian knowledge of the zodiac or cycle of the Precession was derived from the Greeks;

rather it was the other way around. Lockyer was of the opinion that the Temple of Hathor at Denderah was actually erected for the first time around 3200 B.C. and that the 1600 B.C. construction date represents merely the *first re-building*.[21] The reader is referred to the relevant authorities for a fuller discussion of these questions, but the monumental evidence supports the conclusion that the Nile Valley astronomers were well acquainted with the precession, at least by the beginning of the historical period, and used this knowledge to create yet another calendar, one measured by millenia instead of days, months, or years.

What exactly is the Great Year? It is determined by the Precession of the Equinoxes, itself a function of the 23½ degree tilt of the earth's axis. This tilt gives us two north poles, the magnetic north pole defined by the earth's tilted northern axis and the vertical north pole, sometimes referred to as True North or the north pole of the ecliptic. Parenthetically we might note that two-thirds of this axial tilt is caused by the gravitational pull of the moon and the other third by that of the sun. This 23½ degrees of tilt gives the earth a wobbling motion, like a spinning top, as it

WEST OF ORIGIN TRUE SOUTH

TRUE NORTH AXIS OF THE TEMPLE EAST OF ORIGIN

The Zodiac of Denderah, the Egyptian planisphere depicting celestial-zodiacal events going back to 1600 B.C.

rotates and revolves around the sun. As a result of this wobble, the magnetic north pole describes a slow, retrograde circle around the north pole of the ecliptic. Over the slow course of time, this means that the position of the equinoxes against the background of stars gradually shifts in a counter-clockwise movement and the pole-star itself is displaced for another. It takes between 25,860 to 25,920 years for the earth's axis to complete this circle.[22] This is the Great Year and the apparent retrograde movement of the equinoxes relative to the circle of constellations represents the Precession. Once this was discovered, after untold centuries of painstaking observation by pre-historic Kamite astronomer-priests, the heavenly circle was divided into 12 arcs, each dominated by a constella-

1. Aries   2. Taurus   3. Gemini

4. Cancer   5. Leo

6. Virgo   7. Libra   8. Scorpio

9. Sagittarius   10. Capricorn

11. Aquarius   12. Pisces

Egyptian zodiacal figures.

tion associated with a mythic type. Since most of these astro-mythic types were animals, the term "zodiac," from "zoion" meaning "animal," was given to this celestial circle by the Greeks. Each of the 12 arcs of the Precessional circle represents a "month" of 2,155–2,160 years in the Great Year of nearly 26,000 years. Each "month" constitutes an "age" and each age is dominated thematically by its own astro-mythic typology. Since this great zodiacal clock moves continuously and the equinoxes shift from age to age, the elements of astro-mythology change *pari passu.*

It is actually possible to delineate this progression in the events of Egyptian history and its impact on Egyptian chronology cannot be overstated. Along with the Sothic cycle, the Great Year allows us to chart a path through periods in Egyptian history that might otherwise be incomprehensible. Ordinary academic debates on Egyptian chronology dissolve into impenetrable conundra without reference to the Great Year. Having thus handcuffed themselves, academics have settled for the lowest possible date that most can agree on, 3100 B.C.E., then congratulated themselves for solving the dating problem. We can see why Napoleon sardonically opined that history is a set of lies mutually agreed upon.

Gerald Massey believed that the Egyptians' remote Afro-Kamitic ancestors had discovered the Great Year as early as 39,000 years ago.[23] In this, he followed certain ancients such as Martianus Capella who asserted that Egyptians had cultivated the science of astronomy for 40,000 years— an implicit reference to the Kamitic star-gazers who lived in the lands to the south of Egypt.[24] Manetho himself recognized legendary and semi-legendary dynasties going back 36,525 years prior to the time he wrote his history in 241 B.C.E.[25] The Egyptian New Year of the Sothic calendar started at the summer solstice because it coincided with the heliacal rising of Sirius and the onset of the Nile flood 20 days later. The Kamitic Great Year began in the Age of Leo (whose sign encompassed the 30 days following the solstice and the heliacal rising of Sirius) because Leo rose at the time of year when the angle of sunlight upon Egypt, due to the earth's tilt, was most nearly perpendicular.[26] The most recent Age of Leo, and hence the beginning of a *new* cycle of the Great Year, commenced around 10,858 B.C.E. The beginning of the *previous* cycle of the Great Year in the Age of Leo would have been 36,768 B.C.E. Since Manetho was writing in 241 B.C.E. and since he outlines a chronology of Egyptian history going back 36,525 years earlier, his chronology starts in 36,766 B.C.E. Thus the two dates, the beginning of the previous Great Year at 36,768 B.C.E. and of Manetho's chronology at 36,766 B.C.E. are virtually identical, a congruence that cannot be mere coincidence. We are therefore bound to say that Manetho's chronology incorporates all of one Great Year, beginning nearly 39,000 years ago, and part of another, the one in which he was living and writing. This provides additional evidence that the Egyptians knew of the

Great Year and had known of it for millenia before the historical era. Whether *we* believe the early Kamites knew of the Great Year since 37,000 years before our era or not, it is clear that the ancient Egyptians claimed to have received knowledge of it from their remote ancestors and that the world of antiquity accepted their claim.

The second Great Year, by ancient Kamitic time-reckoning, begins around 10,858 B.C.E., nearly 13,000 years ago, again in the Age of Leo. In one of the oldest Egyptian creation myths, the lion-headed Shu and Tefnut issue from the lion-faced Atum. Shu and Tefnut are the primordial male-female Twin-Consorts, divine progenitors of all neters (gods) and humanity. Tefnut represents the principle of moisture and Shu is the airspace between earth and heaven. It is Shu who creates the firmaments by separating heaven and earth, lifting the celestial Nut from the embrace of the terrestial Geb. He, as the air or wind, is the breath of life moving over the face of the waters, personified by his sister Tefnut, the primeval fluid. This "genesis," therefore, is the beginning of a new world cycle in the Great Year.

From the sign of Leo, the equinoxes precessed, after a period of 2,155–2,160 years into the sign of Cancer or Khepera, the Scarab-Beetle in the ancient Kamite cosmo-conception. This age begins sometime between 8702–8698 B.C.E. Khepera is the "self-created one," the symbolic expression of "becoming" or "evolution;" the ideographic sign of the scarab beetle means "to become" or "to come into existence." It is easy to see why. Just prior to the Nile flood, the scarab beetle rolls a ball of dung and mud into a perfect sphere into which it deposits its eggs, then buries the ball in the soil over which the Nile flood waters wash. When the waters recede after three months, the larvae fly up out of the mud where they have incubated. This is a striking ontogenesis from the dark, primeval "ooze" that the Egyptians called Nun,[27] and, in another phase of Kamite myth, an arresting image of life bursting forth from the Cosmic Egg. The birth of the winged scarab beetle in this fashion also evokes the sun emerging from the dark womb of the underworld. Thus Khepera the Scarab is the self-creator, the Author of all becoming. Iconographically, he is depicted as rolling the sun across the heavens; he is one of Egypt's profoundest, most venerated symbols.

Between 6548–6538 B.C.E., the equinoxes precessed out of Khepera/ Cancer and into the sign of the Twins, Gemini. In this age we can just descry the first glimmers of known history. In Egyptian terms, the Twins are Set and Horus, and in pre-dynastic times they "divided" the lower Nile Valley into two or more or less equal patrimonies, Set's Upper Egypt in the south and Horus's Lower Egypt in the north. These were veritably the twin kingdoms, literally designated the "Two Lands." Even after formal political union of the Two Lands under Menes in the fifth millenium

The Set and Horus names of pharaoh Perabsen of the 2nd Dynasty, circa 4000 B.C.

B.C.E., the pharaohs of the first two dynasties insisted on being recognized by *both* Horus and Set ideotypes, a paradigm carrying over from the preceding Age of the Twins. In this era, Set and Horus were complementary, not the belligerent Twins they were to become in the later cosmo-myth. One remarkable pictograph shows a single god with two heads, one of Horus and the other of Set! Thus the epoch immediately preceding the dynastic/historical period of Egypt was clearly dominated by the Twin mythos, defined and determined by the cosmic Age of the Twins (Gemini) in the ever-recurring Great Year.

Between 4393–4378 B.C.E., the equinoxes precessed into the sign of the Bull, inaugurating the Age of Taurus. Egyptian dynastic history begins here with unification of the Two Lands under a single pharaoh, Menes. The historical testimony of Manetho and the iconography of the period irrefutably attest that it is among Menes and his immediate successors that the worship of the Apis Bull is instituted. Menes and his successors are devotees of Ptah, the preeminent Bull-deity of the period, and they dedicate their new capital, Memphis, to his worship. Memphis is therefore the Bull-city, of the Bull-god, in the Age of the Bull. Osiris, whose ascendancy dates from this time, is also a form of the Bull-god who takes many of his attributes from Seker, a form of Ptah in Amenta. Ra—prominent in the 6th dynasty and eventually rising to the pinnacle of the pantheon—also assumes a Taurean aspect by his identification with the Mnevis Bull. The bull is a symbol of masculine power and potency and in the Age of Taurus, the male deities come into their own.

The Taurean Age inaugurates an era in which the celestial powers are incarnated in the pervasive bull symbolism dominating the period, reflected in Egyptian religion, political organization, and social life. In the Afro-Kamitic cosmic scheme, the world below is a mirror of the heaven above.

Armed with these facts, we can begin to appreciate the improbability of 3100 B.C.E. as the date for the beginning of the Egyptian dynastic era. Not only does it contravene the chronology of Manetho—who had access to the ancient Egyptian archives—and not only does it contradict the first verifiable Egyptian calendar date of 4241 B.C.E., but 3100 B.C.E. does not synchronize with the Great Year which guided Egyptian history. That the celestial Great Year was imposed upon history is an alien concept to the modern world but it is impossible to penetrate the ethos of the ancient Egyptians unless we accept their connection to it.

Some of the most distinguished Egyptologists of the early part of this century refused to countenance a dynastic date as low as 3400–3100 B.C.E. William Flinders Petrie, closely following Manetho, initially proposed a First Dynasty date of 5500 B.C.E., though by the end of his life in 1941, he had down-dated its appearance to 4326 B.C.E.[28] E.A.W. Budge's proposed First Dynasty date of 4400 B.C.E. was closer to the latter Petrie date.[29] Petrie and Budge remained the staunchest proponents of the "long" chronology which, until Meyer and Breasted, was the one accepted among Egyptologists.

All being said, we feel justified in assuming that Egyptian dynastic history commences sometime between 4400–4200 B.C.E., with a mean date of 4300 B.C.E. (close to the mean [4309 B.C.E.] between the beginning of the Age of Taurus at 4378 B.C.E. and the beginning of a new Sothic Cycle at 4241 B.C.E.). This is not to imply that Egyptian civilization begins at this time, only that political unification was accomplished then. We already know from the work of Bruce Williams at the Oriental Institute that a pharaonic kingship called Ta-Seti was in place in Nubia some 300 years prior to unification under Menes; this kingdom gave its name to Upper Egypt.[30] But the Afro-Kamitic civilization that flourished in the lower Nile Valley can be traced back 6,000 years or more *prior* to the dynastic period.[31]

Between 2238–2218 B.C.E., the equinoxes precessing into the sign of the Ram, inaugurated the age of Aries. Right around this time, the god Amen and his sacred city Thebes, rose to a preeminent position in Egypt. Amen's symbol is the Ram and Thebes is the Ram-city, showing unequivocally the historical impact of the transit of the Great Year into the Arian epoch. Previously, Menthu, a Bull-god, had been the dominant Theban deity. With the advent of the Age of Aries, however, Menthu was supplanted by Amen. The Ram and its related symbols, the Lamb and the Shepherd, came to dominate the Age; Ram-Lamb-Shepherd symbols abound throughout Egypt in this period. Without reference to the Great Year, the shifting symbols that characterize Egyptian history seem haphazard and unintelligible, but by pursuing their cyclical movements we can delineate and define the permutations of Egyptian culture. We must reiterate: modern hostility to the notion of a great celestial "clock" defining history impedes our understanding of the mind of the ancients. To them, the Great Year was a cosmic Fact, and the story of man enacted a higher reality.

We can conclude our discussion in this chapter by noting that the equinoxes precessed into the sign of Pisces between 83–58 B.C.E. Within 200 years, Egypt was well on its way to conversion to the archetypal religion of the Piscean Age: Christianity. We will now leave the discussion of the Great Year and pick it up again in the following chapters.

Postscript

Waddell points out in his edition of the works of Manetho that the 36,525-year span of the Egyptian chronological system also implies a Great Year comprising 25 cycles of the Sothic year of 1461 years (1461 civil years of 365 days is equal to 1460 sidereal years of 365 one-quarter days). This suggests that the Egyptians operated with at least two synchronized Great Years.

Notes

1. See Pingree, DE, "Astrology," *Encyclopedia Brittanica,* Volume 2, Chicago, Encyclopedia Brittanica, Inc., 1984, p.223.
2. Neugebauer O, *The Exact Sciences in Antiquity,* New York: Dover Publications, Inc., 1957, 1969, p.81.
3. Cited in Schwaller de Lubicz RA, *Sacred Science,* translated by Andre and Goldian VandenBroeck, New York: Inner Traditions International, 1961, 1982, p.279.
4. Calendars based on the cycle of Venus were known among the Chaldeans and the Dogon of Mali. It is possible to demonstrate connections with Nile Valley civilization among both cultures, permitting us to wonder if the Venusian calendar also existed in the Nile Valley.
5. See Tompkins P, *Secrets of the Great Pyramid,* New York: Harper and Row, 1971, pp.113, 211; see also the Appendix of the above book, Stecchini LC, "Notes on the Relation of Ancient Measures to the Great Pyramid." Both the text and the Appendix reveal astonishing facts about the level of Egyptian science, providing a useful antidote to detractors such as Neugebauer.
6. Ibid.
7. The difference between the solar year and the sidereal year is caused by the Precession of the Equinoxes causing the solar year to slip behind the sidereal one at a rate of 20 minutes per year. The re-coincidence of the two years occurs after about 26,000 years. Ibid.
8. The mean difference between the length of the solar and sidereal years is exactly 365.24927 days.
9. See Jones WD, *Venus and Sothis,* Chicago: Nelson-Hall, 1982, pp.73–90, for a lucid short treatment of the role of Sirius in Egyptian chronology.

10. Jones, citing Eduard Meyer, gives a regnal dating in the reign of Senusert III of 1880 B.C.E. Ibid., p.78.

11. Waddell WG, translator, *Manetho,* Cambridge: Harvard University Press, 1940, 1980.

12. See Tompkins, op. cit., p.143.

13. Hoffman M, *Egypt Before the Pharaohs,* London: ARK Paperbacks, 1980, 1984, pp.14–5.

14. Ronan CA, "Hipparchus," *Brittanica,* Volume 8, op. cit., pp.940–1.

15. See de Santillana G and von Deschend H, *Hamlet's Mill,* Boston: David R. Godine, 1977, pp.66–7. The authors are convinced that Hipparchus merely rediscovered the Precession.

16. See Lockyer JN, *The Dawn of Astronomy,* Cambridge: The M.I.T. Press, 1894, 1964, passim; also Tompkins, op. cit., passim.

17. Lockyer, op. cit., p.300.

18. Massey G, *Ancient Egypt,* New York: Samuel Weiser, Volume II, 1970, pp.525–628 and Schwaller de Lubicz, op. cit., pp.285–6.

19. de Santillana and von Deschend, op. cit., pp.66–7; also Stecchini in Tompkins, op. cit., p.354.

20. Tompkins, ibid., pp.173–4.

21. Lockyer, op. cit., pp. 141, 212–3.

22. The actual length of the Great Year can vary from period to period. It can be as short as 25,860 years and as long as 25,920 years. Thus a zodiacal Age, a "month" in the Great Year, can vary from 2,155–2,160 years. Recently, some astronomers have revised the time span of the precession downward to 21,000 years, though this has yet to find widespread acceptance. It is evident, however, that the Great Year utilized by the ancients was (about) 26,000 years long.

23. See Massey, op. cit., p. 582; also *Lectures,* New York: Samuel Weiser, Inc., 1974, p.8.

24. See Massey, *Ancient Egypt,* op. cit., pp.580–628. As the author shows, certain classical writers had some inkling of the extraordinary antiquity of Kamitic star-gazing, as revealed in the comments of Martianus Capella. The ancestral star-gazers of the ancient Egyptians would have inhabited the lands south of Egypt.

25. Manetho (Waddell), op. cit., p.227.

26. "Precession of the Equinoxes," *Brittanica,* Volume VIII, op. cit., pp.183–4.

27. See Obenga T, "African Philosophy in the Pharaonic Period" in *Egypt Revisited,* edited by Ivan Van Sertima, New Brunswick: Journal of African Civilizations, Ltd., 1989, pp. 297–300, for an important exposition of creation out of the primordial waters of Nun.

28. See Jones, op. cit., p.80.

29. Budge EAW, *A History of Egypt,* Volume I, The Netherlands: Anthropological Publications, 1902. 1968, pp.176–7.

30. Williams B, "The Lost Pharaohs of Nubia," reprinted in *Nile Valley Civilizations,* edited by Ivan Van Sertima, New Brunswick: Journal of African Civilizations, Ltd., 1985, pp.29–43.

31. C.A. Diop, in a private conversation, saw no reason to doubt a 10,000 B.C.E. date for the remote origins of what came to be Egyptian civilization.

V

The Nile Valley Sources of the Old Testament

In our previous chapters, we have attempted to lay a foundation, using the Masseyan method of "natural genesis," for discussing the religious themes that came to dominate the history of the Western world. In our approach we have attempted to show the extent to which myth and religion interpenetrate. Myth is, after all, a symbolic or typological means of representing the psychic, cultural, and natural dimensions of reality. Through myth, archaic humanity sought to make tangible the impalpable, to create order from chaos, to give form to the inchoate, and to make the cosmos intelligible in terms of the common experience of humanity. Myth was then, as it is now, the only "truth" that man could grasp because in its pristine forms it achieved for him a synthesis of all reality. Today, the dross of myth as fables, fairy tales, and superstitions—the Märchen of the Germans—is mistaken for the real gold. The debasement of the coinage of myth has led us to equate it with fiction, falsehood, and fantasy. We have steadfastly refused to look beyond the surface structure of myth, seeing only with the empirical eye instead of the intuition to which true myth speaks. Joseph Campbell has called myths "depersonalized dreams" and dreams "personalized myths," and in this he is undoubtedly correct.[1] But myths are not merely epiphenomena of psychic activity; its substrates feed directly into the psyche from concrete external sources organized by the activities, behaviors, and experiences of human beings. We can, therefore, say that there is no religion without myth; in fact, no organized system of thought can escape it. An ostensibly anti-theistic, areligious doctrine such as Marxism still expresses itself in mythic forms and images: to wit, the "sacred symbols" of the hammer and sickle, the "revealed scripture" of *Das Kapital*, or the worship of the dead "sacred kings," Lenin and Stalin, lying in state in Red Square. The "withering away of the state" is merely the Marxist version of utopia, paradise, or nirvana. Even in an anti-mythic age, mythic impulses inform everything we do.

Take myth out of religion and there is no religion. Gerald Massey, in 36 years of mind-bending labor, was able to demonstrate that "revealed" Judaeo-Christian religion, as preserved in the Old and New Testaments, represents but the creation of history out of purely mythical events. Figures and episodes in scripture, meant to be allegorical expressions of an age-old mystery-drama, were gradually transmogrified into real persons and events. The unbelievable and fantastic in the Bible are precisely those elements that were originally mythical, then made historical. Revealed religion is but unrevealed mythology.[2]

In examining the Bible myths, we have no intention of debunking them as mere fictions but of tracing them back to their original condition. We wish to "de-euhemerize" them, that is, chip away the encrustations of a bogus historicity so they can be understood in their original essence. That accomplished, it will become clear and evident that both Testaments are fundamentally Afro-Kamitic at their root. This is not to deny the kernel of historical fact present in many Bible stories, but these facts are so fused with the myths that it is almost impossible to disentangle them. Once the proper keys are applied, however, it is possible to unveil a new Biblical "revelation," one that explains the source and substance of Judaeo-Christian belief.

Beneath the surface narrative of the Bible is a vast subterranean pool of mythic actuality which, in truth, extends its reach. Tapping into this reservoir, the Bible assumes a place in the living stream of Afro-Kamitic wisdom whose beginnings are as old as *Homo sapiens* himself. Kamite wisdom is, Khepera-like, "ever-becoming," and the Bible participates in a continuing sequence of revelation. However, literalistic Bibliolaters can teach us nothing of this and nothing they have to say will serve us here.

To approach the Bible in its "geo-ethnic" context, we must begin by critically examining the term "Semitic" which is conventionally and all-too-loosely employed to describe the peoples and cultures of Western Asia and the Arabian peninsula. The term is derived from the name of the legendary, eponymous ancestor of these peoples identified as Shem in the genealogy of Noah.[3] In modern usage, however, the word has a checkered semantic history; the connotations that arise from it depend on the point to be proved or world-view to be reinforced. Variously, the term can denote a race, an ethnic group, a language, or some combination thereof. The Semites are conventionally held to be a branch of the Caucasian race and the term "Semitic" is regularly invoked whenever antiquarians wish to prove that civilization began in Mesopotamia. It is easy enough to decode the intent behind this approach; it is a way of saying that civilization was created by a Caucasian race. One can readily succumb to this facile way of thinking because the contemporary Semitic group of Western Asia more or less approximates to the Caucasian type and it is easy to suppose that this has always been the case.[4] As we shall see, though, the case was very different in antiquity.

It is important to clarify the Semitic "question" because there is a persistent tendency to view the rise of civilization in Africa as issuing from a Semitic (read: Caucasian) stimulus. Largely, this is based on the perceived affinities between the languages of the civilized peoples of northeastern Africa and the Semitic languages of Western Asia. For scholars of the Semitic "school," this was proof enough that Caucasian invaders from Western Asia stimulated the development of such civilization as Africa produced.

In the definitive monograph, "Processus de Semitisation,"[5] C.A. Diop has shown that, far from being a branch of the Caucasian family as ordinarily assumed, the Semitic type only begins to emerge at the end of the proto-historical period, between 5,000–4,000 B.C.E., as a result of the gradual inbreeding of the autochthonous Blacks of Western Asia with in-migrating Indo-European types. These Blacks belonged to the Natufian culture whose remains, covering most of Western Asia, date back to 10,000 B.C.E.[6] Their cranial remains show them to have possessed obviously Africoid characteristics: dolichocephaly, meaning "long-headed," and prognathism, or "jutting jaw." From what we know about the early migrations of Africans out of the continent to populate the rest of the Old World, there is nothing strange in this aboriginal presence in Western Asia. Western Asia is, after all, geographically adjacent to Africa and therefore a logical conduit through which Africans could migrate. The first cultures of Western Asia, especially those in the Fertile Crescent, arose out of the aboriginal black Natufians.

In Sumer, so often touted as the world's "first" civilization, the African derivation of the original inhabitants is betrayed by their name for themselves, "the black heads," and by skeletal remains which show an extreme "hyperdolichocephalic type."[7] Furthermore, Sumer's first capitol was Kish, the same as the Egyptian KESH, a name for Cush or Ethiopia. The idea of a close ethno-cultural connection between Cush and Sumer was first put forward by Sir Henry Rawlinson, a prominent 19th-century orientalist. Particularly in the realm of language, Rawlinson found that Cushitic and Sumerian betrayed unmistakable affinities.[8] More recently, an indirect line of evidence has appeared in the work of Walter Fairservis, wherein he links the language of Sumer to that of the pre-Aryan black Dravidians who created the Indus Valley civilization.[9] Since we know that the creators of Indus Valley culture originated in Africa and passed through its northeastern corridor into Western Asia on a migration that brought them into northwest India, the links between their language and Sumerian strongly suggest an umbilical African connection. Sumer would have been a way-station, so to speak, on this migration, settled, cultivated, and ultimately transformed into one of the world's early, though not first, civic societies.

Northeast of Sumer was the land of Elam whose capital was Susa, the first pre-Aryan civilized state of Persia. About the race of the Elamites there has not been the slightest doubt since 1894, when Dieulafoy discovered the "Acropolis" of Susa whose walls displayed numerous reliefs depicting a highly-civilized, unmistakably black-skinned, woolly-haired

**Terracotta statuette of the goddess of Astarte from Palestine: 1350 B.C.
(Photo: Chandler)**

FIGURE 1

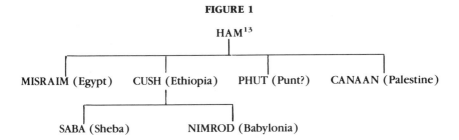

populace. This caused confusion among later Greek chroniclers. They couldn't decide whether the black Ethiopian king Memnon, the nephew of Priam who fought at Troy, came from Cush or Elam.[10]

On the Horn of Africa and in the adjacent southwest corner of the Arabian peninsula, the black Sabaeans created a brilliant "cyclopean" culture famous for it marvelous architecture and its astronomical knowledge. The name of this country, "Saba," is exactly the same as the Egyptian word SBA, meaning "star." This is a reference to the Sabaean reputation for star-gazing.[11] Saba, the Biblical Sheba, is mentioned in the records of at least one Egyptian expedition to African lands to the south. That the Sabaeans were Blacks is attested to in *Genesis* (see below) and in the writings of Josephus.[12]

The Biblical testimony to the early Black presence in Western Asia is found in the genealogy of Noah. Though allegorical or legendary, the genealogy faithfully records ethnic classifications known to the Old Testament writers. For our purposes, we can focus on the lineage of Ham, one of the three sons of Noah, to appreciate the relevant relationships (see Figure 1). Our name "Ham" comes from the Hebrew CHAM which in turn is derived from the Egyptian word KAM, meaning "black."[14] That Ham is the eponymous ancestor of black African peoples is so universally accepted as to require no further demonstration. Thus the Old Testament writers, assuredly eyewitnesses, knew intrinsically that the ancient Egyptians, Cushites, Puntites, and Canaanites all belonged to the same black African family. This is additional confirmation that Canaan, as well as other parts of Western Asia, was originally inhabited by Natufian Blacks, who remained the dominant ethnic type there down to the end of the proto-historical period. We see, moreover, that the Sabaeans were Cushites which conforms to the above-cited testimony of Josephus.

Another important son of Cush in the genealogical diagram is Nimrod, the mighty hunter, best known as the legendary founder of Babylonia. Thus our earlier assertion that Mesopotamian culture was originally Cushitic finds tangible support in the Old Testament. The Biblical writers, in delineating these ethno-historical relationships, were drawing upon more than just hearsay and legend. The Hebrews, after all, spent 70 years in Babylon and since many of them rose to positions of influence, it is not too much to assume they enjoyed access to Babylonian records in the same manner as Berossus.[15] We are therefore drawn inexorably to the conclusion, following Diop's argument, that the Semitic world and its civilization arose on a foundation laid down by the black autochthones of the region.

The business of the Egyptian and Ethiopian languages being "Semitic" now begins to come into proper focus. In 1920, E.A. Wallis Budge proposed that Egyptian was fundamentally an African language. This opinion was ignored until 1973 when Cheikh Anta Diop and his talented colleague, the Congolese scholar Theophile Obenga, demolished once and for all the notion that ancient Egyptian was anything but an African language, at the now-famous Cairo symposium.[16] At this gathering of some of the leading Egyptologists in the world, Diop and Obenga showed that in lexicon, syntax, and grammar, Egyptian was in all respects an African language, allied to tongues as diverse as Wolof and Bantu. But how could Egyptian be an African language and yet retain so many "Semitic" characteristics? The noted linguist, Joseph Greenberg, has provided an answer. He discarded as imprecise and illogical such familiar linguistic categories as "Semitic" and "Hamitic" in favor of a more inclusive category, which he termed "Afro-Asiatic." In Greenberg's opinion, this category was justified by the demonstrable affinities between the Semitic Hebrew, Arabic, Phoenician, Aramaic, and Amharic on the one hand and the northeast African group (formerly "Hamitic"), comprising Egyptian, Cushitic, Chadic, and Hausa on the other. According to Greenberg, the long-dead mother tongue of all these languages would have originated in the highlands of Ethiopia.[17] What this means, in effect, is that the so-called Semitic languages are but branches of an original northeast African parent, of which Egyptian and Cushitic are "charter" members. This interpretation is consistent with Rawlinson's 19th-century assertion that the Chaldean languages were offshoots of Cushitic. Moreover, the Semitic characteristics of Amharic would have evolved from Sabaean antecedents, according to Diop, not from the language of presumed Semitic invaders.[18] We can sum up by saying that the African languages in Greenberg's Afro-Asiatic group were primary and the Semitic languages derivative.

Many, if not most, linguists have accepted Greenberg's model or variations of it but we must now consider an important dissent. In a private conversation, the prominent Congolese linguist, Theophile Obenga, categorically rejected the Afro-Asiatic linguistic classification of Greenberg, insisting that the northeast African language family—formerly "Hamitic"— and the Western Asian one—formerly "Semitic"—are separate and distinct. But Professor Obenga readily agrees that numerous proper names

Egyptian artifacts in Israel: 8th-century B.C.

and other loan words passed from the northeast African language group into the Western Asian group. At a later period, circa 1250–600 B.C.E., loan words and names would have passed back into at least the Egyptian branch of the northeast African group. This bilateral passage of words and names between adjacent linguistic families accounts for the similarities between them, in Obenga's view. The argument is far from settled but, as shall be seen, either approach can be adduced to support the thesis and method that will be developed later in this chapter.

The first Semites in history were in every way "mulattos;" all that we have said up to now points ineluctably to this conclusion. Moreover, for two to three thousand years, at least up to 680 B.C.E., the African states of the lower Nile Valley exerted a kind of hegemony over large sections of Western Asia. The Bible itself offers eloquent testimony to the impact of both Egypt and Cush on the history of Palestine, amounting to a suzerainty in the case of Egypt for the better part of 500 years.[19] Knowing this allows us to register, develop, and clarify the powerful currents of the Afro-Kamitic symbolism and mythos that pulsate through the Bible. It will become evident that the Bible is essentially a Kamitic document and we have tried to set the stage for a definitive proof of its provenance by reference to ethnography, linguistics, and anthropology. But the idea that Africa is the prime source, at least of the Pentateuch (the five Books of Moses), will not go down easily, not even with empiricists who refuse to accept it as the revealed word of God. No matter what our conscious attitude toward the Bible may be, we have been conditioned to look anywhere but to Africa for its origins.

The Hebrew story begins around 2000–1900 B.C.E. when the shepherd Abram migrates from his father's lands in Chaldea, through southern Canaan, and into Egypt during a pre-Hebrew stage of history. Hebrewism as a religion and way of life is predicated on having received and followed the Law given to the Children of Israel by Moses at the foot of Mount Sinai, which didn't occur until 700 years after Abram left Chaldea. Thus *sensu strictu,* we can't call Abram, or Abraham, a Hebrew, and in point of fact, he is the legendary founder of an entire branch of Western Semites. The Arabs, for example, claim descent from Abraham through Ishmael, his son by Hagar, an Egyptian woman, and Ishmael is Abraham's first son. Through his second son Isaac, Abraham is the progenitor of the Edomites through Esau and of the Hebrews through Jacob-Israel. The mixed or "mulatto" character of at least the Ishmaelite branch of Abraham's descendants is obvious since the Egyptian origin of Hagar makes her a black woman.[20] Moreover, Ishmael's wife is also Egyptian, so Ishmael's children have a 75% black ancestry; their descendants go on to become the Arabs of history.[21]

We note here that Ishmael and Isaac are a species of the warring twins whose prototypes are Set and Horus. Just as Set, the elder Twin, is superseded by Horus, the younger Twin, so Ishmael the older is superseded by Isaac the younger. This theme permeates the Pentateuch: in addition to Ishmael and Isaac there are Cain and Abel, Esau and Jacob, Ephraim and Manasseh. In each instance, twins are posed against one another and the younger twin gains the ascendancy. J.G. Frazer calls this "ultimogeniture," contrasted to the earlier "primogeniture."[22] It is indicative of the new epoch in which the younger brother, representing the patriarchate, is made to assume the birthright of the older brother, whose legitimacy derives from the Mother.

To better grasp the historical genesis of the Hebrew nation, we must examine one of the most enigmatic epochs of Egyptian history, the period of Hyksos domination. The Hyksos furnish a point of departure for the modern inquirer searching for a way around the legendary and miraculous events of *Exodus.* Though this is far from certain, they seemed to have achieved dominance in Egypt sometime between 1800–1700 B.C.E. Manetho had this to say about them:

There was a king of ours, whose name was Timaus. Under him it came to pass, I know not how, that God was averse to us, and there came, after a surprising manner, men of ignoble birth *out of the eastern parts* (my emphasis), and had boldness enough to make an expedition into our country, and with ease subdued it by force, yet without our hazarding a battle with them.[23]

It has been assumed as a matter of course that the Hyksos were Asiatic invaders from outside Egyptian territory, but the one Egyptian authority who had access to the archives informs us only that the usurpers were of "ignoble birth" and came "out of eastern parts." Nowhere does he say they were Asiatics or came out of Asia.[24] The Hyksos era is obscure and problematic because contemporary records were ruthlessly expunged by later generations of Egyptian rulers. What does survive leaves very little impression of "foreign" rule; in fact Egyptian culture and political organization apparently flourished without interference. Later conquerors such as the Assyrians, Persians, and Macedonians left distinct traces of their rule on the Egyptian body politic but marks of the Hyksos are barely recognizable.

The one thing that does change is that Set, the oldest of the Egyptian male deities, is re-elevated to supreme status. What evidence we have concerning the period, including the testimony of Manetho, attests to this.[25] This development makes us believe that the "eastern parts" to which Manetho refers might more plausibly be construed to have been Egypt's eastern deserts, home to groups of nomads and shepherds, where Set would have been ascendant. In fact the name "Hyksos" is derived from the Egyptian HIK, meaning either "king" or "captive," and SA or SU, meaning "shepherd."[26] This gives us HIK-SA or HIK-SU which, when Hellenized, is "Hyksos," and means either "shepherd kings" or "captive shepherds." We may well presume that the pastoral peoples inhabiting Egypt's eastern desert were, in effect, Egyptian nationals, or at the very least, "dependents," who pursued their way of life as part of an Egyptian "protectorate." They would have been a constant source of trouble and turbulence to a settled civilization like Egypt and Set, the god par excellence of the desert and desert peoples, would have been their supreme deity. There is nothing strange in assuming that during a period of social and political instability in the Second Intermediate Period, certain desert chieftains could have formed a coalition, seized power in Egypt, and imposed the worship of Set over most of the country.[27] That this usurpation came from within Egyptian national territory rather than from outside is given further credence by Manetho's assertion that political power was seized in what amounted to a "bloodless coup," i.e., "without our hazarding a battle," as he put it. Being in effect Egyptian nationals, these eastern nomads, the Hyksos, would have changed nothing essential in Egyptian life except to re-assert the supremacy of the older Egyptian deity, Set, over the reigning supremacy of Amen and Osiris.

The worship of Set, known as Sutekh in Canaan, was still very pervasive in parts of Egypt, Cush, and Canaan. So dominant was Set-worship in Canaan at the time that the Hyksos established their capital Avaris in the Delta, closer to their co-religionists. Upper Egypt was too completely dominated by Amen and the Hyksos were never able to bring this part of Egypt entirely under their control. Under Hyksos domination, Set or Sutekh-worshippers from neighboring Canaan could find a ready haven in Lower Egypt and filtered into the Delta in numbers. It would have been under these auspices that the clan of Jacob, through the good offices of their kinsman Joseph, settled in Egypt under the pressure of famine. It is hard to know if there really was a Joseph in Egypt, or someone like him, but nothing in the Hyksos period makes his presence there improbable. There would have been no bar to a talented person of Canaanite extraction rising in the service of a Hyksos pharaoh. Be that as it may, there is an undeniably legendary character to the story of Joseph, most likely drawn from two sources in Egyptian literature. The first relates an episode that occurred in the reign of Djoser in the 3rd dynasty. There was a period, so the annals tell us, when Egypt experienced seven consecutive low Nile floods, leading to seven years of famine. Finally Djoser turned to his great prime minister and most trusted advisor Imhotep, who after consulting the sacred books, advised pharaoh to repair to the temple of Khnum, the controller of the floodwaters, in Egyptian Nubia. Khnum appeared to Djoser in a dream describing all that needed to be done to release the Nile floodwaters and relieve famine. Duly following Khnum's instructions, Djoser was able to obtain the release of the flood, bringing the famine to an end.[28] In the *Story of the Two Brothers,* from Egyptian fiction, the younger brother Bata is the faithful servant of his older brother Anubis but catches the amorous eye of his brother's wife. She importunes him for his favors which he stoutly rebuffs, whereupon she goes to her husband to accuse Bata of improper advances. A catastrophic series of events befall Bata, evoking the episode of Joseph's encounter with Potiphar's wife.[29] It seems likely that these two episodes in Egyptian literature served as source material for the Biblical Joseph story. Harold Cooke points out that Joseph, after all, was in all things Egyptian and very likely an initiate into the Egyptian priesthood.[30] We would therefore not be overextending ourselves to say that the story of Joseph is but reworked Egyptian folk material.

The clan of Jacob very likely worshipped Aiu or Yiu, the Golden Ass. Aiu/Yiu stood for both Ra *and* Set: the Ass that pulls the bark of the sun-god Ra across the heavens, or alternatively, that carries Ra between his ears. He is one of the 75 forms of Ra. Set, as we have seen, is also a symbol of the sun. The Egyptian word SET, among its many meanings, gives us "fire" or "burning rays," i.e., the fiery, incendiary aspect of the sun. Ra is the beneficent, life-giving aspect of the sun; Set the burning, dessicating aspect and both are manifested in Yiu, the Golden Ass. That Set and Ra were closely linked is revealed in the *Contendings of Horus and Set,* where Ra is made to take Set's part in the dispute between the warring Twins.[31] There is also a strange story of Set's sexual inversion in which he is made to give birth to the seed of Horus which comes forth from Set as the disk of the sun.[32] Moreover, Ra staves off complete humiliation for Set by finding a place for him in the prow of his solar boat fending off Apap, the Dragon of Darkness.[33] It is interesting to note further that one of the pharaohs of the late Middle Kingdom, Ra-Nehsi ("Ra the Nubian"), was a devout worshipper of Set.[34] Thus we can see a remarkable contrast between the enmity of Set and Osiris on the one hand and the congenial, almost intimate relationship between Set and Ra on the other. These early solar types were mythically linked which is why the Golden Ass could personify one as well as the other.

The clearest representative of the Golden Ass in the Old Testament is Joseph, as Massey relates, whose name in Egyptian may be rendered as YIU-SEFI, meaning either "Yiu, the son" or "the son of Yiu."[35] Several classical writers related that the early Hebrews were worshippers of an ass-headed deity and that even in the period just before our era, a figure of a man seated on an ass received veneration in the Tabernacle.[36] The Jews of the time of Josephus (1st century A.D.) hotly denied such assertions as slanders upon their religion but these were undoubtedly correct insofar as they refer to a pre-Mosaic form of worship among the "proto-Hebrews."[37] In fact J.G. Frazer tells us that asses were exempt from sacrifice because of the veneration paid to them by Hebrews.[38] Samson's destruction of the Philistines with a jawbone of an ass further establishes the connection between the ass type and Hebrew myth, identifying him as a type of Sethian solar power.[39] All this being said, if, as seems likely, Jacob and Joseph's clan were devotees of the Yiu cult, they would have found toleration in the Egypt of the Hyksos, for such worship would have been considered merely a sub-species of Sethian religion.

According to the Old Testament, there were 70 who entered Egypt with Jacob, but more than two million men, women, and children who left during the Exodus.[40] This latter figure is so excessive as to defy all historical possibility but it is safe to say that there was a proliferation. The Bible states that there came a pharaoh "who knew not Joseph," and this must refer to the line of Theban dynasts who surged out of the south and forced the Hyksos from Egypt, 240,000 of whom, according to Manetho, migrated to the Canaanite city of Hierosylyma, or Jerusalem.[41] To the extent that this expulsion is the source of one of the traditions conflated in the Exodus story, the impossibly high numbers given by scriptural writers may partially reflect the massive Hyksos retreat. Still, it is certain, after

Manetho, that a second exodus drove religious dissenters from Egypt at a later time and there may have been as many as 80,000 of these.

The *Book of Exodus* is especially important for internal evidence of the Bible's African origins, but to evaluate it we must look beyond the theological commonplaces that have obscured the whole question for centuries. The first to do this with any success was Gerald Massey in a chapter entitled "The Egyptian Origins of the Jews Traced From the Monuments," in Volume 2 of *Book of Beginnings*.[42] Massey was able to show that in scriptural texts purporting to be veritable history, the germ of historical incident which may be present is so overgrown with mythic foliage that it is almost impossible to obtain a "purified extract" of it. The *Book of Exodus* is no exception and Massey was one of the few courageous enough to consider seriously what the Egyptians themselves had to say about an event that so colored the evolution of western religions.

It is, in fact, a shock to most people to find that there is *any* Egyptian commentary on the Exodus at all, yet the Egyptian scholar-priests, Apion and Manetho, did write about it from their perspective. Unfortunately, only fragments of their commentaries on the subject have come down to us and then only through the eyes of a hostile witness. Flavius Josephus, a Romanized Jewish apologist of the first century C.E., attempted to refute the two Egyptians in an essay entitled "Against Apion."[43] As we have seen, it is Manetho who tells us (after Josephus) that there were at least two exodes out of Egypt.[44] The first consisted of a remnant of the defeated Hyksos and their loyalists, who retreated to the Canaanite city of Jerusalem. The second, a band of downtrodden Egypto-Canaanite dissenters and Hyksos co-religionists, were led into Canaan by an apostate Egyptian priest of the temple of Ra named Osarsiph in the centuries after the Hyksos retreat. We can only assume that if the Exodus story has any historical foundation at all, it reposes in these versions, and it seems evident that the post-Exilic Hebrew writers either confounded or conflated the two events.

Nothing in the Egyptian account of this episode, as recounted by Josephus, makes any mention of the ten plagues, the parting of the waters, or the drowning of pharaohs army nor is there anything in the authentic Egyptian annals that alludes to any of this.[45] These fabulous happenings are certainly legendary and Massey shows they were drawn from the mystery drama of the Ritual and made into literal history by the Old Testament scribes.[46] In fact, Manetho asserts that, far from any plagues being visited upon Egypt, the exiles were driven out because they were "lepers." Manetho then tells us that Osarsiph, after assuming leadership over the deportees, changed his name to Moses, led them into Canaan, and instructed them in an exclusively monotheistic creed whose god was Yahweh. At the dawn of Hebrew history, Yahweh appears for the first time at Mount Sinai; thereafter, He and the Hebrew nation are inexorably bound.

We can now proceed to demystify the events that led to the formation of the Hebrew people, culture, and religion. The 70 who came into Egypt under Jacob were a tiny band of illiterate shepherds settling within the dominant civilization of the time. In the manner of any small, marginal group settling among a culturally superior people, the members of this clan would have lost their language within a generation or two. Inevitably, they took their spouses from among the people in whose country they settled. There would have nothing unusual in that—all the way down to the 6th century B.C.E., the Children of Israel freely intermarried with neighboring peoples and this tendancy would have been more pronounced among the early patriarchs, whose numbers were few. Abraham, Ishmael, and Joseph all took Egyptian wives. Following this pattern, the descendants of Jacob would have become ethnically indistinct from the surrounding population within three or four generations. The Bible reckons 430 years from the time of Jacob's entry into Egypt until the Exodus, so those led out of Egypt under Moses-Osarsiph in the 13th century B.C.E. were, by then, racially, culturally, and linguistically black Egyptians. While it is true that a "mixed multitude" inhabited the eastern Delta, that element descended from the clan of Jacob-Israel had to be black and Egyptian.

The idea that a group of Blacks constituted the core people of the Exodus is a radical notion today, given our familiar suppositions about the racial milieu of the Old Testament, but it was an accepted idea in antiquity. Celsus, Plutarch, Tacitus, Eusebius, and Diodorus all recorded the received tradition that the original Hebrews were a group of Ethiopians and Egyptians who were forced to leave Egypt and migrate to Canaan.[47] Thus when we echo the assertions of scholars of the caliber of Diop and Massey by affirming that the historical Semites, including the original Hebrews, evolved out of the African world and were originally black-skinned, we are insisting only on facts known and attested to by the ancient authorities who wrote on the subject. Manetho's history, the only surviving one from an identifiable Egyptian historian, corroborates this impression. Thus we must reiterate: if Jacob's clan was not black when it entered Egypt, it certainly was when its descendants departed in the group organized and led by Moses-Osarsiph. To the extent that there were any literate persons among them, apart from Osarsiph himself, their written language and literature would have been Egyptian, at a time when the Hebrew language didn't even exist.

This brings us to the imposing figure of Moses, the human centerpiece of the whole Exodus. Sigmund Freud in *Moses and Monotheism* proposed that the original Moses was in fact an Egyptian priest who, in taking the part of a downtrodden group of serfs in Egypt, was influenced by the ideas and example of Akhenaten, who lived at least 100 years earlier.[48]

Wall relief of negroid Jewish captives: 660 B.C. (Photo: Chandler)

Freud may have arrived at his conclusion regarding the Egyptian origin of Moses after reading the essay "Against Apion" by Josephus, but whatever the case, he was undoubtedly correct. The story of Moses being born of a poor Israelite family and then being adopted by a female member of the royal house of Egypt has all the earmarks of poetic fantasy, a fable manufactured to create a Hebrew provenance for the great founder of the Hebrew nation. In Egypt, the royal bloodline was sacrosanct; the notion that a royal daughter, through whom the very legitimacy of that bloodline depended, would adopt a child of serfs, putatively foreign ones at that, is contrary to all reality. We cannot imagine a royal house in modern Europe allowing something of this nature and such a scenario would have been even more unthinkable during Egypt's 18th dynasty. Indeed, Amenhotep III was obliged to tell a foreign king who wished to take to wife an Egyptian princess of the blood, that never in all the history of Egypt had a royal daughter married a foreigner.[49] If a dynastic marriage with a foreign prince was unthinkable, we can imagine what would have been thought of the adoption of an Israelite foundling by a royal daughter. If there is a grain of truth is Moses's royal connection, it could only be that Moses was himself Egyptian. The *Book of Exodus* and the *Book of Acts* (New Testament) both insist that Moses had acquired all the knowledge and wisdom of the Egyptian priesthood, assertions explicitly confirmed by Manetho.[50]

Since the priests were mostly recruited from the aristocracy, many of whom had royal ties, Moses could have been the scion of such a family.

Other writers have been led to the same conclusion as Freud. Harold Cooke in his *Osiris: Studies in Myths, Mysteries, and Religion* also advances the opinion that Moses was a "high-grade initiate" in the Egyptian temple. His marriage to a Cushite woman makes sense, too, since both the royal and high-born families of Egypt were in the habit of contracting dynastic alliances with the Cushite aristocracy. Miriam's objection to the marriage is a later interpolation.

That Moses-Osarsiph may have been clandestinely influenced by the posthumous teachings of Akenaten is certainly plausible. Akenaten was the first to institute monolatry, the worship of a single, exclusive deity whose symbol was Aten, the disc of the sun. He was the first to insist that God not be represented by "graven images." We cannot say, strictly speaking, that Akenaten was the first monotheist, because Egyptians had recognized the existence of a single creator from time immemorial, but he was the first to do away with the multiplicity of images of the deity. It is difficult to avoid the conclusion that Akenaten was the true source of what came be called Hebrew monotheism. We can summarize by saying that Moses-Osarsiph was an Egyptian nobleman, with possible links to the royal house, trained as a priest of Ra who, inspired by the example of Akenaten, took up the cause of certain native pariahs, led them into Canaan, taught them the new worship of a single deity, and provided them with their first laws.

The people of the Exodus had undergone proscription of their religion, itself Egyptian, because fundamentally they had been worshippers of the deity Set, the great Son of the Mother. There were several forms of this Set worship and Jacob's descendants very likely followed that of Yiu, the Golden Ass, who, as we have seen, was both Ra and Set. And, as we have seen, even Aten, the sun-disk, was closely connected to Set.[51] To orthodox worshippers of Osiris and Amen during the 18th dynasty, Set was a sort of "anti-Christ," and when Amen-worshippers regained power under the energetic leadership of a dynasty of Theban princes with close ties to Napatan Cush, they systematically destroyed all traces of the regime of Set raised up by the hated Hyksos. The Hyksos and their allies were anathemized in Egypt as "lepers" not necessarily on account of alien or marginal nationality but because of cultic allegiance to Set in his many forms. At the high tide of the 18th dynasty, the Set-worshippers were hated as remorselessly as any foreigner, in a manner not unlike the sectarian strife of the present day. We will return to this theme later on.

We have exerted substantial effort to establish solid ground for a radical re-examination of the Old Testament through the prism of ancient Kamite culture and language. Our method was first demonstrated in the course of a private conversation with Cheikh Anta Diop; it requires that we trace the meaning of Old Testament words and names back to their Egyptian cognates. To do this, we must first transliterate these names from Hebrew then show their correspondences to related words in the old Kamite tongue. The relationships thus revealed are really quite astounding and allow us to uncover content and connections in these names heretofore completely hidden. Since Hebrew is descended from the Egyptian, or at least from the African linguistic family to which Egyptian belongs, and since we know that Egyptian myths worked their way repeatedly into Hebrew sacred writings, the premise makes perfect operational sense. Even if we subscribe to Obenga's opinion which places Hebrew and Egyptian in separate and distinct language families, our method would still be sound because we know that numerous names and loan words passed from the Egyptian into the Hebrew across the linguistic barrier. These "new" etymologies, many anticipated by Massey in the last century, unlayer a hidden history to which conventional theology and philology seem oblivious. The results are sure to surprise and outrage.

In *Genesis,* the Hebrew ADAM or ADM is the first man in the image of God, the father of mankind, the namer of all things, and the completion of creation.[52] He is also the Egyptian ATM or ATUM, defined conversely as the first god in the image of Man and the father of mankind.[53] The root of ATM is TM (TEM/TUM), which has several meanings, among them "mankind" or "people" and "completion." ATUM is no less than the complete or perfect Divine Man. A cognate root of TEM is DEM and this means "to

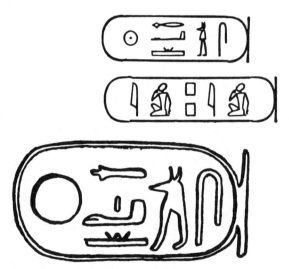

Cartouche of Hyksos pharaoh APEPA of the 15th dynasty—circa 1650 B.C.—whose name is that of the Sethian dragon.

name." Thus, the most elementary and indisputable etymological analysis demonstrates that all the attributes of the Egyptian deity Atum are embraced in the Hebrew Adam. We might note in passing that Genesis represents not merely the creation of the cosmos but also a new cosmic time cycle. The Great Year begins in the sign of Leo the Lion; ATUM is not only God-as-Man but additionally the lion-faced one who creates Shu and Tefnut, also represented in lion-forms. Hence Leo the Lion *is* ATUM and since the genesis of the Great Year is in the Lion-sign, the Biblical *Genesis,* logically enough, begins with ADAM.

ADAM (Heb.)	ATM (Eg.)
1. Father of Mankind.	1. Father of Mankind
2. First man in the image of God.	2. First god in the image of Man.
3. Completion of creation.	3. Root TM means "completion."
4. Namer of all creatures.	4. Cognate DM means "to name."

The female consort of ADAM is EVE, whose Hebrew name can be rendered as CHAVVAH* or HAVVAH. Eve is seduced by the Serpent in the Tree of Life, who bids her to pluck the fruit from the Tree of Knowledge in direct violation of God's command. There are two ways in which we can unravel the etymological strands of Eve's name: on the one hand CHAVVAH can be derived from the Egyptian HFA or HEFA, one of the names of the Great Mother Serpent of the World, and/or it can be derived from HWA or HEWA, meaning "fruit." Ernest Busenbark Busenbark informs us that HAVVAH is another form of the Aramaic word HAWWE which means "serpent."[54] As HEWA, the Fruit, Eve is also identified with the fruit-bearing Tree of Life.[55]

EVE/HAVVAH (Heb.)	HEFA/HEWA (Eg.)
1. Suborned by the Serpent.	1. HEFA is the Great Mother Serpent.
2. Plucks the Fruit of the Tree.	2. HEWA means "fruit."

This imagery comes straight out of the Egyptian funerary Ritual where the Manes, passing through Amenta, reaches the place where Hathor, the Lady of the Sycamore, offers fruit to the tired soul to refresh and revitalize him.[56] As we saw in Chapter II, the Serpent, Tree, and Fruit are all aspects of the Mother that have been separated and then re-linked in *Genesis.* Primitively, Eve *is* Serpent, Tree, and Fruit who succours the Manes but

---

* The Hebrew "CH" is pronounced like a gutteral "H."

Osiris Ani and his wife in the Garden of Peace and Plenty in Amenta.

who in *Genesis* is made to violate God's command by offering the Fruit to Adam.[57] The fruit that Hathor, the Lady of the Sycamore, offers to the Manes is also that of the Tree of Knowledge because it is knowledge and knowledge alone that allows the Manes to successfully negotiate Amenta. In the Ritual, however, such knowledge is the reward of virtue; in *Genesis* it is the cause of Original Sin.

In prehistoric Africa, the snake, because of its ability to shed its skin, was a symbol of renewal, and since the python in particular was so often a tree-dweller, serpent and tree were linked in a composite symbol that signified life, growth, and renewal. Originally, all of this typology would have been feminine and maternal, of which Eve is but a late expression. What is all the more interesting is that the snake is also one of the forms of Atum, representing that which surges or rears up out of the primeval NUN in the first act of Kamite creation.[58] Adam and Eve can both be seen as humanized aspects of the Great Cosmic Serpent who contains all forms, incorporates both masculine and feminine elements, and is depicted as the Snake with its tail in its mouth, signifying the totality of all existence.[59]

The Garden of Eden imagery is also straight out of the Ritual, where it is depicted as a great enclosure of luxurious plantlife and flowing waters, an oasis of peace, plenty, and coolness to delight the Manes after their harrowing journey through the terrors of Amenta. The root of the Biblical

EDEN/ADN (Heb.)	DN/DEN (Eg.)
1. The paradisiacal garden of Genesis represented as a great enclosure in religious motifs.	1. DN means "enclosure."

word Eden, the Hebrew ADN, can be found in Egyptian as DN or DEN which means "enclosure." Much of medieval religious painting depicted the Garden of Eden, with its Tree of Life, as such an enclosure, but the image itself is very old. When Adam and Eve are driven from Eden they settle in the Land of Nod. In Egyptian, this word is NUD and it means "outside of" or "away from," perfectly describing Nod as a place "outside of" the Garden. It is the place set aside for them when they are driven "away from" Eden.

NOD/NWD (Heb.)	NUD (Eg.)
1. NOD is the land, "east of Eden," where Adam and Eve settle when driven away from the Garden.	1. NUD means "outside of" or "away from."

The first two children of Adam and Eve are CAIN and ABEL, and with them we first meet in the Bible the myth of the warring twins. Cain is the cultivator of the crops; Abel is the shepherd. The sacrifice of Abel's first-ling lambs in a holocaust to God is more pleasing to Him than are Cain's first fruits. We can at least partially understand this episode by reference to the Great Year. The Hebrew religion emerges during the Age of Aries, the Ram, starting around 2218–58 B.C.E., and this accounts for the pervasive metaphors of the Ram, Lamb, and Shepherd permeating the Old Testament. The Lamb is the zootypical saviour of the Age of Aries, the sacrificial victim whose flesh and blood renews life and evokes the blessings of God. That is why Abel's lamb sacrifice was more pleasing. The lamb is in fact the alter ego of Abel himself who, when struck down by Cain, becomes a sacrificial victim in true Osirian fashion. Abel is thus a Biblical type of the "sacred king" who is killed in his prime in a rite of fertility and regeneration. He is the sacrificial lamb whose flesh and blood in the Arian Age renew life, making him a type of saviour.

Cain is a Sethian type from the older dispensation. Cain's name in Hebrew is QAYIN, equivalent to QN or QEN in Egyptian. The word QEN means literally "to strike down" or "to overcome," exactly describing the salient deed of Cain's life. In Hebrew, Abel is HABL or HABEL; the Egyp-

CAIN/QAYIN (Heb.)	ON/QEN (Eg.)
1. Strikes down his brother Abel in the first murder.	1. QEN means "to strike down."

tian form is HAB-IR*: HAB means "feast" and IR means "ceremony" or "rite." HAB-EL as HAB-IR therefore refers to the "ritual feast" which is Abel's food-offering of a lamb to God. We know that in times long anterior to the epoch of the Bible, "Dionysian" revels would end in a sacrificial "king" being torn limb from limb and then eaten by the participants. In this sense, then, Abel himself is the "ritual feast."[60]

ABEL/HABEL (Heb.)	HAB-IR (Eg.)*
1. Abel makes a food-offering of a lamb to God and is killed by Cain.	1. HAB means "feast." 2. IR means "rite." * HAB-IR is thus the "ritual feast."

After Genesis, the Fall, and the First Murder, the next major mythical event in the Old Testament is the Flood. In this myth, Noah, who survives the Flood in a great ark, is established as the Master of the Flood. More than that, he is the first cultivator of the vine and thus the earliest type of Gardener or Cultivator.[61] Noah's name in Hebrew is NUACH, also NH. In Egyptian, this is equivalent to NU-AKH and also NUH. The Egyptian Nu personifies both heavenly and earthly floodwaters. The annual Nile inundation, so completely dominating Egyptian life, is the arcehtypal Flood of the earth and therefore a manifestation of Nu. The heavens were imagined as the celestial "floodwaters," across which sailed the boat of the sun, and therefore constituted the heavenly Nu.[62] The Egyptian word AKH means "fertile field," "garden," or "irrigated lands," so NU-AKH is the (Nile) flood which irrigates and fertilizes the cultivated fields. This is why Noah is both the Master of the Flood *and* the Gardener: as NUACH/NU-AKH, he is the flood that fertilizes and rejuvenates the fields and gardens. The ark of Noah, in one sense, is but a replica of the boats that Egyptians used to move about in during flood season, but since the Flood is also celestial, there are other modes of rendering the ark. In the stellar mythos, the ark is polar and zootypically is Draco, i.e., Ta-Urt, the celestial Hippopotamus, who floats on the northern circumpolar heaven. In the lunar mythos, the

---

* R and L are linguistically interchangeable so that the Egyptian HAB-IR can be read as HAB-IL, practically the same as HAB-EL.

NOAH/NUACH/NH (Heb.)	NU-AKH/NUH*
1. Survives the Flood, and is the Master of the Flood.	1. NU is the Great Flood of heaven and earth.
2. Master Cultivator as grower of grapes.	2. AKH means "garden" or "irrigated fields."
3. Imbibes and becomes drunk from wine.	3. NUH means "drunkenness."
	* NU-AKH is the flood irrigating the fields.

ark is the barque of the moon which sails across the "flood" of the night-time heavens on its nightly and monthly travels. Finally, in the solar mythos, it is the boat of the sun on its daily course that is pulled along the great waterway of heaven by the Golden Ass.

Noah and his three sons, together with their wives, represent the eight original ancestors of man that are met with in the Ogdoad of Hermopolis and the eight original Nommo of the Dogon.[63] The two birds sent out of the ark by Noah, the raven and the dove, indicate the two-fold division of the cosmos into darkness and light, exemplified by Set and Horus. The olive branch, according to Massey, is a type of time representing the completion of one time cycle and the beginning of another. When, in the course of the Precession, the pole star moves or "falls" from its position it

Mer, a form of Nu and Hapi, god of the Inundation.

is said, metaphorically, to sink into the floodwaters of the northern heavens.[64] The "submerged" pole-star is replaced by another, signalling the end of the Flood and the beginning of a new time-phase in the Great Year, symbolized by the olive branch.[65] The Mount Ararat upon which the ark comes to rest is none other than the primal mound of Atum that rises out of the waters of the void at the beginning of creation.[66] This mount or hill can also be construed as the "new" pole that is erected or rises up in a new era within the Great Year. For the ancient Kamite mythographers of inner Africa, time, eternity, and creation were cyclical; creation was re-enacted at the end of every cycle of time, dictated by the movements and activities of the heavenly bodies.*

Noah can also be NUH in Egyptian, where it means "drunkenness." The Bible states that Noah, after descending from Mount Ararat, cultivated a vineyard, fermented a beverage from grapes, and succumbed to drunkenness. Fermented beverages, because of their intoxicating properties, were the original "soma" of the gods. Wine-drinking was a privilege initially limited to the priesthood who, as mediators between gods and men, would imbibe the intoxicating liquor as a mode of "communing" with the gods or ancestral spirits. This is why alcoholic beverages today are called "spirits" and the drunkenness of Noah can only be appreciated in this light. Certain customs among the Dogon clarify this point. On certain ritual occasions, the elders of the Dogon community get drunk on millett beer and stagger around the village making oblique references to the needs of the departed ancestral spirits. The refrain of these intoxicated elders, "The dead are starving to death," is sure to unsettle those who have been neglecting their sacerdotal duties of providing food and drink offerings to their ancestors.[67] This reminder from those closest to the ancestral spirits—under the influence of spiritous liquors—spurs the delinquent families to perform their ancestral obligations, lest they invite trouble upon themselves. The association of Noah with wine-making is another attribute which assimilates him to Osiris on the one hand and Dionysus on the other.

Having earlier advanced an etymology for the name Ham,[68] we can easily do likewise for Noah's other two sons. In Hebrew, SHEM is SEM, the mythical and eponymous ancestor of the Semites. In Egyptian, the equivalent word is SM or SEM, meaning "traveller," "wanderer," or "nomad." When the Egyptians first encountered the people we today call Semitic, they were nomadic shepherds. Other synonyms used by the Egyptians for these Asiatic pastoralists were AAMU and SHASU. JAPETH is the designated ancestor of the Indo-European peoples; his name transliterates

---

* For the Egyptian prototype of the Biblical Flood, see Appendix III at the end of this chapter.

SHEM/SEM (Heb.)	SM/SEM (Eg.)
1. Ancestor of the semitic peoples whom the Egyptians first encounter as nomadic shepherds.	1. SEM means "traveller," "wanderer," or "nomad."

from Hebrew as YAPHET. In Egyptian, this is YA-PET, which can be broken down as follows: YA means "islands" and PET means "heaven;" therefore JAPETH/YA-PET is the "islands of heaven." From a celestial point of view, heaven was centered around the north pole so that the "islands of heaven" are also the "islands of the north." These Boreal islands might well have been the Aegean Islands of the pre-classical Greek world, or just possibly, the islands of the North Atlantic. We know the Phoenicians operated a tin-mining colony in the British Isles and traded extensively in the north; since they acted as Egypt's merchant marine, we can assume that the Egyptians were familiar with these northern Atlantic islands. The Bronze Age Britons may have been considered the prototypical Indo-Europeans, reflected in the Egyptian YA-PET.

JAPETH/YAPHET (Heb.)	YA-PET (Eg.)*
1. Considered the ancestor of the Indo-European peoples.	1. YA means "islands."
	2. PET means "heaven," situated around the north pole.
	* YA-PET thus means "islands of heaven" or the "islands of the north."

Returning to the figure of Abraham from our earlier discussion of him, we can arrive at etymologies for his name and those of his immediate descendants. He is the first of the patriarchs directly ancestral to the Hebrews as well as other western Semitic tribes. He is originally a Chaldean shepherd named Abram who, in the course of his wanderings, leads his clan into Egypt. The events that befall him there are probably not historical per se but are nevertheless crucial to understanding his subsequent history. His marriage to his half-sister Sarai (Sarah), for example, appears to be of the same type as the brother-sister marriage practiced among Egyptian royalty.[69] When he finally does leave Egypt, he seems to undergo transformations that change the whole character of his life. By his Egyptian consort Hagar, be begets Ishmael, who eventually becomes the founding ancestor of the Ishmaelites or Arabians. Hagar's ability to conceive arouses the jealousy and ire of Sarai who torments her, finally causing Hagar to run away. In the wilderness on the way to Shur, she is confronted by an angel of the Lord who says: "You are with child and will bear a son. You shall name him Ishmael, *because the Lord has heard of your affliction*" (italics added).[70]

ISHMAEL in Hebrew is YSMAAL which in Egyptian can be rendered YS-MAIR. The word YS in Egyptian means "place" and MAIR means "affliction," so that ISHMAEL/YS-MAIR means literally "the place of affliction." Hagar's affliction, i.e., her persecution by Sarah, is expressed in the name of her son. In this same encounter, Hagar is also told that Ishmael will become a "wild ass of a man" and this evokes the pre-Mosaic worship of Yiu, the Golden Ass, a form of both Ra and Set.

ISHMAEL/YSMAAL (Heb.)	YS-MAIR (Eg.)*
1. The son conceived by Abraham through Hagar, causing her affliction through Sarah's jealousy.	1. YS means "place." 2. MAIR means "affliction."
2. Ancestor of Arabs.	* YS-MAIR is thus "the place of affliction."

When Ishmael reaches age 13, God instructs Abram to perform the rite of circumcision upon himself and all male members of his clan as a sign of His new covenant. Following this covenant-by-circumcision, Abram is granted a new identity as ABRAHAM. In Hebrew, this name is given as ABRHM and its equivalent in Egyptian can either be AB-RA-IM or AB-RA-HEM. The Egyptian word AB can be "heart," "will," "desire," or "wisdom;" RA is the Egyptian sun-god; IM means "fire" or "light;" HEM means "servant." Thus ABRAHAM as AB-RA-IM is either "the desire for the light (or fire) of Ra" or "the light of Ra's wisdom." ABRAHAM as AB-RA-HEM is "the servant of Ra's will." This etymology reveals a direct link between Abraham and Ra, irrespective of whether the Egyptian episode was legendary or historical. Whatever deity Abraham worshipped when he left Chaldea, he became a worshipper of Ra in Egypt. *A fortiori* RA, as Atum-

---

ABRAHAM/ABRHM (Heb.)	AB-RA-IM/AB-RA-HEM (Eg.)*
1. The first patriarch of a branch of Semites; includes Hebrews and Arabs.	1. AB means "desire" or "will." 2. RA is the Egyptian sun-god. 3. IM means "fire" or "light." 4. HEM means "servant."
2. After stay in Egypt, establishes circumcision as sign of covenant with God.	* AB-RA-IM is "the desire for the light of Ra;" AB-RA-HEM is "the servant of the will of Ra."

Ra, is the Egyptian god of circumcision, the mode of creating through himself alone.[71] Thus Abraham's convenant-by-circumcision with God categorically proves his relation to Ra. We might even say that Abraham was a humanized version of Ra himself. As we shall see, the particular form that this Ra-worship took among Abraham's descendants was that of Yiu, the Golden Ass.

The Ra-connection among Abraham's descendants is further substantiated in the case of Isaac. Isaac in Hebrew is YSAK and we remember that Isaac was to be offered as a sacrificial burnt offering, or offering by fire, to God by Abraham. God prevented the sacrifice by sending a lamb as a substitute offering, the same as Abel's lamb sacrifice. Both sacrifices are typical of the Ram Age where the sacrificed "saviour" takes the form of a lamb. Whatever the case, since fire is the sacred element of Ra, ISAAC/YS-AKH is related to Ra by his connection to fire.

ISAAC/YSAK (Heb.)	YS-AKH (Eg.)*
1. Was to be sacrificed as a burnt offering to God by Abraham.	1. YS means "place."
	2. AKH means "burnt offering" or "offering by fire."
	* YS-AKH thus means "place of the burnt offering."

It is interesting to note that Isaac's marriage to Rebecca like that of Abraham and Sarah, also seems to have been a species of brother-sister connubium. When Isaac migrates with his wife Rebecca to the country of Abimelech, she is induced to pass herself off as his sister.[72] In the "common source" material from which this story is drawn, Issac and Rebecca, like Abraham and Sarah, would have in fact been brother and sister but this relationship, in deference to incest taboos, was modified in the Old Testament story.

The entire line of Abraham seems to have been linked to Ra as priests, devotees, or human personifications. Isaac's son Jacob is no exception. His name in Hebrew is YAQB or YAQUB, whose Egyptian equivalent is YA-QB or YA-QEB. This name is susceptible of more than one interpretation. On the one hand, YA may be the diminutive of YAI, a name of the Golden Ass and a form of Ra, and QEB means "circuit." YAQUB AS YA-QEB is, therefore, the "circuit of the sun," that is to say, Ra moving on his heavenly path as the Golden Ass. On the other hand, YA may be the diminutive of YAH, a name of the deified Moon in Egyptian mythology, who may be Thoth, Khonsu, or Osiris. Therefore, YAQUB/YA-QEB may be the Moon YAH on

JACOB/YAQUB (Heb.)	YA-QEB (Eg.)*
1. Younger twin of Esau.	1. YA may be diminutive of YAI, Ra as the Golden Ass.
	2. YA may be the diminutive of YAH, the deified Moon.
	3. QEB means "circuit"
	* YA-QEB may be either the heavenly circuit of Ra as Yai or the Moon as Thoth, Khonsu, or Osiris.

his monthly peregrinations through the nighttime sky. This reflects the dominant lunar mythos extant among the peoples of Western Asia in early antiquity, a point to which we will return later.

Jacob's name changed to ISRAEL in the wake of two events: (1) the vision of the ladder permitting angels to go back and forth between heaven and earth and (2) the wrestling match with an Angel wherein Jacob was said to have "seen the face of the Lord."[73] In its Hebrew form, ISRAEL is YSRAL and in Egyptian is YS-RA-IR. YS means "place," RA is the creator sun-god, and IR means "create." Thus, YS-RA-IR means "the place that Ra created," a reference to the place in Amenta where souls, having been justified by Osiris, climb a ladder to the boat of Ra to join the beatified elect. Jacob's ladder and the ladder of Ra are one and the same. There is evidence that the emergence of the place name Ys-ra-ir, assuming that the Exodus did not occur until nearly the end of the 13th century B.C.E., may have preceded the founding of that country by the Hebrews. The stele of Merneptah, circa 1230 B.C.E., mentions Ys-ra-ir as one of the league of Asiatic peoples laid to waste by Merneptah's armies:

Ysraar (Israel) is wasted, his seed is not.[74]

ISRAEL/YSRAL (Heb.)	YS-RA-IR (Eg.)*
1. Experienced the vision of the Ladder upon which the heavenly hosts moved.	1. YS means "place."
2. Wrestled with the Angel and "saw the face of the Lord."	2. RA is the sun-god and Creator.
	3. IR means "create."
	* YS-RA-IR means "the place that Ra created."

Or, this might refer to the forcible expulsion of the Children of Israel and their co-religionists under Moses-Osarsiph, as related by Manetho. In any event, Jacob-Israel represents yet another of the 75 forms of Ra and the continuation of an unbroken Ra-tradition extending back to Abraham.

The fourth member of the Ra-worshipping quartet of pre-Mosaic patri-archs is JOSEPH. Transliterated from Hebrew, his name is rendered as YUSUPH, the favored son of Jacob-Israel, a form or devotee of Ra. In Egyp-tian, this name can take three forms: YU-SEFI, YIU-SEFI, or YU-SEP. YU means "to come" and SEFI means "child" or "son," making YU-SEFI a type of the "ever-coming Son." This is Horus, who dawns every day as the morning Sun and is, therefore, the prototype of the ever-coming Son of Ra. Since YU can also be YIU, YIU-SEFI is the Son of YIU, the Golden Ass, a type of RA. SEP is a name of Osiris so that YU-SEP is "Osiris, the Coming One," who in this guise is really Horus. Each of these derivations assimi-lates Joseph to the Ra cycle and thus all of the patriarchs from Abraham to Joseph must either have worshipped or personified Ra—in most instances as Yiu, the Golden Ass—whose visible emblem was the sun.

JOSEPH/YUSUPH (Heb.)	YU-SELI/YU-SEP (Eg.)*
1. The favored son of Jacob/Israel, a Hebrew form of Ra.	1. YU means "to come" 2. YU can be YIU, the Golden Ass. 3. SEFI means "child" 4. SEP is a name of Osiris. * YU-SEFI is "the coming child or son;" YIU-SEFI is the "son of Yiu," the Golden Ass; YU-SEP is "Osiris, the Coming One."

None of that outlined above is incompatible with our prior assertion that the pre-Exodus "proto-Hebrews" were largely a group of Egypto-Canaanite Set-worshippers. This seeming paradox is resolvable with the typological key. Set is merely the reverse aspect of the life-giving Ra as the solar fire. He is also that aspect of the Golden Ass depicted as carrying the disk of the sun between his ears. Thus we repeat: the pre-Mosaic proto-Hebrews in northeastern Africa, comprising elements from Egypt, Ethiopia, and Canaan, were worshippers of Yiu the Golden Ass, perceived as both Ra and Set. But with the triumph of the House of Thebes and the expulsion of the Hyksos, the worship of Set fell into disrepute. Because of the association of the Ass with Set, it fell into disuse as a Ra symbol. Cer-tain peoples in Lower Egypt clung to the worship of Yiu-Set and for this reason suffered a proscription against their religion, rendered in the Old Testament as the persecution of the Children of Israel. In effect, a schism occurred in the old solar worship—where originally Ra and Set were two aspects of the same deity—under the impact of forces both religious and political. This deity, as Yu, was a type of the "ever-coming son," and though the Hebrews in the centuries following the Exodus came to worship an exclusive Father, this was emphatically not the case with their pre-Mosaic ancestors. The classic dichotomy between Judaism and the Christianity that arose from it is ordinarily posed as clash between the exclusive Fatherhood versus an eschatological Sonship. This dichotomy is more apparent than real. It was Massey's opinion that had Judaism in some way retained the original Sonship, it might have pre-empted the later claims of Christianity.[75]

The typology of fertilization, death, and rebirth explored in earlier chapters also crops up in the Old Testament. The curious story of Onan— destroyed by God for spilling his seed on the ground instead of impregnating his dead brother's wife—is of this character, revealing itself through an Egyptian etymology. In Hebrew, ONAN is AUNAN, AU-NEN in Egyptian. AU means "ground" and NEN means "to anoint," so that ONAN/

ONAN/AUNAN (Heb.)	AU-NEN (Eg.)*
1. He who spilled his seed on the ground and was consequently struck down by God.	1. AU means "ground." 2. NEN means "to anoint." * AU-NEN means "to anoint the ground."

AU-NEN means "to anoint the ground." This refers to Onan spilling his seed on the ground through premature withdrawal and reveals him as another form of the sacred king who fertilizes the Mother, in this instance Mother Earth, with his semen and then, typically, is destroyed. He can also be a form of Ra as UN-AN: UN means "to create" and AN means "to turn back on oneself," thus "he who creates out of himself." This is clearly Atum-Ra, who created mankind out of a masturbatory act, a divine onanism as it were, thereby becoming the masculine figure of the god who creates out of himself. Once again, the conundrums of the Old Testament are illuminated by the light of the phenomenal typology of old Kemit.

ONAN	UN-AN
1. Spilled his seed on the ground through masturbation or premature withdrawal.	1. UN means "to create" 2. AN means "to turn back o oneself." 3. UN-AN is "he who creates out of himself"

We can now proceed to examine the etymology of the name of Moses, who of all Biblical patriarchs, is probably the earliest with some claim to historicity. Our evidence has already led us, after Manetho, to identify him with the apostate priest of Ra, Osarsiph; to look for the historical Moses anywhere else is to pursue a phantom. That he was a remarkable individual is evident; that his persona was eventually overshadowed by mythic qualities is also beyond question. It is readily admitted that the name MOSES was never Hebrew to begin with but Egyptian, allowing for a seamless etymological connection. The Hebrew form of Moses is MSHH or MUSHEH and in the Exodus story, he assumes a number of attributes: (1) as an infant, he is carried down the river in an ark of bulrushes, (2) he is found in a "sea of reeds," i.e., a papyrus swamp, by pharaoh's daughter, and (3) he becomes a type of Hebrew saviour. In Egyptian, his name has two forms: (1) MU-SHA and/or (2) MU-SAH. MU means "sea" or "pool" and SHA means "reeds," so that MU-SHEH/MU-SHA is literally the "sea of reeds," the Egyptian way of designating a papyrus swamp. Thus the name of Moses refers to his nativity and since the infant Horus also was born in a papyrus swamp to conceal him from his enemies, we may say that Moses is a type of Horus. We also know that just as Horus is a type of Egyptian saviour, so is Moses a Hebrew analogue. In the second form, SAH means "to obtain" or "draw from," so that MU-SAH means "to draw from

Akhenaton, the world's first true monotheist and probably forerunner of Moses.

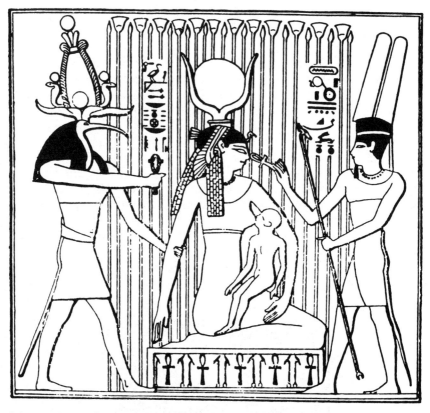

Isis nursing infant Horus in the "sea of reeds" with Thoth and Amon in attendance.

the water." We will remember that in *Exodus* the daughter of pharaoh bestowed the name MOSES on the foundling because, as she put it, "I drew him from the water."[76] Recalling Manetho, Moses was originally OSARSIPH, meaning "son of Osiris,"[77] another datum connecting him with Horus, himself the son of Osiris. Thus, from every conceivable angle,

MOSES/MUSHEH (Heb.)	MU-SHA/MU-SAH (Eg.)*
1. Carried in an ark of bulrushes as an infant.	1. MU means "sea" or "pool."
2. Found in a sea of reeds.	2. SHA means "reeds."
3. Becomes a type of Hebrew savior.	3. SAH means "to obtain" or "to draw from."
	* MU-SHA means "sea of reeds;" MU-SAH means "to draw from the (pool of) water."

the Egyptian provenance of Moses is corroborated. With good reason, Freud insisted that Moses must have been an Egyptian.

The brother of Moses is AARON, the Hebrew AHRN, who is the fashioner and high-priest of the Golden Calf. In Egyptian we get AH-RN or AH-REN. AH means "bull" and REN means "child" or "calf," making AARON/AH/REN the "Bull-Calf." Thus Aaron as AH-REN *is* the Golden Calf, a youthful type of the Celestial Bull from the Age of Taurus whose mother would have been Hathor, the heavenly Golden Cow. AH-REN is a type of Taurean saviour who, at the time of the Exodus, had long been superseded, in the course of the Precession, by the Ram-Saviour of the Arian Age. The anger of Moses when he descends from Mount Sinai is not directed against the image of the Golden Calf per se, but against the attempted re-establishment of a zootypical avatar whose time had passed, and who had been replaced, in the inexorable course of the Great Year, by another in the guise of the Lamb. But the people had berated Moses for having removed them from the familiar comforts of Egypt and, as Harold Cooke relates, the worship of the Apis bull that they bid Aaron resurrect was one indication of their discomfort and disorientation.[78] But after all, it was the blood of the Lamb that had saved the Children of Israel from the Angel of Death,[79] but when in the course of the Precession one Age gives way to the next, the type and symbol of the earlier Age, though losing its place, nonetheless lingers into the succeeding Age. That is why cow, calf, and bull symbols frequently crop up in the Old Testament. We need only recall the Seven Cows—the Seven Hathors—in pharaoh's dream, Aaron's Golden Calf, and the red bulls sacrificed as sin offerings in the *Book of Leviticus.* However, the whole Passover theme expresses the role of the zootypical saviour who, when sacrificed, ensures the salvation of the believers. Thus, the blood of the Lamb protects the Children of Israel from death and ensures their national rebirth in Canaan.

AARON/AHRN (Heb.)	AH-RN/AH-REN (Eg.)*
1. The fashioner and high-priest of the Golden Calf.	1. AH means "bull."
	2. REN means "calf."
	* AH-REN is literally the "Bull-Calf."

The most crucial episode in *Exodus,* apart from the flight itself, is the sojourn of the Children of Israel at the foot of Mount Sinai. It is here that the old worship of the Golden Calf is briefly resurrected, then discredited, and the new dispensation of the Arian Age firmly ensconced. Here the Laws are given that transform an amorphous congeries of Afro-Canaanitic peoples into the Hebrews of history. Thus Hebrew history proper begins

SINAI/SYNY (Heb.)	SY-NY (Eg.)*
1. The volcano or "fire mountain," whence issued the "firestones" and where the Law was given by Moses to the Hebrews.	1. SY means "stone." 2. NY means "fire." * SY-NY means "stone of fire" ("firestone").

at Mount Sinai. SINAI in Hebrew is SYNY, identical to the Egyptian SY-NY. SY means "stone" in Egyptian and NY means "fire" which gives "stone of fire" or "firestone." Sinai, being a volcano, a "fire mountian," often spewed forth "firestones" from its interior. God himself appeared on Sinai surrounded by fire and it was his "finger of fire" which etched the Commandments on the stone tablets [80]; on these "stones of fire" the Law was writ. We might add that the Ten Commandments bear more than a passing resemblance to the so-called 42 Negative Confessions from the *Ritual of the Coming Forth By Day* (Book of the Dead). At least six of the Commandments seem to have been taken almost verbatim from the Negative Confessions:

TEN COMMANDMENTS[81]	NEGATIVE CONFESSIONS[82]
1. Thou shalt not take the name of God in vain.	1. I have not cursed the god.
2. Thou shalt not kill.	2. I have not slain man or woman.
3. Thou shalt not steal.	3. I have not committed theft.
4. Thou shalt not bear false witness.	4. I have not set my mouth in motion against any man.
5. Thou shalt not covet thy neighbor's wife.	5. I have not defiled the wife of another man.
6. Thou shalt not covet they neighbor's goods.	6. I have not defrauded the oppressed one of his property.

This correspondence between six of the Commandments and a like number of the Negative Confessions should cause no surprise when we realize that Moses-Osarsiph, as a fully-trained priest of Ra, would have known by heart all 190 chapters of the *Book of the Coming Forth By Day.* But, as Ernst Busenbark makes plain, the promulgation of the Law on the stone tablets at Mount Sinai marked the beginning of a new worship, substantially different from the pre-Exodus religion.[83]

It is at Sinai that the Hebrews first learn of the name of the deity that they are being called upon to worship: YAHWEH. He explicitly tells Moses, "I appeared to Abraham, Isaac, and Jacob as God almighty but I did not let myself be known to them by my name Jehovah."[84] The worship of Yahweh, therefore, is given to the Hebrews by Moses; their ancestors knew nothing of him.[85] As J.H. Breasted says, concerning this matter: "Through the influence of Moses the Hebrews cast out their ancient ēls and adopted Yahweh as their sole god."[86]

As before, we can recover the hidden meaning of the name of this new deity through an Egyptian etymology. The name YAH in Egyptian is that of the Moon deity, whether as Thoth, Khonsu, or Osiris.[87] The word WAH in

JEHOVAH/YAHWEH (Heb.)	YAH-WAH (Eg.)*
1. The God of Moses, introduced to the Hebrews at Mount Sinai. 2. Became the sole and exclusive God of Israel.	1. YAH is the Moon deity as Thoth, Khonsu, or Osiris. 2. WAH means "to grow" or "increase." * YAH-WAH is the "increasing Moon," ie, Osiris, the New Moon who increases to fullness.

Egyptian means "to grow" or "increase." Thus YAHWEH as YAH-WAH is the "increasing Moon," i.e., a form of Khonsu-Osiris who represents the

Osiris-Yah, the Egyptian prototype of Yahweh.

youthful male Moon in his growth phase from the New Moon. In the words of Ernst Busenbark: "... the Eduth or Testimony must have been a male image, probably of unhewn stone, representing *Jahveh the increaser,* the generator of life (italics added)."[88]

Lunar religion was very much older than the solar and lingers even to the present day in Africa and Asia in the form of traditional new moon festivals and the Muslim lunar calendar. Nowhere was the lunar mythos stronger than in Canaan and under Moses, the lunar Osiris, YAH, was installed as the worship of Yahweh at the foot of Mount Sinai. For the Children of Israel it was a new worship but Yah was not a new god. He had long pre-existed the foundation of the Hebrew nation as an Egyptian deity. Moreover, he was known by the name YAH in South Arabia, Samaria, and even in the 6th-century B.C.E. Jewish community at Elephantine in Upper Egypt.[89] In the Bible itself we find that Yahweh is referred to simply as Yah no fewer than 25 times.[90] We know that the moon was originally feminine in character, so Yahweh, at least early on, would have partaken of this attribute: "... the name appears to derive from Yaw or Yah, a prehistoric title of the male-female moon-god among Semitic tribes of South Arabia. The Jews added the female root, making the word Yahweh or Jahvah."[91] We cannot doubt then that YAHWEH, the national god of Israel, derives from an older, pre-extant lunar deity known throughout northeast Africa and Western Asia. Another clue to the immersion of the ancient Hebrews in the lunar cult can be detected in the word JEW, which in Hebrew is YAHUDY. This is almost exactly the same as JEHUDY, the Egyptian name of Thoth, the chief lunar deity. These facts show that the God of Abraham and the God of Moses were not precisely the same. The Atum-Ra-Yiu that Abraham worshipped and the Yah-Osiris that Moses worshipped issue from the same culture-complex but manifest variant yet complementary aspects of the godhead.

JEW/YAHUDY (Heb.)	JEHUDY (Eg.)
1. Name of one of the 12 tribes of Israel (Judah) influenced by the lunar mythos.	1. JEHUDY is the name of Thoth, the most important Egyptian lunar deity.

We can now attempt to weave all the strands we have traced out so far into one identifiable fabric. Three, perhaps four, threads of Kamitic thought were stitched together to create the cloth of Hebrew religion. These were separate but related strands that ramified into the historic Hebraic religion out of Africa through Egypt. Osarsiph, being a hierophant, would have absorbed the entire corpus of Egyptian religion, committing the whole system—with its rituals, mythology, symbols, philosophy, metaphysics, and ethics—to memory. His immediate disciples and the successive priesthoods would have continued the teaching through oral instruction alone for nearly 300 years until the great prophetess Deborah, an early Judge, authorized the first book of the Torah to be written. The remainder of the Torah was written bit by bit over a period of 500 years; the redactions and rescensions constituting the final product were not completed until the 5th century B.C.E. By then details of the original Kamitic thought had been lost, Chaldean traditions had been introduced during the Babylonian Captivity, purely historical events were interwoven, and the totality of the writings had been edited to conform to the tastes and sensibilities of the 5th century Jewish nation.

Modern Biblical scholarship recognizes at least three schools of thought interwoven into the Old Testament: the Priestly or P tradition, the Elohistic or E Tradition, and Yahwistic or J tradition.[92] Though the J writings are chronologically the earliest, the P and E traditions appear to be closer to the original common source material and it is from these that we can discern a goodly measure of the founding mythos. This is especially the case with the E tradition, for in the Torah the Elohim are made responsible for Creation. The Elohim are, by definition, plural and their presence permeates *Genesis;* it is the Elohim who say, "Let *us* make man in *our* own image."[93] Further on, after the generations of Adam, it is the *sons* of the *gods* who intermarry with daughters of men.[94] Finally, in the face of the rising Tower of Babel, the Elohim induce a babble of mutually unintelligible languages so that men "may not be like *us.*"[95] There is nothing monotheistic about *Genesis.* The J tradition, on the other hand, is anachronistic, bent on imposing strict monotheist orthodoxy on the earliest Torah. As the written corpus of the Torah evolved, the J redactors sifted through the E writings with minute care and while they did not utterly deface these traditions, they did insert Yahweh into parts of Scripture where theretofore he had not been mentioned. Wherever in the Old Testament there is any reference to a pre-Mosaic worship of Yahweh, it is the hand of the orthodox, anachronistic J redactors at work. We are not asserting anything out of the ordinary when we say that the Old Testament is a patchwork quilt of many traditions.

If the Old Testament is a pool fed by many streams, at least four of them debouch into it from Africa. The oldest tradition is the Sethian, the one from which all others derive. Cain, Ishmael, Esau, and Samson are four such Sethian types. But the long, looming shadow of the Mother, whose Divine Son and Sacred King Set is, informs this tradition. Though the Mother's presence in the Bible is not always obvious, it percolates through in certain undercurrents, camouflaged as Eve, Lilith, Deborah, and Delilah. The second tradition is that of Atum-Ra, personified in Adam, Abraham, Isaac, and Israel. The Atum-Ra tradition fuses with that of Set in the figure of Yiu, the Golden Ass, who appears in the Old Testament as Ishmael, Jacob, and Joseph. Then there is the Osirian tradition that, in its lunar guise, is expressed in the person of Yahweh himself but is also embodied in Abel and Noah. Lastly, we must mention a Horus tradition, one that is but an extension of the Osirian, and that is manifested most powerfully in Moses.

Strictly speaking, Hebrew religion begins with Moses-Osarsiph, who, like so many religious reformers, merely wanted to purify the existing Kamitic faith. Inspired by his predecessor and model, Akenaten, the protest of Moses-Osarsiph emerged as a reaction to the overweening power, with its attendant abuses, of the priests of Amon. The unprecedented military and political successes of the 18th-dynasty pharaohs had brought untold wealth and power to the Temple of Amon. Inevitably, such an immense concentration of resources brought corruption in its wake, so much so that the Ammonian priesthood had begun to encroach even upon the prerogatives of pharaoh. Amen-hotep III had made tentative efforts to curb the Ammonian priests but a true reformation, the "Amarna revolution," had to await the succession of his son Akenaten, that most remarkable, and peculiar, of Egyptian monarchs. Akenaten, who began the process of attempting to reform the existing cult practices, ended by creating an entirely new religion, whose offspring was Hebrewism. There was a strong fundamentalist impulse running through this effort because Moses-Osarsiph turned to an older cult, the lunar one, to establish a "purer" conception of the godhead. Ironically, though spawned from an older, lunar tradition, Yahweh evolved into a single, exclusive Father-deity whose qualities and powers closely resembled those of all-powerful solar types like Amen-Ra, against whom the initial reaction had occurred. Conceptually, Amen-Ra had triumphed.

With respect to the Bible and Hebrew religion, we might well ask ourselves what happened to Set as a result of all this? Set became SATAN. This was by no means an instantaneous occurrence and we find that in the Old Testament, certainly down to the time of the Captivity, Set as the Devil is more troublesome than wicked. The metamorphosis of Set into a demonic SATAN really transpires after the Babylonian Captivity. During this epoch, and in the centuries that followed, Judaism fell increasingly under the influence of Persian ideas which divided all Creation into Absolute Good, personified by the Light, and Absolute Evil, personified by Darkness.[96] In the Persian schema, the two forces were utterly unreconcilable and waged a perpetual war for supremacy neither could win. The profound impact of this extreme dualism on Judaeo-Christian thinking was to lead to the demonization of Set as SATAN. Thus SATAN would be SET-AN in Egyptian: SET of course is the Great Adversary, the Evil One, and AN means "to repeat" or "again." This means that SATAN is really "the second manifestation of Set." The metamorphosis of Set, the cosmic miscreant, into a figure of evil seems to have been completed in Egypt also by the late dynastic period (after 300 B.C.E.). Set was perhaps not wholly demonic there but it is clear that he had become the paradigm of all that was baneful in Egyptian life, no longer exhibiting any extenuating or redeeming qualities that permitted an even grudging veneration.

SATAN (Heb.)	SET-AN (Eg.)*
1. Satan is the Biblical personification of absolute Evil.	1. SET is the Egyptian Great Adversary, the Evil One.
	2. AN means "again."
	* SET-AN is the "second manifestation of Set."

We have already had occasion to say that Set remains one of the most enigmatic deities in the Egyptian pantheon. His manifold permutations are keys to understanding the evolution of religion in the Kamite world and in the surrounding lands that came under his influence. In view of this, we could pose the question of why Osarsiph, "the son of Osiris," would become the leader of a group of Sethians whose god was the veritable Archenemy of Osiris? As always, the pristine genius of Kamite typology points the way to an answer. Pre-dynastic Afro-Kamite mythotypes, and the complex religions that grew out of them, contain the power of resolving paradoxes and reconciling opposites. Reviewing the eschatology of the Ritual, we see that one of the important ministers to the souls of the dead is Babai, a form of Set. He is, in one manifestation, "the eater of the dead," like the jackal-headed Anubis, yet like Anubis, he is also the Guide of Souls. But what is surprising is that Babai is also the son of Osiris: thus, he too was "Osarsiph."[97] Set/Anubis was the very first Guide of Souls and Judge of the Dead, even before Osiris. But in the conservative fashion typical of the Egyptians, when the Osirian eschatology took control, all that came before was assimilated to the new dispensation, and Set-Anubis as Babai became the son of Osiris. Egyptians of the 18th-dynasty very likely looked upon the Set-worshippers of Lower Egypt who followed Moses-Osarsiph into Canaan as outcasts; in effect they were ritually "dead" in Egyptian eyes. Thus it would be entirely consistent that they should be led by a "son of Osiris," who as Babai-Set, was the "eater of the dead." The Jews of a later time read the rites of the dead over the names of those who had departed from the fold of orthodoxy; on the threshold of their own history, they may likewise have been expelled from the "congregations of the righteous."[98]

Continuing our etymological analysis of some other post-Mosaic Old Testament names, we find that the Hebrew conqueror Joshua is also a crypto-Kamite. His Hebrew name is rendered as YAHUSHUA, YAH-USH-UA in Egyptian. YAH is the Egyptian original of Yahweh, USH means "adore," and UA means "one," giving "the one whom Yahweh adores." YAHUSHUA is the true Hebrew name of Jesus as well and we will note in passing that such an etymology is in perfect keeping with the most important attribute of Jesus, about whom we shall say more in the next chapter.

JOSHUA/YAHUSHUA (Heb.)	YAH-USH-UA (Eg.)*
1. Joshua is the successor of Moses and the first Hebrew conqueror.	1. YAH is the Egyptian YAHWEH. 2. USH means "adore." 3. UA means "one." * YAH-USH-UA means "one whom YAH(WEH) adores."

The second king of Israel is David, DAUD in Hebrew. This is DA-WD (DA-UD) in Egyptian and is derived from Da meaning "to smite" and WD meaning "to fling." Thus DA-WD means "to smite by flinging," an obvious reference to David's successful combat with Goliath whom he killed with a stone flung from a sling. Solomon's name is equally fascinating. Solomon

DAVID/DAUD (Heb.)	DA-WD (Eg.)*
1. Killed the giant Goliath with a stone flung from his sling.	1. DA means "to smite." 2. WD means "to fling." * DA-WD means "to smite by flinging."

in Hebrew is SELMEH, which in Egyptian gives us SER-MEH. SER means "chief" or "princely" and MEH is the Egyptian word for "cubit." SER-MEH is literally the "chief cubit." This "chief cubit" is the "royal cubit" of 20.62 inches, the standard unit of measure used by the architects and masons of ancient Egypt in the construction of all public buildings. It was called the "royal cubit" because it was initially established by measuring the forearm of an early pharaoh from the elbow (Latin: cubitum) to the tip of the hand, then standardizing this measure at 20.62 inches. Exactitude was an obsession with the ancient Egyptian priests; all measuring sticks had to conform precisely to a black granite measure exactly 20.62 inches long, maintained and guarded in Memphis. The god Ptah, the Divine Architect, is pictured as standing on a cubit measure; thus the cubit was the sign of builders and architects. The outstanding accomplishment of Solomon's reign was the construction of the Temple, making him the Hebrew type of Supreme Builder, as shown in his name SELMEH. James Henry Breasted states, in fact, that Solomon's Phoenician architect, Hiram, designed the Temple on the ground plan of an Egyptian temple.[99] Thus Solomon, through Hiram, was connected to the sacred guild of Egyptian architects. Again, we can see why the "royal cubit" or "chief cubit" was embodied in his name.

SOLOMON/SELMEH (Heb.)	SER-MEH (Eg.)*
1. Solomon was the builder of the Temple, thus the Hebrew Great Architect.	1. SER means "chief."
	2. MEH means "cubit."
	* SER-MEH means "chief cubit."

We cannot end this chapter on the Egyptian etymologies of Old Testament names without considering some of the important female figures. By the time the Torah had reached its final form in the 5th century B.C.E., Hebrew religion was so staunchly patriarchal as to have virtually eradicated all matriarchal influence. It was for this reason that Godfrey Higgins was able to assert that "the Jews hated the female principle."[100] He was correct insofar as it concerned post-Exilic Judaism, but the extraordinary pull of the Great Goddess is revealed in the famous reply of the Hebrew women to Jeremiah concerning the worship of the Queen of Heaven.[101] The thunderous anathemas and invective of the prophets were directed against Her because she posed the direst of threats to Yahweh. For 600 years, Hebrews in numbers participated in the worship of the Queen of Heaven, making one legitimately wonder if Judaism as we know it would have survived if the Exile, which provoked the Jews to turn to Yahweh exclusively as a national rallying point, had not occurred. Despite the unconditional triumph of the patriarchal Yahweh, the matriarchate adumbrates the Old Testament like a shade that refuses to depart.

It is in the female figures of the Old Testament that Kamite typology most readily manifests itself. As we know, this typology was so hoary that portions of it were obscure even to the dynastic Egyptians. So much of the Old Testament was drawn from Afro-Kamitic source material that the typology of old Africa would naturally have crept into it, particularly in the persons of Biblical females, though in a way that is totally camouflaged without the etymological key.

We can begin this phase of our analysis by considering the name of SARAI, the wife of Abraham. SARAI is SA-RY in Egyptian: SA means "son" and RY means "opening" or "abode." SARAI/SA-RY is thus "the abode of the son," the Mother who gives birth to the Son, in this case Isaac.[102] As we have seen in earlier chapters, the Mother-Son primal pair is one of the fundamental precepts of the mythotypes undergirding all theology.

SARAI (Heb.)	SA-RY (Eg.)*
1. As the wife of Abraham is an early type of Hebrew Mother.	1. SA means "son." 2. RY means "opening" or "abode." * SA-RY is "the abode of the son."

Sarai's daughter-in-law is Rebecca, REBEQAH in Hebrew and RE-BEQ-AH in Egyptian: RE means "opening" or "mouth," BEQ means "to be pregnant," and AH may mean either "cow" or "moon." The cow and the moon are always identified with one another in Kamite typology as co-types of Hathor-Isis. RE-BEQ-AH is therefore a type of the original lunar Mother or Cow-goddess, manifested as the Full Moon, who brings forth through the birth canal, "the opening."

REBECCA/REBEQAH (Heb.)	RE-BEQ-AH (Eg.)*
1. Wife of Isaac and the mother of the twins Esau and Jacob.	1. RE is "opening" 2. BEQ is "to be pregnant." 3. AH is either "cow" or "moon" * RE-BEQ-AH is "the opening of the pregnant cow (or moon)."

Rebecca's daughter-in-law is Rachel, whose name in Hebrew is REKH-AL and whose Egyptian form is REKH-ER: REKH means "wise" and ER means "word" or "speech." So Rachel as REKH-ER translates as she who is "wise of speech," making her the typical oracular priestess or wisewoman of primeval times who became "the witch" of a later era. In this caste of wise women, the original priestesshood, was reposited the secular and sacred lore of the community. They were credited with occult knowledge of the forces of nature, later designated as "magic." The gods spoke through them and the oracular function of these priestesses was so ingrained in the popular mind that even such militantly patriarchal cultures as Greece and Rome could not dislodge them. The most famous oracles of the northern Mediterranean, Delphi and Dodona, were under the control

RACHEL/REKHAL (Heb.)	REKH-ER (Eg.)*
1. Rachel, the wife of Jacob, seizes the gods of her father's house.	1. REKH means "wise" 2. ER means "speech" * REKH-ER means "wise of speech."

of women, black women at that.[103] Rachel's attachment of the gods of her father's house shows that they spoke through her, so that wherever she went, the gods went with her.[104] It was for this reason that her father Laban was so reluctant to part with his daughters in the first place.

Joseph's Egyptian wife, Asenath, is none other than AS-NIT, or Isis-Neith, the ancient Virgin Mother goddess of Sais, whom the Greeks identified

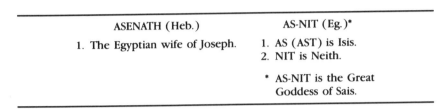

ASENATH (Heb.)	AS-NIT (Eg.)*
1. The Egyptian wife of Joseph.	1. AS (AST) is Isis.
	2. NIT is Neith.
	* AS-NIT is the Great Goddess of Sais.

with Athene. Moses's sister MIRIAM is MER-YAM in Egyptian: MER is "pool" and YAM means "tree." Miriam as MER-YAM is the "tree in the pool." This is the primeval Tree of Life, situated in a pool and identified with Hathor-Nut, the Mistress of the Waters, shown pouring water from a Tree to the thirsty Manes in Amenta. This may also be a figurative North Pole, the Tree rising up from the Waters of the Heavens. All such imagery is derived from the annual floodtime of the lower Nile Valley, where the trees of the countryside stand for weeks in pools of floodwater, which in Egypt revive and nourish all life.

MIRIAM (Heb.)	MER-YAM (Eg.)*
1. The sister of Moses.	1. MER means "pool."
	2. YAM means "tree."
	* MER-YAM is the "tree in the pool."

The astronomical aspect of the allegory is reinforced by the figure of Deborah, the earliest of Israel's Judges, and the reputed author of the first written book of the Torah. Her Hebrew name is DEBURAH, the Egyptian DEB-UR-AH: DEB is the great female hippopotamus, UR means "great," and AHA is a cycle or circuit of time. Thus Deborah is DEB-UR-AHA, "the great time cycle of the female hippopotamus."

Now Ta-Urt is the Egyptian hippopotamus goddess and absolutely the oldest deity in the pantheon. In the northern planisphere of Egyptian sky-maps, Ta-Urt was situated in the constellation we now call Draco so that the north pole of the ecliptic passed through her right udder. We know

DEBORAH/DEBURAH (Heb.)	DEB-UR-AHA (Eg.)*
1. The first Judge of Israel; author of the first book of the Torah.	1. DEB is the great female hippo. 2. UR means "great" 3. AHA is a cycle of time. * DEB-UR-AHA is "the great time cycle of the female hippopatamus."

that the Great Year was determined by the revolution of the magnetic north pole around the north pole of the ecliptic,[105] thus the "great time cycle of the female hippopotamous" is nothing but the Great Year of 26,000 years. Deborah is just the humanized Hebrew version of the vastly more ancient Ta-Urt, the first Great Genetrix, the determiner of creation, time, and eternity. We might also note in the Great Year at the time of Deborah, the magnetic north pole was situated at the base of the celestial Jackal in the Egyptian planisphere; this Jackal is SAB, the Egyptian word for "judge." The SAB-Jackal is indubitably a type of Set, the primeval Son and Consort of Ta-Urt. We can see again why Deborah, therefore, would have been the first Judge; not only was she the Judge (Regulator) of Time, but we might say that she was the "Mother of the Judges" of Israel. It is also entirely fitting that she should be the author of the first book of the Torah. TORAH in Egyptian is TER-AHA: TER means "time" and AHA means "cycle," so that the Torah as the TER-AHA is a "cycle of time." Thus the Torah is the Book of the Celestial Cycles of Time authored by Deborah who, as a form of Ta-Urt, would be the determiner of heavenly time. We might also point out that TER can also means "tree" so that TER-AHA can be the "cycle of the Tree," i.e., the North Pole over which Ta-Urt presides.

Gerald Massey states that ancient prophesy consisted of knowing the Cycle of the Great Year, because in so knowing, the characteristics of every Age could be revealed beforehand. The Old Testament has come down to us as, on the one hand, a book of Judgement and on the other, a book of Prophecy. But, at least initially, this Testament was neither the judgement of a truculent deity over the mundane affairs of man nor the inspired predictions of his future. Judgement resided first in the Celestial Genetrix and in Set, the Celestial Son, who jointly ruled those ineluctable heavenly moments which governed the quotidian earthly affairs. Prophecy was the natural unfolding of cosmic Fate tied to the inexorable clockwork of celestial time cycles presided over by the Judge(s). We seem to be back to where we began, at the feet of the Mother and Son, the typological source of all high theology.

Appendix I

THE QUOTABLE MASSEY: EXCERPTS FROM THE *BOOK OF BEGINNINGS* (VOLUME II)

Gerald Massey dedicated the last 36 years of his life uncovering the Kamite origins of world culture and religion, amassing enough evidence to fill nearly 3500 pages in six volumes. He mined every scrap of information from ancient and modern sources he could lay his hands on, establishing a rock-solid foundation of proof for his assertions. For Massey believed,

A Deep, unfathomed, dark and dumb,
Is left in Africa to plumb.

In *Book of Beginnings,* Massey clearly enunciated the mission of his obsessive labor. He subtitled the book "Containing an attempt to recover and reconstitute the lost origines of the myths and mysteries, type and symbols, religion and language, with Egypt for the mouthpiece and Africa as the birthplace." Volume II of the work was dedicated to plumbing the "Egyptian Origines in Hebrew, Akkado-Assyrian, and Maori." In particular, he subjected Hebrew scripture and belief to an exhaustive examination and came to the conclusion that the Hebrews were but the latest branch of what he termed the ancient Sut-Typhonians of inner Africa from which all myth, symbol, and religion derived.

It is beyond the scope of our present work to explore the Massey material in detail but the following quotes will evoke his fathomless erudition and make clear why he was a powerful inspiration for this book:

According to Josephus, the Egyptian writer Apion most strenuously insisted that the Jews were of Egyptian origin. He affirmed that when they were cast out of Egypt, they *still retained the language of that land.* (page 23)

... the phenomenal origin and descent of the male divinity can be more or less traced from the genitrix Jehovah, goddess of the seven stars, whose son as a star god is Sut ... (page 345)

The African mintage of the earliest current coin of the male divinity is manifest forever in the image and hue of the black god of the negroes, Sut-Nahsi. (page 346)

To this origin in the negro god, and this line of descent throuugh the black star-god, the black-and-golden Sun-and-Sirius god, and the black god who was the sun of the darkness, the Typhonians remained devoutly attached, no matter whether they worshipped Sut-Nahsi in Nubia, or Sutekh in Syria ... or Jah in Israel. (page 346)

The solar triad represented by Shem, Ham, and Japhet is repeated in Abram, Isaac, and Jacob ... (page 349)

... apparently, very few of those who came out of Egypt could have understood the real purport of the writings carried off from the temple of Heliopolis; and, as these died out, the Jews of Palestine became more and more a people without a clue to their own Scriptures, so the true mythos was lost to the Rabbins of the

Haggadah on the one hand, and, on the other, it was restored as history under the renaissance of Ezra. (page 360)

There is no new creation to be found in the most ancient Hebrew writings, language, imagery, allegories, or divinities. They are wholly of Egyptian origin, to be read by Egyptian, to be interpreted and valued as Egyptian of the Typhonian cult. (page 361)

For the Hebrews, who collected and preserved so much, have explained nothing. There is evidence enough to prove the types are Egyptian, and the people who brought them out of Egypt must have been more less Egyptian in race, and of a religion that was Egyptian of the earliest and oldest kind. (page 361)

Undoubtedly, there is some very slight historic nucleus in the Hebrew narrative, but it has been so mixed with myth that it is far easier to recover the celestial allegory ... than it is to restore the human history. (page 363)

As to the Hekshus names, Dr. Birch has remarked, "They unfortunately throw no philological light on their origin. They are neither Semitic or Aramaean, and would, except for other considerations, pass for good Egyptian Pharaohs. They (the Hekshus) did not disturb the civilization." (page 365)

Typhon is Taurt, Khepsh, Rerit, or Teb ... the first and oldest genitrix pourtrayed as the suckler. Her children and worshippers were the detested MENAT. The orthodox Egyptians looked on them as the fanatical Protestant does on the emasculated Mariolator. The name of the AATI was hurled at them. The word signifies the unclean, the leprous, miserables, accursed. (page 365)

In the religious sense Aahmes the Pharaoh [1st king of the 18th dynasty] was a king who knew not Joseph, and the eighteenth dynasty arose as the opponent and conqueror of the worshippers of Sutekh, or Sut the child ... Aahmes married an Aethiope woman, apparently the daughter of some royal house ... (page 365)

... Sut was the god of the Nahsi, and the Aten sun was especially worshipped by the Aethiopians. It breaks out in the person of Amenhept III, whose mother was a black, and whose features show the Aethiopic type. The monarch introduced afresh the Aten disk of the sun, designated Aten-Nefer, or youthful solar god. This, when rightly understood, was no new thing in Egypt. (page 405)

The Hebrew record asserts that the Egyptian princess called the child Moses because she drew him out of the water. Now the typical child of Egyptian mythology was the water-born; was drawn out of the water. So ancient is the imagery of this subject, that the ideograph of SU, the child, is the water-reed (page 418)

The worshippers of "Iu," whether as the dual Sut, Sut-Horus, the ass-headed Iu, the bull-headed Iu, or Iu-em-hept, were all Jews according to religious origines, but they were Egyptians also by race ... (page 431)

On the religious line of descent the Jews are as old as Iu (the Ass) ... whose type was the star Joudi, and on the ethnical line they might rightly claim to be not only affiliated to the exiles of the later revolts, the Hekshus and the emigrants during the reign of Isis; not only to be a branch of the Egyptian vine, for there must be a rootage beyond the branch that struck deep in the Aethiopian and Upper African soil long before it fructified in the alluvial land of the Nile; they might go back and back, and claim kindred at last with the black Jews of India who emigrated with the original complexion of the African progenitors of the Egyptians. (page 432)

Appendix II

African Origins of the Early Hebrews: Quotations from Classical Writers

Josephus: "[Ragmus] had two sons, the one of whom, Judadas, settled the Judadaeans, a nation of Western Ethiopians, and left them his name . . . "

Plutarch: "Those, however, who say that Typhon's [Set's] flight from the fight [against Horus] on an ass lasted seven days, and that after reaching a place of safety he begat sons—Hierosolymus [Jerusalem] and Judaeus—are instantly convicted of dragging Judaic matters into the myth."

Tacitus: "Many consider them [Jews] to be the progeny of the Aethiopians, who were impelled by fear, and by the hatred manifested against them, to change their settlements in the reign of King Kepheus . . . "

Eusebius (citing the Greek philosopher Polema—died 273 B.C.E.): "In the reign of Apis, the son of Pharonaeus, a portion of the Egyptian army deserted from Egypt and took up their habitation in . . . Palestine . . . These were the very men who went out with Moses."

Celsus: "The Jews were a tribe of Egyptians who revolted from the established religion."

Diodorus: ". . . the nation of the Colchians on the Pontus, and that of Jews lying between Syria and Arabia, were also settled by certain expatriates from Egypt. This explains the traditional circumcision of male children practice among these races, an age-old custom imported from Egypt."

Strabo: "This region [Judaea] lies towards the north; and it is inhabited in general, as is each place in particular, by mixed stocks of people from Aegyptian and Arabian and Phoenician tribes . . . But though the inhabitants are mixed up thus, the most prevalent of the accredited reports in regard to the temple at Jerusalem represents the ancestors of the present Judaeans, as they are called, as Aegyptians."

"Moses, namely, was one of the Aegyptian priests, and held a part of Lower Aegypt, as it is called, but he went away from there to Judaea, since he was displeased with the state of affairs there, and was accompanied by many people who worshipped the Divine Being."

Appendix III

An Egyptian Flood Story

As James George Frazer showed in *Folklore of the Old Testament*, stories of a universal flood are legion in the mythologies of the world. The Biblical Flood is ordinarily thought to derive from the flood stories of Mesopotamia; it is not commonly known that a flood story that could have been the source of the Hebrew one existed in ancient Egypt at least since the 13th century B.C.E. We will quote excerpts from this story which appeared in E.A. Wallis Budge's book *From Fetish to God in Ancient Egypt* (pp. 197–98):

> What is it that hath happened to those who have become like the children of Nut. They have fought fights, they have upheld strifes, they have done evil, they have created hostilities, they have made slaughter, they have caused trouble and oppression. Verily, in all their doings they have made the great to become feeble in all our works. O Great THOTH, declare strongly that what TEM hath commanded shall be performed. Thou shalt not see iniquity, thou shalt not be pained, for their years are nothingness, and their months are drawing to an end, even whilst they are working mischief.
>
> [Lord TEM says] I am going to blot out everything I have made. This earth shall enter into the watery abyss of NU by means of a raging flood, and will become even as it was in primeval time. I myself shall remain together with OSIRIS, but I shall transform myself into a small serpent which can neither be apprehended or seen.

This version appears to be only half of the Biblical story but it seems likely that this NU-OSIRIS was the prototype of the Biblical Noah.

Notes

1. Campbell J, *The Hero With A Thousand Faces,* Princeton: Princeton University Press, 1948, 1973, p. 19.
2. Massey G, *Lectures,* New York: Samuel Weiser, 1974, p. 262.
3. Genesis 10: 21–31.
4. Despite the predominance of fair-skinned Semitic types in the northern parts of Western Asia, there is a distinct "mulatto" strain that can be seen in the southerly regions of Western Asia even today.
5. Diop CA, "Processus de Semitisation," in *Parente Genetique de L'Egyptien Pharaonique et des Langues Negro-Africaines,* Dakar: IFAN-Les Nouvelles Editions Africaines, 1977, pp. XXIX-XXXVII.
6. Ibid., p. XXIX.
7. Cited in Rashidi R, "Africans in Early Asian Civilizations: A Historical Overview," in *African Presence in Early Asia,* edited by Ivan Van Sertima and Runoko Rashidi, New Brunswick: Journal of African Civilizations, Ltd., 1985, 1988, p. 15.
8. Cf. Rawlinson G, *The Seven Great Monarchies of the Ancient Eastern World,* Volume I, New York: John B. Alden, 1885, pp. 31–7.
9. Fairservis W, "The Script of the Indus Valley Civilization," reprinted in Van Sertima and Rashidi, op. cit., pp. 64–77.
10. Cf. Snowden F, *Blacks in Antiquity,* Cambridge: Harvard University Press, 1970, 1971, p. 151.
11. Cf. Rashidi, op. cit., pp. 22–9. The ancient kingdom of Saba encompassed both southwestern Arabia and the horn of Africa.
12. Whiston WP, translator, *Josephus: The Complete Works,* Grand Rapids: Kregel Publications, 1867, 1981, pp. 32; 180–1.
13. Genesis 10: 7–10.

14. Budge EAW, *An Egyptian Hieroglyphic Dictionary,* Volume II, New York: Dover Publications, Inc., 1921, 1978, p. 787.

15. Berossus was the Mesopotamian counterpart of Manetho who wrote a history of Mesopotamia for Ptolemy in the 3rd century B.C.E.

16. UNESCO, *The Peopling of Ancient Egypt and Deciphering of the Meroitic Script,* 1978, pp. 65–103. See also Diop, op. cit., passim.

17. Greenburg JH, "African Languages," in *Peoples and Cultures of Africa,* edited by E.P. Skinner, Garden City: Natural History Press, 1973, pp. 70–80.

18. Cf. Diop, op. cit., p. XXXV.

19. Cf. Whiston/Josephus, op. cit., p. 31.

20. Genesis 16: 2–3.

21. Genesis 21: 20–21.

22. Frazer JG, *Folklore in the Old Testament,* New York: Tudor Publishing Company, 1923, pp. 172–5.

23. Whiston/Josephus, "Against Apion," op. cit., p. 610–1.

24. Ibid. Manetho cites an opinion, to which he did not subscribe, that the Hyksos were originally Arabians. It is not unlikely, however, that certain Arabian tribes might have seasonally inhabited Egypt's eastern desert during the period in question.

25. Ibid.

26. See Budge, op. cit., Volumes I and II, pp. 512–3; 586–7; 592.

27. Whiston/Josephus, op. cit., p. 611. The name "Apophis," which belonged to an important Hyksos ruler, was another name for Set.

28. Cf. Budge EAW, *From Fetish to God in Ancient Egypt,* London: Oxford University Press, 1934, pp. 480–6.

29. Lichtheim M, *Ancient Egyptian Literature,* Volume II, Berkeley: University of California Press, 1976, pp. 203–11.

30. Cooke H, *Osiris: A Study in Myths, Mysteries, and Religion,* Chicago: Ares Publishers, 1931, 1979, p. 95.

31. Cf. Budge, op. cit., p. 445.

32. Ibid., p. 453.

33. Ibid., pp. 127; 456.

34. Cf. Budge EAW, *A History of Egypt,* New York: Humanities Press, Inc., Volume III, 1902, 1968, p. 104.

35. Cf. analysis of Joseph's name later in this chapter.

36. Epiphanius, Apion, Diodorus, and obliquely Plutarch, all reported traditions concerning the veneration of an ass-headed deity by the Jews. Gerald Massey had this to say concerning this phenomenon: "...the ass was not a god whether of the Egyptians or the Jews, the Gnostics or Christians. It was but a type of the power that was recognized first as solar, the power that was divinized in Atum, who was Ra ... and whose son was the ass-headed Iau ... or Iu" (Massey G, *Ancient Egypt,* Volume I, New York: Samuel Weiser, 1970, p. 507).

37. Cf. Note 36.

38. Frazer JG, *A Dying God,* London: MacMillan & Co., Ltd., 1911, p. 173.

39. "Striking parallels of features of Samson's career with the various roles of the sun have been enumerated: benevolently, his hair was the sun's rays giving daily agricultural life ... malevolently, the fox-tail firebrands were the sun-withering blight on agricultural crops ... " (Buttrick GA, editor, *Interpreter's Dictionary of the Bible,* Volume 4, Nashville, Abingdon Press, 1984). Clearly, Samson was a solar figure of the Sethian type.

40. The actual number given in *Exodus* is 600,000 men but if wives and children are counted, we arrive (minimally) at the impossibly high figure of 2.4 million. Exodus 12: 37–38.

41. Whiston/Josephus, op. cit., p. 611.

42. Massey G, *Book of Beginnings,* Volume II, London: Williams and Norgate, pp. 363–442.

43. Cf. Note 23.

44. Whiston/Josephus, op. cit., pp. 610–8.

45. Cf. Brier B, *Ancient Egyptian Magic,* New York: Quill, 1980, p. 270. There are all sorts of precedents in the experiences of the Egyptians for the miraculous happenings attributed to Moses. In one Egyptian tale, a magician sets one side of a lake upon the other. In the realm of natural phenomena, at the onset of the flood season the Nile turns blood red from suspended silt.

46. Massey, op. cit., pp. 176–227.

47. Cited in Massey, ibid., pp. 426–32.

48. Freud S, *Moses and Monotheism,* translated by Katherine Jones, New York: Random House, 1967.

49. Cf. Budge, *A History...* , op. cit., Volume IV, p. 189 for the letter from Kallima-Sin to Amenhotep III, requesting a wife from the Egyptian royal house.

50. Whiston/Josephus, op. cit., p. 618.

51. "And Thoth said, 'Come forth from the crown of his head.' And it came forth as a Disk of Gold (i.e., the solar disk) on the head of Set... " (Budge, *From Fetish...* , op. cit., p. 453). This passage shows that the Aton disk was related to Set which means that there was a palpable Sethian element in the so-called "Atonian heresy" of Akenaten. This is consistent with Massey's assertion that Akenaten had "resurrected," so to speak, an ancient symbol—with definite Sethian overtones—to serve as the "new" paradigm of worship.

52. All of the following material on Hebrew names is taken from Buttrick's *Interpreter's Dictionary of the Bible* (five volumes). See Note 39 for full reference.

53. All of the Egyptian language material is taken from Budge's *Egyptian Hieroglyphic Dictionary* (two volumes); see Note 14 for full reference. Many consider parts of Budge's orthography out of date but this has little impact on our transliteration. We do, however, follow the modern usage by using "y" where Budge places an "å"

54. Busenbark E, *Symbols, Sex, and the Stars,* New York: Truth Seeker Co., 1949, p. 186.

55. See Budge EAW, *Book of the Dead: The Theban Rescension,* New York: E.P. Dutton & Co., 1928, pp. 202; 204.

56. Cf. Massey, *Ancient Egypt,* Volume I, op. cit., pp. 447–52, for a further elucidation of this subject.

57. Genesis 3: 6–7.

58. Clark RTR, *Myth and Symbol in Ancient Egypt,* London: Thames & Hudson, Ltd., 1959, 1960, p. 36.

59. Clark, ibid.; cf. also Neumann E, *The Origins and History of Consciousness,* translated by R.F.C. Hull, Princeton: Princeton University Press, 1954, 1973, pp. 5–38.

60. In this aspect, then, Abel is an Osirian type.

61. Genesis 9: 20–21.

62. Nu is thus the "waters above," the "upper firmament" of *Genesis.*

63. Griaule M, *Conversations With Ogotemmeli,* London: Oxford University Press, 1965, 1975, pp. 24–8

64. Reiche HAT, "The Language of Archaic Astronomy," in *Astronomy of the Ancients,* edited by Kenneth Brecher and Michael Feirtag, Cambridge: The M.I.T. Press, 1979, 1980, pp. 154–60. In this essay, the author discusses the archaic mythical imagery employed to describe the celestial "Fall" and "Flood," occasioned by certain stars dipping below the horizon in the course of their heavenly movements. The author also seems to accept the conclusion of de Santillana and von Dechend that the Precession was known by the ancients before the time of Hipparchus (c. 150 B.C.E.).

65. Cf. Massey, op. cit., Volume II, pp. 545–628, passim. The palm branch in Egypt was a symbol of time-keeping or time-cycles; this became the olive branch in the flood story.

66. Clark, op. cit., pp. 35–40.

67. Griaule, op. cit., pp. 179–83.

68. Cf. Note 14.

69. Genesis 20: 12–14.

70. Genesis 16: 12.

71. Atum-Ra was said to have slit his penis, or circumcised it, causing blood to flow, then masturbated to produce the mix of semen and blood necessary for the creation of life. In so doing, He bypassed and superseded the Mother.

72. Genesis 26: 7–8.

73. Genesis 32: 30–31.

74. Petrie WMF, *A History of Egypt,* Volume III, London: Methuen & Company, 1905, p. 114; cf. also Budge, *A History . . . ,* Volume V, op. cit., pp. 104–6.

75. "If the Jews had only held on to the sonship of Iu, the su or the sif, they might have spoiled the market for the spurious wares of the "historic" Saviour, and saved the world from wars innumerable . . . But they let go of the sonship . . . with the growth of their monolatry . . . " (Massey, op. cit., Volume I, p. 523).

76. Exodus 2: 10.

77. OSAR is Osiris; SIPH is the same as SIF, meaning "son" in Egyptian, giving "son of Osiris."

78. Cooke, op. cit., p. 102.

79. Exodus 12: 1–36.

80. Exodus 19: 17–18.

81. Exodus 20: 7–17

82. Budge, *Book of the Dead,* Volume II, op. cit., pp. 366–71.

83. Busenbark, op. cit., p. 170.

84. Exodus 6: 2–3.

85. The pre-Exodus Israelites used generic terms like EL to denote "God" and ADON to mean "Lord." The Semitic EL is the same as the Egyptian IR(IL) which means "creator." ADON is derived from the Egyptian ATEN or ATON, i.e., God personified as the Disk of the Sun. N.B. Note 51.

86. Breasted JH, *Dawn of Conscience,* New York: Charles Scribner's Sons, 1933, p. 356.

87. Budge EAW, *Gods of the Egyptians,* Volume I, New York: Dover Publications, Inc., 1904, 1969, p. 412 and Volume II, pp. 33–8; also Budge EAW, *Osiris: The Religion of Resurrection,* Volume I, New Hyde Park: University Books, 1961, p. 389.

88. Busenbark, op. cit., p. 170.

89. Ibid., pp. 108; 351.
90. Cf. Buttrick, op. cit., Volume II, p. 409.
91. Busenbark, op. cit., p. 108.
92. Buttrick, op. cit., Volume II, pp. 1; 777 and Volume III, p. 617. A fourth "school" of Biblical writing is termed the D or Deuteronomy tradition. The epochs of the three main schools are: J Tradition—ninth century B.C.E., E Tradition—eighth century B.C.E., and P tradition—sixth century B.C.E.
93. Genesis 1: 26.
94. Genesis 6: 4.
95. Genesis 11: 7–8.
96. In Persian cosmogony, Ahura-Mazda was the Light principle and Ahriman the Dark principle.
97. Budge, ... Hieroglyphic Dictionary, Volume I, op. cit., p. 200; cf. also Budge, Gods..., Volume II, op. cit., pp. 91–2.
98. Cf. Massey, Book of Beginnings, Volume II, op. cit., pp. 363–441.
99. Breasted, op. cit., p. 383.
100. Higgins G, Anacalypsis, Volume I, New Hyde Park: University Books, 1833, 1965, p. 433.
101. "... the crowds of women standing by answered Jeremiah, 'We will not listen to what you tell us in the name of the Lord ... we will burn sacrifices to the Queen of Heaven and pour drink-offerings to her as we used to'" (Jeremiah 44: 15–17, italics added).
102. Sarai's name was changed to SARAH; SAR in Egyptian means "to bring" and AH means "affliction." SAR-AH thus means "to bring affliction," consistent with Sarah's treatment of Hagar.
103. Cf. Herodotus's discussion of the Egyptian origin of the Oracle of Dodona, cited by C.A. Diop in "Origins of the Ancient Egyptians," reprinted in Great African Thinkers, edited by Ivan Van Sertima, New Brunswick: Journal of African Civilizations, Ltd., 1986, p. 43. The Oracle of Delphi, on the other hand, was named after Delphos whose mother was Lamia, an African queen. Delphos is frequently depicted by Greek artists as a Negro and we have every reason to believe that his oracle priestesses were likewise African women. Cf. Snowden, op. cit., pp. 150–1.
104. Genesis 31: 19–35.
105. Tompkins P, Secrets of the Great Pyramid, New York: Harper & Row Publishers, 1971, p. 173.

VI

Osiris, the Egyptian Funerary Ritual, and the Birth of Christianity

Having explored the Afro-Kamitic sources of the Old Testament, we may now elucidate the Afro-Kamitic roots of Christian religion. Christian apologists have expended enormous energy creating the impression that Christianity sprang up suddenly and miraculously as a New Order ordained by Jesus Christ, the Son of God. The "Good News" of the Gospels is considered the latest and last dispensation of the Almighty. Christian roots in the Old Testament are readily acknowledged, but Christianity is seen to hold pride of place as the highest and holiest dispensation, literally God's last word. Christianity took from ancestral Judaism all that was needful to it, rejected the rest, and then turned on its progenitor in a fury of anathema and repression. Frequently in history, the followers of the older religion, though giving birth to the new one, are branded with a demonic and unholy aspect by the new devotees. Such was the fate of the followers of Sethian religion vis-à-vis the worshippers of Osiris and Amon. Similarly, the followers of the Hebrew religion founded at Mount Sinai cursed and abjured pharaonic Egypt out of which their religion emerged; Egypt came to epitomize evil and godlessness. Thus Christian hostility toward its parental Judaic religion had ample historical precedent.

Given the prestige of Greek culture in late antiquity, it is not surprising that Greek philosophy, particularly that of Plato, also exerted a formative influence on nascent Christianity. Since Greek was the *lingua franca* of the Roman empire, it became the chief means by which the written dogma of Christianity was promulgated. In the western Church, a significant amount remained in the liturgy even after Latin became the sacred language of Christianity and in the Eastern Church, Greek remains the sacred language to this day.

There is yet a third root of Christianity, all but unacknowledged to the present, and it is Afro-Kamitic. So much basic Afro-Kamitic material reposes in the Old Testament that certain of these ideas would have crept into Christianity indirectly. Other Platonic ideas derived from Afro-Kamitic metaphysics, notably that of the "Logos," also drifted into Christianity. But we are not concerned here with the oblique infusions of such thought into Christian dogma but with the direct, tangible, unattenuated borrowings.

It is a matter of history that the early church, ignored or persecuted elsewhere in the Mediterranean world, found a nurturing haven in Egypt. The early desert fathers, such as black Saint Anthony and countless like him in Egypt, were the first to hammer Christian doctrine into distinct shape. The Egyptian hermits were the founders of Christian monasticism. The Church's earliest saints and bishops were Egyptian; in fact the tradition of African sainthood would exert a formative influence on European Christianity. One of Europe's earliest martyrs was Maurice, the black captain of the Theban legion of the Roman army stationed in central Europe. He accepted death rather than execute Christians,[1] becoming the patron saint of Switzerland and Germany.

The capital of Christendom up to the time of Constantine was Alexandria; its bishops were instrumental in creating the organizational structure of the patristic Church. Moreover, the Egyptians were among the first as a people to accept Christianity; Egypt was securely Christian before Greece or Rome. These Kamite people of late antiquity took so readily and naturally to the "new" doctrine because they perceived it to be an unbroken continuation of their old religion. Early Christian teaching contained nothing alien to Egyptians; Christianity *was* Egyptian in their eyes.

The Christ myth, instead of being a spontaneous upsurge of a new divine dispensation, was traced back by Massey some 10,000 years in Africa.[2] That historical Christianity is largely a reworking of Afro-Kamitic religious ideas has to come as a profound shock, but once we look beneath the shroud of "heresy" cast over its early non-canonical elements, the validity of this conclusion will become self-evident.

We cannot untangle all the threads that lead out of the matrix of old African symbols into modern Christianity; the energetic reader, desiring a more comprehensive picture, is referred to the boundless Massey material. We must focus on the Osirian myth, which forms a bridge between Christianity and pre-extant Kamite symbols. An exploration of the Osiris drama will allow us to unravel the phenomenal origins of the Christhood. Plutarch will aid us immeasurably in this task because his is the only coherent narrative of the Osiris story we possess.[3] Plutarch was perhaps the Greco-Roman world's most reliable authority on Egyptian mythology, particularly the Osiris cycle, a cool observer of impressive learning, and an initiate in the Delphic mysteries. His primary source material undoubtedly was the writings of Manetho, the Egyptian historian who lived during the Ptolemaic period. The authenticity of Plutarch's version of the Osiris myth is almost completely corroborated by Egyptian monumental inscriptions. It must be said, however, that Plutarch was a Greek of the philosophic type and he may not have understood the substructure of phenomenal typology underneath Egyptian myth. He was more at home

with the metaphysical explanations fashionable among Neo-Platonic phi-
losophers. But his cogent rendering of the Osiris myth stands alone—
even surviving Egyptian literature lacks such a narrative.

As we saw in an earlier chapter, the Egyptian name of Osiris, ASAR or
WOSIR, means "begotten of Isis," making him a son of Isis and thus a type
of the Son-Consort. This means that Horus and Osiris are aspects of one
another. Classical mythographers echoed traditions that revealed the
mother-son relationship between Isis and Osiris:

> Lactanius tells us . . . the priests, with their shaven bodies, beat their breasts and
> lamented, imitating the sorrowful search of Isis for *her lost son Osiris,* and how
> afterwards their sorrow was turned to joy when the jackal-headed god Anubis,
> or rather a mummer in his stead, produced a small boy, the living representa-
> tive of the god who was lost and was found (italics added).[4]

Osiris, the son, is the principle of growing vegetation, either as grain or
tree. This vegetative Osiris is sometimes depicted in green color. Plutarch
tells us, "Osiris is buried when the sown corn is hidden by earth, and
comes to life and shows himself again when it begins to sprout."[5]

We see that Plutarch has preserved the old agrarian typology, originally
dominated by the Great Mother. Osiris in his vegetative aspect sacrifices
himself as the harvested grain, from which bread is made to be eaten as
"real food" for regeneration.[6] His rebirth occurs in the new sprouts of the
succeeding spring. As we have already noted, certain traditions assert that
Osiris was killed by a scorpion and this refers to the harvest that occurs
in the sign of Scorpio. We can reaffirm here that the earliest type of saviour was he (originally she) who gave himself as food so that the community might live.

In the Plutarch narrative, a tree grows up around the coffin of Osiris
when it lands in Byblos, the country of reeds.[7] This is another manifestation of the growth or re-growth principle: the dead god is reborn as a
tree, a kind of symbolism legion among the ancients that explains the custom in many cultures of burying the dead in the hollows or branches of
trees. This was effectively the sign-language of resurrection and the tree is
later stylized as the cross, as in the symbol of the Tet or Djed whose
raising signified the re-arising Osiris.

Osiris was also the god of grape cultivation and wine-making. This was
one reason, among many, that the Greeks considered him the prototype of
their own Dionysus. As we have seen, the intoxicating properties of wine
gave it a mysterious and sacred role in certain rites, for the imbibing of
wine enabled the priest to assimilate with the ancestral spirits and forces
of nature. Plutarch informs us that,

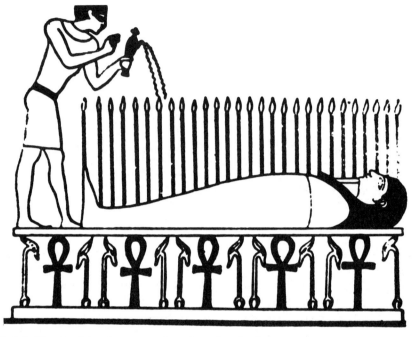

Osiris-Nepri with wheat growing from his body.

> The kings used to drink it, though in certain measure according to the sacred writings, as Hecataeus has narrated, for they were priests (as well).[8]

Since Osiris, the Great Ancestor, was identified with the grape, wine, the blood and spirit of the grape is his blood and spirit as well. In priestly ritual, to drink wine was to drink the blood of Osiris.[9] The lives of Egyptian kings were diving reenactments of the life of Osiris, whose blood was rendered symbolically as wine.

Osiris was also prominent as a lunar deity, presiding over the moon's 28-day (29½ days conventionalized) cycle. According to Plutarch, Osiris ruled Egypt 28 years before spreading civilization to the rest of the world:

> And eight-and-twenty is the number of years which some say Osiris lived, and others that he reigned; for this is the lights of the moon, and it rolls out its own circle in this number of days.[10]

The son-consortship of Osiris to Isis is also played out in this lunar drama:

> By thus placing the power of Osiris in the Moon, they mean that *Isis consorts with him while being (at the same time) the cause of his birth* (italics added).[11]

With rare exceptions, modern mythographers have failed to recognize the Isis-Osiris mother-son relationship, though there are intimations of it in Egyptian rituals and Plutarch categorically declares it.

Earlier, we noted that Set, the dark side of the moon, cuts Osiris's body into fourteen pieces. As Plutarch explains,

> ... the tearing of Osiris into 14 pieces they refer enigmatically to the days in which the luminary wanes after the full moon up to the new moon.[12]

Thus the war of the Twins is incorporated into lunar mythology. But there is a linkage here between agrarian and lunar typology: the sacred king submitted himself to death and dismemberment in an act of fertility and regeneration. The dismembered moon is regenerated as the new moon; thus, the dismemberment of the moon and that of the sacred king are functionally the same.

No matter what the imagery employed, it was the death and resurrection of Osiris that accounts for his unique position in Egyptian religion for 4,000 years. But the resurrectional drama steadily evolved. First it was Isis, his mother-sister-wife, who revived and reconstituted the dead Osiris.

Osiris, personification of viticulture, sitting under bunches of grapes.

Isis, as the maternal type of resurrecting agent, is found in both the Egyptian Ritual and Plutarch's narrative. She is the one who gathers all the parts of Osiris's dismembered body, knits them together, refashions the missing phallus, then fans the breath of life into the inert body. After reviving him, Isis begets the child Horus from the resurrected Osiris. In a significant twist on the old theme, Isis is fertilized by Osiris, the sacred king, *after* she has resurrected him. But his phallus, in effect, still belongs to her; it is Isis who refabricates the lost member of Osiris and impregnates herself with it. But we find that in the last phase of this evolving eschatology, Osiris's son Horus assumes the role of resurrector, the one who calls Osiris forth from death. Anubis, the primeval guide of souls, now assists Horus in his role as embalmer and reconstituter of the dead. But all worshippers, in *imitatio Osirii,* could hope for resurrection after death.

As noted, Isis is the second principal in the Osirian drama, whose rites of resurrection devolve from her own. Her name in Egyptian is AST, meaning "seat," "abode," or "throne." It also means "womb," "tomb" or "chapel." Thus the etymology of her name makes Isis both the womb and the tomb of Osiris. In dynastic times, she became the supreme goddess of the pantheon, embodying all the positive feminine attributes of deity. She is the latest, and perhaps sublimest, form of the Kamitic Great Mother as gestator, bearer, nurturer, and protector. She is the Virgin Mother of Horus, recalling the ancient Mother who conceived and brought forth alone. The Son of this primal Mother is represented as imperfect, as lame or blind, in contrast to the perfected Horus, the son of Isis *and* Osiris. In his manifestation as the Son of the Mother alone, he is Heru-pa-Khart, Horus-the-lame. Plutarch says of him:

> . . . Harpocrates is brought forth about the winter solstice imperfect and infant in the things that sprout too early.[13]

In the Osirian drama, Isis is the true and faithful consort who, with her sister Nepthys, mourns the dead Osiris and searches tirelessly for his dead and dismembered body. She is the feminine counterpart of Osiris as an aspect of the grain and other growing things, originally in the feminine domain. She presides over the making of beer, the oldest of the fermented beverages. Her zootype is the Great Cow, identifying her with Hathor, and this also makes her a type of the full or "pregnant" moon. In addition, she is, as noted, the star Sirius, the herald of the flood; the annual Nile inundation is said to originate from her teardrops. Thus she is REMI, the Weeper, which also alludes to her sorrows in the wake of the murder of Osiris. Finally, she is the "Queen of Heaven," a form of Nut.

The third divine actor in the Osiris drama is Horus, whose Egyptian name, HERU, is derived from the root HER, meaning "face." Horus as

Heru is the "face of heaven," and thus originally a sky-god. He has a rather protean parentage: in one aspect he is the son-consort of Hathor whose Egyptian name, HET-HER, means "mansion of Horus;" in another, he is styled the son of Ra, making him a type of rising sun. As the "face of heaven," his right eye is said to be the sun and his left eye the moon. In lunar guise he is Khonsu. He is best known, of course, as the son of Isis and Osiris, the highest type of Divine Child. Finally he is the twin, and ultimately the antagonist, of Set. As the younger Twin, he overthrows and supersedes Set, which in celestial typology represents Light triumphing over Dark. Horus is therefore the emergent sun who, in rising, slays the Sethian or Typhonic Dragon of Darkness. Horus is the prototype of all later heroes of mythology who, one way or another, are depicted as slaying the Dragon in its multifarious guises. Horus's Egyptian name, HERU, is the likely source of the Greek word HERO. His most important zootype is the Golden Hawk, also a type of Ra, whose golden color, keen eyesight, and soaring ability made it a ready solar zootype. As a bird of prey, often feeding on snakes, the golden hawk was a symbol also of the martial Horus, i.e., in his warring capacity against the Sethian Dragon or Serpent. In the Taurean Age, Horus is the bull-god Menthu of Thebes, who also has a martial aspect. Most fundamentally, however, Horus is the resurrected Osiris, who has triumphed over death.

We have already dealt at some length with Set, the fourth divinity in the Osiris cycle. To reiterate, he is the oldest male deity, the first Son of the

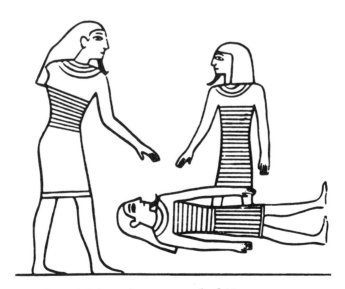

Horus arising from Osiris at the command of Atum.

Mother, and the embodiment of the earth, the tail, the solar fire, the pole star, Sirius, the storm, thunder, and desert. He is at various times Black Set, Golden Set, and Red Set, this last in his evil persona. He is at first a benevolent and powerful deity who, under the impact of the Osirian ascendancy, turned into the Great Adversary. In this he is similar to Lucifer, the first and greatest of God's angels, who rebels and is cast out of heaven. In fact the name "Lucifer" means "light-bringer," analogous to the solar aspect of Set. The Greek counterpart to Lucifer, and also to Set, is Prometheus who stole the sacred fire of Olympus and brought it down to men. We should mention parenthetically that though Egyptologists do not usually connect Set to the solar fire, that least impeachable of witnesses, Plutarch, confirms the relationship:

> ... some of the Mathematic (doctrines) derived from star-lore, think that the solar cosmos is called Typhon* and the lunar Osiris. For (they think) that the Moon, in that its light is generative and moistening, is favourable both for the breeding of animals and the sprouting of plants; whereas the Sun, with untempered and harsh fire, burns and withers up (all) that are growing ... and with fiery heat renders the major part of the earth entirely uninhabitable ...[14]

Whatever his manifestation, Set developed a reputation at the close of Egyptian history so inimical that both red and gold, two colors associated with him, became taboo in certain rituals.[15] All his zootypes took on a negative character to varying degrees. In the Osirian drama, he is preeminently the Evil One who murders his good and kingly brother Osiris and threatens the life of the infant son of Osiris, Horus. He is the prototype of Satan.

Reviewing the attributes of the principal characters of the Osirian drama, certain parallels to the Christian Gospels immediately stand out. The composite figure of Osiris-Horus is the archetype of the Gospel Christ. Like Jesus, Osiris-Horus was born of a Virgin, contended against the Adversary in the desert, died, and was resurrected to become the Judge of the Dead. Isis, like Mary, was the Queen of Heaven and Virgin Mother of the Divine Child. Set was the original Satan: one of his zootypes was the goat, complete with horns, tail, and cloven hooves. Moreover, Set's color was red. But the links between the Osirian mythic structure and Gospel Christianity are much closer than these superficial, though striking, similarities.

The Nativity itself is an Egyptian import. In the Temple of Amon at Luxor, first built around 1700 B.C.E., there is a panel of four vignettes depicting the birth of the infant pharaoh, who as the god-king was the

---

* Typhon, frequently portrayed as a dragon, was the Greek name of Set.

avatar of Horus on earth. In the 18th dynasty, the pharaohs, to more fully assert their divine prerogatives, insisted on their descent from Amon-Ra through their mortal mothers. The birth of a pharaoh, therefore, was a divine nativity, one of which was portrayed on the wall of Amon's temple at Luxor more than 1500 years before the birth of Jesus. In the first scene, Thoth the Messenger, corresponding to Gabriel in Matthew's Gospel, announces to the royal mother the impending birth of a divine child who, as the son of Amon-Ra, will reign as the divine king over Egypt. The royal mother's name is MUT-EM-UA which means "mother of the one," just as Mary is the mother of the "one to come" who will be King of Israel.[16]

In the second scene at Luxor, the enceinte royal mother stands before Hathor, the mistress of childbirth, while Nef, the personification of the Divine Breath, holds the ankh, the symbol of life, to the mouth of Mut-em-ua. Nef, as the divine breath, is veritably the Egyptian Holy Spirit, and by holding the ankh to the mouth of the royal mother, he signifies that she is conceiving by the power of the Holy Spirit. This is echoed in Matthew's Gospel where Mary also conceives "by the power of the Holy Spirit."[17] In the third scene, Mut-em-ua is sitting on the birthing chair; adjacent to her sits the new-born royal babe, shown as the Child Horus holding his finger to his mouth. This is the Egyptian version of the Divine Child who, in Matthew, is born in Bethlehem.[18] In the final scene at Luxor, the heavenly hosts of the Egyptian pantheon gather around the newborn Child to pay him homage. In front of the Child stand three divine personages proffering gifts. In Luke's Gospel, the heavenly hosts of angels gather over the Christ Child to praise and adore him; the Three Kings or Magi come before him offering precious gifts.[19] Hence, in these mural scenes from the Temple of Amon we have, 1700 years beforehand, all of the essential elements of the Gospel Nativity: the Annunciation, Conception, Birth, and Adoration of the Child. The only difference is the Palestinian, as opposed to Nile Valley, setting.

Throughout the Gospels, Jesus is referred to as the "light of the world" and the "sun ... to shine on those who sit in darkness..."[20] In point of fact, the Gospel Jesus assumed the attributes of the solar gods of antiquity of whom Horus was the prototype. In his solar form, Horus was HERU-NEB-IAKHU, meaning "Horus, Lord of Light," in every way comparable to Jesus as the Light of the World. That Jesus was a solar type derived from Horus is seen in the canonical birthday of December 25th. That is the birthday of Horus and all other solar gods of antiquity such as the Persian Mithra, whose story also closely parallels that of Jesus.[21] As we have seen from Plutarch, Harpocrates, that is Horus the Child, is brought forth around the time of the winter solstice. Now, in late antiquity, the sun reached its apparent nadir, the winter solstice, on or about December 22nd. It appeared to remain stationary in this position for about three

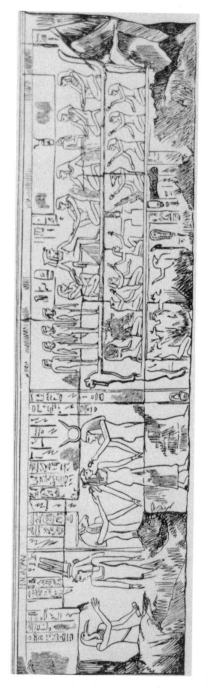

Pharaonic Nativity at Luxor: the Annunciation, Conception, Birth, and Adoration of the Child.

days and then just after midnight on December 25th, the sun began its ascent on the ecliptic, reaching its zenith at the summer solstice on June 22nd.[22] The beginning of the sun's ascent on December 25th was, metaphorically, its "birth" and since this ascent began in the deepest hour of darkness on the morning of December 25th, the sun was said to be born in a "cave," just as certain extra-Gospel traditions place the birth of Jesus in a cave.[23] As Ernest Busenbark informs us,

> According to the Alexandrian astronomer Sosigenes, who revised the calendar for Julius Caesar in 46 B.C., the winter solstice took place... on December 25th at 1:30 a.m. It was reckoned the nativity of the sun because the day then begins to lengthen.[24]

In the pre-Christian era, the constellation Virgo, the celestial Virgin, was positioned due east on the horizon as the sun started (on December 25th) its annual ecliptic ascent. Thus we can say that the sun was born "of a Virgin" in a "cave" on December 25th. We are further informed by Busenbark that high in the western sky on December 25th stood the sign of Taurus—and that

> Within the sign of Taurus there is also a small group of stars called the Stable (Aurega). This is the same Stable of Augeas which Hercules mythically cleansed as his sixth Labor and Justin Martyr proudly boasted that Christ was born on the very day when the sun takes his birth in the Stable of Augeas in the sign of the Goat...[25]

The Gospels place the birth of Jesus likewise in a manger.[26] The Church fathers consciously assimilated the old solar deities to Jesus by changing his original birth date of January 6th, an old Roman festival, to December 25th instead.[27] The Roman Church converted January 6th to the Epiphany, when the Three Wise Men or Magi were said to have visited the Christ Child. Such were the tactics of the early Christian proselytizers: co-opt the worshippers of the older gods, especially of the solar type, by Christianizing "pagan" customs and feast days.

That the Epiphany is also astronomical is alluded to in the Gospel of Matthew, which describes the "star in the east" guiding the Three Kings to the manger of the Christ Child.[28] According to Edward Carpenter, this star was none other than Sirius which, as he relates,

> stood on the southern meridian (and in more southerly lands than ours this would be more nearly overhead); and that star—there is little doubt—is the Star in the East mentioned in the Gospels. To the right, as the supposed observer looks at Sirius on the midnight of Christmas Eve, stands the magnificent Orion, the mighty hunter. There are three stars in his belt... which lie in a

straight line pointing to Sirius ... A long tradition gives them the name of *the Three Kings* (italics added.)[29]

At a time far anterior to the advent of Christianity, the year in Egypt was reckoned to begin at the summer solstice, coinciding with the rise of the Nile flood and the heliacal rising of Sirius. This made Sirius the herald of the flood and the new year. Since Osiris was often represented as the fertilizing efflux of the Nile, Sirius, in its heliacal rising, was also the herald of Osiris. Now Sirius, the "Dog Star," was also Set-Anubis, the earliest type of guide-by-night in the heavens as in Amenta. The Three Kings following the Star in the East are the three stars in Orion's belt "following" Sirius or Set-Anubis, the heavenly guide and herald of the sun. The stellar Three Kings which derive from Orion's belt are also related to Osiris because the Egyptian name for Orion is SAHU, the spiritual or resurrected body of Osiris. The Nativity, as its astronomical antecedents show, is as much a rebirth as it is a new birth. Consequently, a whole ensemble of meanings attaches to Sirius as the Star in the East that serves as the heavenly Guide. In its celestial phase, the entire Kamitic mythos was originally stellar before becoming incorporated into the solar mythos and re-manifesting in Christianity. From the summer solstice, the new year was retroverted six months to the winter solstice, becoming the new birth date of Osiris-Horus in the solar mode. Thus, the Afro-Kamitic mythos was natural first, celestial second—in three phases—and resurrectional last. All features of this evolution are detectable in Christianity.

Astronomical mythology can aid us further in revealing the solar character of Jesus Christ. After its "nativity" on December 25th, the sun's ascent on the ecliptic for the next three months represents its "infancy" and "childhood." The progressive lengthening of the day reveals the "growth" of the sun. At the spring equinox, the sun reaches the halfway point on the ecliptic, intersecting the celestial equator (the terrestial equator projected into space) where the lengths of day and night reach perfect equality. The equinox exerted a powerful effect on the symbolic imagination of the ancients and many peoples, such as the Hebrews and early Romans, began their new year at the vernal equinox. The Christian Easter and the Jewish Passover (Pasach) out of which it comes are both equinoctal celebrations. Thus the Passover only contingently represents the angel of death "passing over" the homes of the Children of Israel in Goshen, protected by the blood of the lamb; more fundamentally it is the sun "passing over" the celestial equator at the spring equinox, resulting in the equalizing of day and night. At this time, the sun undergoes a "second birth" as the length of day—and therefore the duration and power of the sun—begins to exceed that of night. The equinox is therefore a celestial Passover of the solar type or, using Christian imagery, a celestial "crossing."

The intersection of ecliptic and equator at the equinox represents a "cross" in the heavens and as the sun appears to remain stationary at this point for nearly three days, the sun can be said to be suspended on the cross or "crucified" for three days.[30] Moreover, the celestial equator forms a broad arc through space that can be figuratively imaged as a "mount" or even a "calvarium," Latin for "skull." The celestial equator, then, would seem to be the heavenly Mount Calvary upon which the sun is "crucified" at the equinox.

The delineation of an astronomical foundation of the Easter celebration permits us to discern other Afro-Kamitic types associated with it. The Easter Bunny, for example, is susceptible to an interpretation revealing its Kamitic provenance. We find that all over Africa the hare is a lunar animal. Hor-Apollo explained this by saying that the hare never appears to close his eye, making him a type of full-moon.[31] The hare is *also* an important zootype of Osiris: as one who jumps or leaps up, he is a figure of the resurrected Osiris in the act of rising up from the dead. The hare is an Egyptian ideograph which transliterates as UN, meaning "to be" or "being." Osiris was known as UN-NEFER, meaning "the good being." Now the Christian Easter is derived from Passover, celebrated on the 14th of Nisan by the old lunar calendar and later, on the 15th of Nisan by its solar counterpart.[32] This day represents the closest possible co-incidence of the spring equinox and the full moon, showing that the Passover, originally a lunar festival, became a soli-lunar festival. Easter too is a soli-lunar festival and today it is a moveable feast that always occurs on the first Sunday *after* the first full moon *after* the equinox. The Easter Bunny, therefore, is an incarnation of Osiris as Un-nefer, in both lunar and resurrectional guises.

The Easter Egg is another peculiar symbol of this equinoctal festival and its Kamitic antecedents are also recoverable. In Egyptian astro-mythology, the resurrected Osiris is manifested either as Horus, the Golden Hawk, or the Bennu Bird, the Egyptian phoenix. In addition, the Golden Hawk and the Bennu Bird are types of Ra and are said to rise out of the solar egg at the fiery dawn as light triumphing over darkness. The Easter Egg is therefore the "Great Egg" of Egyptian solar mythology and the Easter Chick that hatches out of it represents the newly-emerging Bennu Bird or Golden Hawk. This is Osiris-Horus-Ra born again, like the sun, out of the Great Egg.[33] The Greeks called the Bennu the Phoenix and claimed that this marvelous bird died and rose from its own ashes in heavenly fire every 500 years at Heliopolis, the City of the Ra. This fiery rebirth is but the light of the sun as it dawns on the morning of the equinox.

Certain extra-religious Easter customs also become intelligible. The Easter Egg hunt, which is restricted to children, recalls the part of Plutarch's narrative wherein he relates that it was children who told Isis where to look for the body of Osiris;[34] consequently, it is children who have the honor of searching for Osiris, the hatchling of the "Great Egg." The golden egg, the prize of the hunt, is nothing more than the aforementioned solar Egg; the other prize, the silver egg, symbolizes the full moon of the Easter festival. Another Easter tradition, hot-cross buns, evokes the celestial Mount Calvary upon which the solar "crossification" takes place.

The solar character of Easter week is also revealed in the Palm Sunday celebration. Palm Sunday commemorates the "ascent" of Jesus into Jerusalem on the back of an ass, his way strewn with palm branches, in preparation for the Passover feast.[35] This procession into Jerusalem admits of a three-fold interpretation: (1) it identifies Jesus with the Egyptian Ra-Yiu or Yu-sa who, as the Golden Ass, is one of the zootypes of the sun, (2) it evokes the pre-Mosaic worship of Ra-Yiu by the ancestors of the Israelites, and (3) it symbolizes the power of Jesus over Satan, who in his original Set-form was ideographed as an Ass. Among the ancient Egyptians, the palm branch was regarded as a time-symbol and its bifurcated leaf represented the equinox with its equal demarcation of day and night. The Palm Sunday procession, therefore, symbolizes Jesus the sun, in the form of Ra-Yiu, preparing to "pass over" or "cross" the celestial equator on his ecliptic ascent at the equinox.

Further investigation into the Afro-Kamitic sources of the Christ concept requires that we return once again to a discussion of the Great Year. In chapter four, we saw that the Great Year is nearly 26,000 years long and is determined by the retrograde precession of the equinoxes which moves them every 2,155–2,160 years into the adjacent zodiacal sign to inaugurate a new age. We have shown that Egyptian dynastic history begins in the Age of Taurus, circa 4368 B.C.E., when the celestial Bull and its analogs reign supreme. Biblical times, on the other hand, begin in the Age of Aries, around 2230 B.C.E., when ram, lamb, and shepherd symbols become paramount. Speaking of this time, Edward Carpenter says,

> ... the point where the Ecliptic crossed the Equator was, as a matter of fact, in the region of the constellation of Aries or the he-Lamb. The triumph of the Sungod was therefore, and quite naturally, ascribed to the influence of Aries. The *Lamb became the symbol of the risen Savior,* and of his passage from the underworld to the height of heaven (italics added).[36]

Christianity, on its part, is inextricably a product of the Age of Pisces, the Fishes.

We have already noted that the dominant celestial zootype of the preceding age lingers, much diminished in influence, into the succeeding age. Thus the Piscean avatar, Jesus, is also styled "the Good Shepherd" and the "Lamb of God," residuals from the preceding Age of Aries. The Egyptian Christ, Osiris-Horus, is the archetypal Savior, so it is not surprising that he is embodied in each succeeding zootypical avatar as one age transits to another. In the Taurean Age, Osiris-Horus is the typical Bull, in the Arian Age, the Ram, and in the Piscean Age, the Fish.

About 68 B.C.E., the equinoxes precessed into the sign of Pisces. We know that this event exerted a powerful impact on world imagination because the Jews were only one of many peoples raised to a fever pitch of excitement over the expectation of the advent of a new World Savior. Certain powerful men of the era, i.e., Julius Caesar, Augustus Caesar, and Herod Agrippa were not above taking advantage of this atmosphere to advance their own fortunes.[37] Whoever Jesus Christ may have been as a man, he was made to personify the Piscean Age, to take on all the attributes of the expected Piscean Deliverer:

> ... in the quite early years of Christianity the *Fish* came in as an accepted symbol of Jesus Christ. Considering that after the domination of *Taurus* and *Aries,* the Fish (*Pisces*) comes next in succession as the Zodiacal sign for the Vernal Equinox, and is now the constellation in which the Suns stands at that period, it seems not impossible that the astronomical change has been the cause of the adoption of this new symbol.[38]

Horus in Pisces.

Evidence for this interpretation abounds. Early Christians called themselves Pisciculi, e.g., "Fishes." Fish symbols permeate the Gospels and the
Apostles are veritably "fishers of men." In the episode of feeding the mul-
titudes with loaves and fishes, it is Jesus, as the mystic Fish, who is actually being offered up as "real food" for the salvation of the masses. The
Fish has replaced the Lamb as the sacrificial meal, the eating of which
becomes sacramental because the Fish is Jesus. Pisces is a dual sign represented as two fishes; the above Gospel miracle appropriately enough
involves two fishes.

The narrative of Plutarch is, once again, valuable for its insights into the
Egyptian provenance of Christian fish symbolism:

> As to sea fish, all (Egyptians) abstain generally (not from all fish but) from
> some—as, for example, those of the Oxyrhynchus nome from those caught
> with a hook, *for they venerate the sharp-snouted fish* ... while those of the
> Syene nome (abstain from) the "devourer," for it seems that it appears together
> with rising of the Nile, and that it shows their growth to those in joy, seen as a
> *self-sent messenger* (italics added).[39]

In unmistakable language, we see that Egyptians of at least two nomes
venerated certain types of fish as savior-messengers. The sacramental
overtones of this veneration are attested by Plutarch:

> Their priests, upon the other hand, abstain from all; and (even) on the ninth of
> the first month, when every one of the rest of the Egyptians *eats a broiled fish
> before his front door* ... (italics added)[40]

This may be compared to the passage in Luke where the resurrected
Jesus, after showing himself to his afrighted apostles, asks for something to
eat:

> They offered him a piece of fish they had cooked which he took and ate before
> their eyes.[41]

We may say that the Pisciculi were Egyptian, in the nomes of Oxyrhynchus and Syene, centuries before they were Christians in Rome.

Jesus has four major disciples among the 12 he calls "fishers of men"
and these are Peter, John, James, and Andrew who are analogous to the
four who are fishers for Horus in the *Book of the Dead.*[42] In the narrative
of Plutarch, the story of Diktys is mentioned, whom the author calls the
"nursling of Isis," identifying him as a type of Horus. The name DIKTYS
means simply "the Netter" and he is also styled "the Fisherman." Diktys,
in effect, is the Piscean manifestation of Horus, i.e., Horus the Fisherman,
and the aforesaid Fishers of Horus are those in Amenta whose nets cap-

ture all the wrongdoers. To the Manes are attributed these words as he progressess through Amenta:

> Hail, ye who lay snares, and ye who work the nets, and ye who are fishers... know ye that I know the name of the great and mighty net?[43]

By this declaration, the Manes is vouchsafing his innocence to those who "fish" for wrongdoers in their nets. The apostolic Fishers likewise "fish" for sinners or wrongdoers on behalf of Jesus.

Jesus himself removes all doubt about his identification with the Piscean Age when the Pharisees demand of him a sign:

> This is a wicked generation. It demands a sign, and the only sign that shall be given it is the *sign of Jonah* (italics added).[44]

By this reference to Jonah, the Fish-Man of the Old Testament, Jesus is affirming that he is the Spirit or Avatar of the Piscean Age. Jonah of the Old Testament is the same as the Chaldean Oannes, who is but the great Fish AN of Kam. In Chaldean lore, Oannes was half-man, half-fish who every day emerged from the waters to stand on the shore and impart knowledge to men, returning to the deep each night. There is a comparable episode in the Gospel of Luke:

> One day as he stood by the Lake of Gennesaret, and the people crowded upon him to listen to the word of God, he noticed two boats lying at the waters edge... When he had finished speaking, he said to Simon, 'Put out into deep water and lower your nets for a catch.'[45]

Here the Gospel writer has Jesus impersonate Oannes; the connection to the archetypal Fish that both he and Oannes represent is alluded to by the lowering of the nets for a catch.

The idea of a savior symbolized by a fish-messenger is found also among the Dogon of Mali. Among these people is preserved much of the old Afro-Kamitic mythos that originated along the Nile. In fact, a study of the

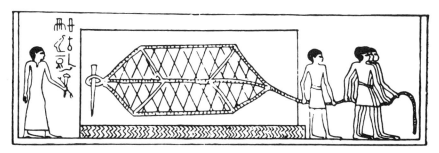

The Four as Fishers for Horus.

Dogon system, as expounded with admirable clarity by Griaule and Dieterlen, sheds light on much that is obscure in the old Egyptian version. The Dogon describe the NOMMO ANAGONNO as the "first living thing created by AMMA," who is God:

> The word for silurus*, *annagonno,* breaks down into *ana,* "rain," and *gonno,* "to sinuate," *ana* also designates "man" (vir), whose seed, on the mythical plane, is associated with the fertilizing rain and fresh water. The word can also be translated as "sinuous rain" or "male (who walks by) sinuating." The sinuous walk belongs to the fish, or to the rain and to fresh water. But the term *ana* foretells that the living being created will become "man"...[46]

There are four ancestral "fish-beings" or nommo anagonno in the Dogon system who, with their syzygies, make eight. It is the third of these nommo anagonno who is of interest here:

> The third (annagonno) is called *o nommo,* "Nommo of the pond." It will be sacrificed for the purification and reorganization of the universe after the wicked deeds of its twin... It will resurrect in human form and descend to Earth on an ark with the ancestors of man...[47]

O Nommo is both the Dogon Oannes and Piscean Dogon Christ, i.e., the messenger Fish-Man who is sacrificed, resurrected, and brings back with him the Word of God to man.

Given the entrenched, orthodox views of the Gospel, most Christians will find the astro-mythical character of Jesus and his ministry difficult to accept, but the truth of it is forthrightly acknowledged by Jesus himself in Luke's Gospel:

> *Portents will appear in the sun, moon, and stars.* On earth, nations will stand helpless, not knowing which way to turn from the roar and surge of the sea, men will faint with terror at the thought of all that is coming upon the world; for the *celestial powers will be shaken* (italics added).[48]

The changes wrought by the precession are what is meant by "the celestial powers will be shaken." What is called the "end of the world" is really the end of a world-age, when the old celestial order makes way for the new. This is what the Magi perceived by their reading of the stars that announced the birth of the new World Savior. Moreover, Jesus's own words make it certain that his advent, and the religion founded upon it, was fundamentally a celestial, hence zodiacal, event.

---

* The silurus is a member of the catfish family of which there are numerous species in the lakes and rivers of Africa.

We can see now that the nature of the Christhood is supratemporal, meaning that it transcends time and operates on multiple planes. The mythos of the old Kamite world teaches us that the Christhood is not embodied merely in a single human figure appearing at a specific moment in history, but is co-existent with humanity itself. Indeed, Jesus alludes to this when he tells the Pharisees, "Before Abraham and Adam were, I am."[49] In Massey's phrase, Jesus the Christ is the "ever-coming One," manifesting and re-manifesting in the cycles of celestial time. Christ, therefore, pre-exists Christianity.

The cross too was a venerable Afro-Kamitic symbol long before the emergence of Christianity and the Tree was the earliest natural type of cross. Not only it is typologically the nurturer and protector, but it is also a type of growth and stability. That Osiris is identified with the Tree is clear from Plutarch's narrative, where a tree grows up around his coffin, emblematic of his resurrection. Iconographically, the Tree is the Tet or Djed cross, "the backbone of Osiris," whose raising enacts his re-arising. The cross is both a figure of the dead, i.e., those who have "crossed over," *and* the raising of the dead to new life. Notably in West Africa, the crossroads is a place charged with numinous power as the point where the material and human meets the spiritual and divine. The West African guide of souls, Eshu or Legba, is the warder of the afterlife and guardian of the crossroads—the dead can only be admitted to the company of the ancestors through his intermediation. In the cross, then, a number of related elements merge. For example, the crucifixion of Jesus encapsulates the fusion of his divine and human natures, making him the Christ. Further, it is the cosmic moment of his death *and* rebirth. This is why he informs his disciples that his crucifixion and death are necessary, unavoidable, and pre-determined; there is no Christhood apart from the crucifixion. If the cross carrying the dying savior is not raised on the Mount of Calvary, there is no union of God and man, no dissolution and re-creation of the divine man, and therefore no hope for universal resurrection. This "crossification" operated primarily on the plane of myth and symbol even for the early Christians:

> In early Christian dogma, it was the blood of the Lamb of God which took away the sins of the world. Long after the beginning of Christianity, however, many people continued to believe that, instead of being accepted as a historical fact, the crucifixion should be viewed ... symbolically ... (the Church) for almost seven centuries ... forbade the placing of Christ's figure on the cross. None of the paintings in the Roman catacombs shows him on the cross and, in the holy sepulchre, the savior is represented by a figure of a lamb.
>
> At the Council called *In Trullo,* held at Constantinople in 692 A.D., this policy was finally reversed and thereafter all crucifixes bore the figure of Jesus ...[50]

Nailing to the cross is merely one type of crucifixion, one employed by the Romans. Hanging from a tree or gallows was another. In fact, in the Book of Acts it is stated that Jesus was hanged from a gibbett.[51] The Hanged Man of Tarot is of the same order as this hanged Jesus. Another remarkable parallel is revealed in the Shango cycle of Yoruba mythology.[52] Shango is the first king of the Yoruba nation of Oyo who is eventually persecuted by his own subjects and driven from the throne. In his despair, he hangs himself from a tree after which he falls into a deep hole. Eventually he ascends into the sky on a chain and becomes one of the most powerful orishas, the controller of thunder and lightning. His emblem is the axe and his zootype the ram.[53] There are a number of curious mythic parallels between Shango and Jesus: (1) each is styled a king, (2) each suffers persecution by his people, (3) each dies by hanging, (4) each descends into the nether world,[54] (5) each is resurrected, ascends into heaven, and is translated into a divine immortal, and (6) each exhibits a zootypical identification with the Arian Ram. This is further evidence that the Church fathers drew on long-standing, ubiquitous mythic material.

The more sedulously the relationship between Kamite religion and the Christian Gospels is probed, the more evident is their affinity. The Egyptian story relating the works and deeds of a marvelous child, entitled *The Veritable History of Satmi-Khamois,* illustrates the truth of this assertion:

> Now Satmi slept one night and dreamed a dream. One spoke to him saying: "Mahituaskhit thy wife, who has conceived by thee, the infant that she shall bear shall be called Senosiris, and many will be the wonders that he will perform in the land of Egypt." When Satmi awoke from his dream after having seen these things, his heart rejoiced greatly. When the months of pregnancy were fulfilled... Mahituaskhit brought into the world a man-child... And it came to pass, when the little child Senosiris was one year old, one would have said, "He is two years old," when he was two, one would have said, "He is three years old," so vigorous was he in all his limbs... he was sent to school; in a little time he knew more than the scribe who had been given him as a master. The little child Senosiris began to read the books of magic with the scribes of the Double House of Life in the Temple of Ptah, and *all who heard him were lost in astonishment...*
>
> *When the little boy Senosiris was twelve years old, there was no scribe or magician in Memphis who equalled him in reading books of magic* (italics added).[55]

Judging from his name, Senosiris obviously *is* Osiris. The word SEN in Egyptian means "image" or "likeness" so that Senosiris means literally "the image of Osiris." His father's prophetic dream sent by divine agency is repeated in Matthew 1:20–23, where the angel of the Lord tells Joseph in a dream of the impending birth of divine child conceived in his wife Mary by the power of the Holy Spirit. Senosiris, the marvelous youth of

12, whose learning and wisdom outstrips those of his masters, is encountered again in Luke 2:41–52, where the 12-year old Jesus is found in the Temple discoursing with all the learned doctors, wise men, and priests, astounding them with his knowledge. The near-identity of two stories cannot be co-incidental.

It is further related that Jesus cured a blind man by rubbing spittle into his eyes, exactly paralleling events in the Osiris drama that portray Horus, blinded by Set, having his sight restored by Thoth, who rubs spittle into his eyes.[56] In Mark 7:8–9, the evangelist relates the story of a deaf and dumb man who has his hearing and speech restored to him.

> They brought to him (Jesus) a man who was deaf and had an impediment in his speech ... He took the man aside away from the crowd, put his fingers into his ears, spat, and touched his tongue. Then looking up to heaven, he sighed, and said to him, "Ephphatha!" Which means "Be opened."

This may be compared to passages in the *Book of the Dead* describing the resurrectional ceremony known as the "opening of the mouth:"

> Horus hath opened thy mouth ... "Thy mouth was closed up ..." Kher-heb says: "Open the mouth and the two eyes ..."[57]

In the ancient conception, to be dead was to be deaf and dumb, to be without the Word that called everything into being. In fact the dead Osiris is called "silent and dumb" in the Ritual.[58] It is the action of the Word that restores life, as illustrated in the "Chapter of Giving a Mouth to Osiris Ani:"

> I rise out of the egg in the hidden land. May my mouth be given unto me that I may speak therewith in the presence of the great god ...[59]

This relationship between the Word and resurrection is further exemplified in the Ritual in the "Chapter of the Opening of the Mouth of Osiris:"

> May the god Ptah open my mouth, and may the god of my city loose the swathings, even the swathings which are over my mouth.[60]

By loosening the swathings, the dead person breaks out of his mummy bandages and comes back to life.

In the Memphite theology, Ptah was the great god who made creation by uttering the thoughts of his Divine Mind. His name means "to open;" the god Ptah is therefore "the Opener (of the mouth)." As we've seen, the Aramaic word meaning "be opened" is "ephphatha" whose root, PHATH, seems to be similar to, if not derived from, the Egyptian word PTAH. By saying "ephphatha," Jesus seems to be performing the "opening of the mouth" ceremony upon the deaf and dumb (and therefore "dead") suppliant.

The Egyptian idea of the Word personifying the Divine Mind is captured again in John 1:1–3, where the evangelist writes, "In the beginning was the Word, and the Word was with God, and the Word was God." In the 14th verse of the first chapter, John tells us that Jesus Christ was "the Word made flesh." It is usually asserted that this "Logos" came into Christianity through the influence of the Neo-Platonic schools of philosophy, but Plato himself studied in Egypt for 13 years and the idea of the Word being the active principle of creation is an age-old one in the Afro-Kamite world. Wallis Budge informs us that Osiris was the Great Word, i.e., "the word of what cometh into being . . ."[61] Moreover, as Budge tells us,

> Osiris, the Word, spake the words through which all things in heaven came into being from non-existence.
>
> Because he was the first man who raised himself from the dead, he became the type and symbol and hope of every dead man.[62]

Osiris, by his command of the Word, held the power of creation, life, and re-birth. In the funerary ritual, the Kher-heb priest says over the deceased, who seeks immortality through identification with Osiris, "Thy voice shall never depart from thee, they voice shall never depart from thee."[63]

Christianity was founded on the messiahship of Jesus Christ, but worship of his prototype, Osiris-Horus, antedates him by at least 42 centuries. The term MESSIAH is nominally Hebrew, signifying the "anointed one," the expected king and deliverer. After the second destruction of Temple at the hands of the Romans in 70 A.D. and the consequent failure of the Jews to establish an earthly kingdom under the Messiah, the early Christians, originally a marginal Jewish sect, were able to re-direct this hope to that of a heavenly kingdom under the messiahship of Christ:

> There is no doubt that after the destruction of Jerusalem (in A.D. 70), little groups of believers in a redeeming 'Christ' were formed there and in other places, just as there had certainly existed, in the first century B.C., groups of Gnostics, Therapeutae, Essenes, and others whose teachings were very similar to the Christian . . .[64]

The word MESSIAH may, as Massey says, come from the Egyptian word MESSU meaning simply "to anoint." On the other hand, the Egyptian root MES means (1) "to give birth," (2) "child," or (3) "son." One of the titles of Horus is "Mes," making him "Horus the Son." MES-IAH in Egyptian means "the Son of Yah," Yah being the Egyptian Yahweh. Earlier we found that the Hebrew name of Jesus, Yahushua, means "the adored one of Yahweh;" as the Messiah he is, naturally, "the Son of Yahweh." To paraphrase Massey, the Messiah is the Ever-Coming Son of God who, as either Iu or Horus, is euhemerized in Hebrew history as the expected historical avenger of the Hebrew nation, and further euhemerized in historical Christianity as God made man, then killed and resurrected as the historical savior of the world.

Jesus the Messiah is Jesus the Christ. Our word CHRIST comes from the Greek KRISTOS, which also means "anointed;" thus it is a direct translation of MESSIAH:

> The "Messiah" means ... the Anointed One. The Hebrew word occurs some 40 times in the Old Testament; and each time in the Septuagint ... translation ... the word is translated ... Christos, which again means Anointed ... the idea or the word "The Christ" was in vogue in Alexandria as far back certainly as 280 B.C.[65]

But this Greek KRISTOS is really the Egyptian KRST (KARAST), the Osirified being who is anointed and mummified. In the Ritual, the body of Osiris is bathed and anointed in oils, resins, and spices to preserve his body against decay. It is then carefully swathed in linen bandages to create his mummy and then set upright to symbolize resurrection. The Osirified body was anointed to prepare for the re-awakening.[66] The Christ was the Karast before there ever was Jesus, historical or otherwise. This idea of the Karast as the prototype of Christ was incorporated into the Gospel of John:

> They took the body of Jesus and *wrapped it, with spices, in strips of linen cloth* according to Jewish burial customs. Now at the place where he had been crucified there was a garden, and in the garden a new tomb not used for burial. There, because the tomb was near at hand and it was the eve of the Jewish sabbath, they laid Jesus (italics added).[67]

Here we have, in the New Testament itself, a description of a mummified Jesus that, in effect, turns him into the Karast. Since this is described as a Jewish burial custom we can only surmise that it was brought out of Egypt by the Children of Israel! Even the garden imagery of this passage is Egyptian: in several places in the Ritual, the soul of the dead man, the manes, is depicted in a garden or oasis, symbolic of the paradisiacal condition to which he aspires. The Egyptian Sekhet-Aarru, the "Fields of the Blessed," is such a garden. In John 20:15, Jesus is called a "gardener," evoking scenes in the *Book of the Dead* where the Osirified soul, having reached Paradise, is free to tend its garden.[68]

Seti I anointing the face of Osiris.

The identification of Jesus with Osiris-Horus is further exemplified in the story of Lazarus, John 11:1–44. Lazarus is the recently deceased brother of two mourning sisters, Martha and Mary. Approaching Jesus, they prevail upon him to come and minister to the corpse. In doing so, Jesus tells the two sisters, "I am the resurrection and the life." Upon reaching the home of the dead Lazarus, Jesus calls to him, "Rise and come forth," and the reawakened Lazarus rises from his funeral bier swathed in linen bandages, i.e., in "mummified" form. This episode is directly parallel to the story of Osiris in the Ritual, the dead brother of the two mourning sisters, Isis and Nepthys. He is shown lying on his bier wrapped in the linen bandages of a mummy. His son Horus stands before him and re-animates him by saying "Rise up!" Upon command, Osiris reawakens and rises to an upright position, fully alive. The important elements of each story are identical—and this identity is further confirmed by the etymology of Lazarus's name. LAZARUS can be broken down to its component parts: L-AZAR-US. The L is the Semitic article "al" or "el" meaning "the." The root of the name is AZAR, the same as ASAR, the Egyptian name of Osiris. The terminal US may be related to the Egyptian IS or AS, meaning "to call" or "to summon." Thus Lazarus is "the Osiris" or "the Osiris called."

One other example of the interconnection between the Karasthood and the Christhood may be considered. The first and fourth Gospels tell the story of a woman who came to anoint Jesus:

> ... a woman came to him with a small bottle of fragrant oil, very costly; and as he sat at the table she began to pour it over his head. The disciples were indignant when they saw it. "Why this waste?" ... Jesus said ... to them, "Why must you make trouble for the woman? It is a fine thing she has done for me ... When she poured this oil on my body it was her way of preparing me for burial."[69]

As Jesus makes clear, he is being anointed for death in preparation for Karasthood, the prefigurement of "Christification." The funerary Ritual also evokes baptism and anointment as features of the process of rebirth when the deceased says:

> I have washed myself in the water wherein the god Ra washeth himself when he leaveth the eastern part of the sky. I have anointed myself with *bat* unguent (made from) cedar.[70]

The anointer and baptizer in this part of the Ritual is the Divine Lady known variously as the "Lady of Tremblings," the "Lady of Offerings," and the "Lady of Splendour." This echoes an earlier time when the Mother was the anointer and resurrector of the sacrificed savior; the primitive

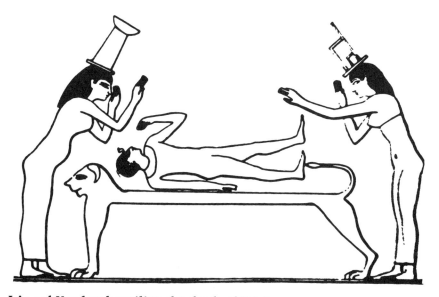

Isis and Nepthys bewailing the death of Osiris.

Osiris arising at the command of Horus, who says "Rise up!"

Karast-type was reborn through her. In the Gospels, she is manifest as the woman who anoints Jesus in preparation for death and resurrection.

A central rite in Christian religion is Jesus's eucharistic sacrifice that purifies and renews the life of his followers. He gives his body and blood as bread and wine "so that sins may be forgiven" and death transcended. For Jesus says:

> ... the bread which I give is my own flesh; I give it for the life of the world. My flesh is real food; my blood is real drink. Whoever eats my flesh and drinks my blood dwells continually in me and I dwell in him.[71]

Jesus incorporates within himself the primitive mode of salvation; the savior whose body and blood are given up for food and drink to sustain life. This ethos of bodily sacrifice is consecrated and formalized in the Catholic Mass, the whole thing fairly palpitating with Osirian imagery. Thus it is said in the *Book of the Dead*:

> Horus is both the divine food and sacrifice. He hath passed on to gather together (the members of) his divine father; Horus *is his deliverer* ... Horus hath sprung from the water of his divine father ... (italics added)[72]

Our word MASS comes from the Old French MES, in turn derived from the Latin MISSUS, meaning "meal." The Mass commemorates the Last Sup-

per and is derived, via Latin, from the Egyptian word MES or MIS, meaning "bread" or "evening supper." Thus our MASS, the recurring Last
Supper, is the Mes, or evening meal/bread of old Kam. One of the most
arresting images emanating from the depiction of the Last Supper is Jesus
washing the feet of his disciples. This scene, too, devolves from the Ritual,
making the Gospel Last Supper seem but a paraphrasis, to wit:

> ... thou eatest the cakes upon the cloth which the goddess Tait herself hath
> prepared; thou eatest the haunch of the animal; thou takest boldly the joint
> which Ra hath endowed with power in his holy place; *thou washest thy feet in
> silver basins which the god Seker* ... *hath wrought* ... Thou *eatest of the
> baked bread* ... (italics added)[73]

Osiris, as we have already shown, is veritably the Bread of Life, whose
body, as the Mes, is broken into 14 pieces just as the eucharistic host is
broken in preparation for communion. The changing of the eucharistic
bread into the body of Christ is accompanied by the changing of wine into
his blood. As the mystic bread was originally the body of Osiris, the wine
was his blood because he personified the grape and viticulture. The
water-into-wine transubstantiation also appears in the Ritual, which says,
"The water of the scribe Nebseni is the wine of Ra."[74] Indeed, the Egyptian provenance of the bread-and-wine imagery is further revealed in the
rubric of the 99th chapter of the *Book of the Dead:*

> ... (the deceased) shall come forth into Sekhet-Aarru (the Fields of Peace), and
> bread and wine and cakes shall be given unto him at the altar of the great
> god ...[75]

Thus is the "Mass" enacted by the Osirified Manes in Amenta.

The attributes shared by Osiris-Horus on the one hand and Jesus on the
other are multifarious. In John 14:6, Jesus tells Thomas, "I am the way, I
am truth, and I am life; no one comes to the father except by me." Two of
the many titles of Osiris are NEB-MAAT, "Lord of Truth," and NEB-ANKH,
"Lord of Life." Moreover, as the Judge of Souls, he justifies the virtuous;
through him they ascend to Father Ra, sailing in his solar barque across
the heavens. Even the teachings that open up the path toward justification
in the afterlife are nearly verbatim in the Gospels and in the Ritual. In
Matthew 25:34–37, Jesus, describing the way toward salvation, says,

> You have my Father's blessing; come enter and possess the kingdom that has
> been ready for you since the world was made. For when I was hungry, you
> gave me food; when thirsty, you gave me drink; when I was a stranger you took
> me into your home; when naked you clothed me; when I was ill you came to my
> help; when in prison, you visited me.

The Ritual says:

> O grant ye that I may come to you, for . . . I live upon right and truth, and feed
> upon right and truth. I have performed the commandments of men (as well as)
> the things whereat are gratified the gods, I have made the god to be at peace
> (with me by doing) that which is his will. *I have given bread to the hungry
> man, and water to the thirsty man, and apparel to the naked man, and a
> boat to the shipwrecked mariner* (italics added).[76]

In John 8:12, Jesus calls himself the "Light of the World." As he instructs
his apostles,

> He who journeys in the dark does not know where he is going. While you have
> the light, trust to the light, so that you men may become men of light.[77]

In the Ritual, the Osirified soul says,

> I have come to give light in darkness, which is made light and bright by me. I
> have given light in darkness . . .[78]

When the beatified soul has been justified by Osiris, he ascends to the
barque of Ra and becomes one of the IAKHU or "sons of light," exactly
the same as the "men of light" that are described in the above passage
from John's Gospel.

In John 19:5, the soldiers, in a cruel parody of kingship, cloak Jesus in a
purple robe and set a crown of thorns upon his brow. Then they mock
him as the "King of the Jews." But in fact, the kingship of Jesus is a recurring *leitmotiv* of the Gospels so the purple robe is not without significance. In the ancient Egyptian paraphrenalia of kingship, purple was the
royal color, worn only by the pharaoh himself. The special dye was obtained in minute quantities from a rare snail and was therefore prohibi-
tively expensive. The cloaking of Jesus in a purple robe was a tacit
indication of his kingship by the Gospel writer.

Other figures in the Gospels are also drawn from the pre-extant Kamite
mythos. We have already noted that the Virgin Mary is but a late form of
the Virgin Isis, but even Mary's name has an Egyptian etymology. The
equivalent word for MARY in Egyptian is MERI, meaning "love" or "beloved," and one of the forms of Isis is MERI-F-UA, a guardian of Osiris
whose name means "his beloved one." Isis is also closely linked to the
goddess Hathor, known as HATHOR-MERI. HATHOR in Egyptian is HET-
HER meaning "mansion of Horus" or "temple of Horus." She may have
been an earlier mother-consort of Horus than even Isis and one of her
zootypes is the dove.[79] In John 1:32–33, the Baptist tells us that he saw
the Holy Spirit coming down on the head of Jesus in the form of a dove.
Trinitarian ideology aside, the Holy Spirit, as the Dove, was not originally

masculine but a form of the Mother, giving a more natural trinity closer to the Egyptian triune Holy Family of Osiris, Isis, and Horus. Massey states that the Hathor dove is a type of "rebegetting spirit" and says,

> In the *Legenda Aurea,* at the assumption of Mary, the Christ addresses his mother as his dove, and says, "Arise my mother! My dove! tabernacle of glory, vase of life, celestial temple."[80]

This "tabernacle of glory," this "celestial temple," is none other than Hathor whose Egyptian name means "temple of Horus," as we have seen. She is also the Mother-Dove that Jesus invokes at the assumption of Mary.

In the Gospel of Luke, both Mary and her kinswoman Elizabeth receive divine visitations which result in their impregnation. Elizabeth gives birth first, to John, who in his adult career becomes the "voice crying in the wilderness" proclaiming, "Prepare a way for the Lord, clear a straight path for him."[81] He is, in effect, the Gospel Anubis who, as Up-uat in the Ritual, is literally the "opener of the way." Thus in the Ritual, Anubis/Up-uat is called upon to

> Open the way in Restau, ease the pain of Osiris, embrace that which the balance has weighed (the heart); make a path for him in the great valley, make light to be on the way to Osiris.[82]

John opens the way for the coming of Christ on earth, Anubis (Up-uat) opens the way for Osiris in Amenta. The character of John appears twice in the Gospels, once as the Baptist, again as the Evangelist; they are two versions of the same character. In the Osiris myth, Isis adopts Anubis as her son; in the Gospels, Mary adopts the apostle John when Jesus, from the cross, points to John and says, "Mother there is your son."[83]

We have tried in a factual manner to present the aggregate of evidence connecting Christianity to the mythos of old Kam, evoked in the *Book of the Dead* and the drama of Osiris. The number of parallels overwhelm mere coincidence; the correspondences are tantamount to identity in many instances. There is an umbilical link between the two religious systems and since the Afro-Kamitic one is millenia older, it must be the parent. We have already referred to the "incubation" of Christianity in Egypt, where the Desert Fathers and Alexandrian bishops took the lead in formalizing the doctrinal and administrative apparatus of the early Church. In the second century A.D., Egyptians converted to Christianity virtually en masse. The lure of Christian monastic life in the western desert proved so strong that it created a manpower shortage in certain parts of the country! Christianity at that time was so close to the Egyptian religion of old as to be almost indistinguishable from it. In a famous letter, the emperor Hadrian avowed that the Christian bishops followed the rites of

Serapis because his worship was identical to that of Christianity![84] Serapis represented a Hellenistic syncretism of two Egyptian gods, Osiris (Asar) and Apis (Hapi) and, according to Hadrian's testimony, Christians had adopted the rites of Serapis as their own. Thus, the living cord connecting Osiris and Christ, far from being shocking or apostatic, is natural and appropriate. Furthermore, there is nothing sacrilegious in the assertion that the New Testament is fundamentally an Afro-Kamitic document, reworked surely, but whose antecedents are recoverable with the proper keys.

It seems fitting that the first gentile ever baptized, according to Acts 8:26–39, was the Ethiopian minister of Candace, who received the rite from the Apostle Phillip. Prior to this baptism, Christianity was but a marginal Jewish sect; thenceforth it could make some incipient claim to universality, making this African black man the world's first true Christian. It is striking that some of the earliest purely human figures of the Christ surviving from Coptic religious art, display the physical features of a black man. This applies also to the portraits of the Black Madonna and Child, which have an Egyptian provenance. Black Isis, always shown holding the black infant Horus, became the source of one of the most influential cults in the Roman empire.[85] Frescoes at Pompeii show Black priests, natives of Upper Egypt and Nubia, performing her rites. Roman legions carried Black Isis and Horus all over Europe, where numerous shrines to her were established. So venerated were these shrines that Christian prosyletizers, upon penetrating into Europe, converted the figures of Black Isis and Horus into the Black Madonna and Child.[86] They remain the holiest icons of Catholic Europe.

We will close this chapter with a brief discussion of the historical Jesus because it might be inferred we impute a purely mythical character to Jesus the Nazarene. No. What *is* mythical is the Gospel Jesus. Outside the Gospels themselves, there is no authentic, independent record or witness to the actual existence of Jesus or the events described in the Gospels for nearly a century after the received date of his putative crucifixion.[87] Philo, Tacitus, Plutarch, and Josephus—all writers contemporary with the Gospel events and all dealing extensively with the religious currents of the first century—are uniformly silent about any person or event remotely similar to those described in the Gospels.[88] Philo and Josephus, both Jews, lived in and around the area where the Gospel events were supposed to have taken place, yet know nothing of them. We cannot possibly hold up the Gospels themselves as bona fide historical records; they were written by enthusiasts bent on promoting a new faith. Doubtless, there are strands of historical verisimilitude in the Gospels, but as we have seen elsewhere in the Bible, they are so interwoven with demonstrably mythical material that it is hardly possible to tease them out. G. R. S. Mead, writing about the historical Jesus, sums up the dilemma by saying,

"The very existence of Jesus appears to have been unknown" in the first century.[89]

To locate the historical Jesus, we must leave Christian literature and search through Jewish writings to catch a glimmer of the man. Talmudic and Mishnaic writings lead us closer to the subject.[90] In this literature we find several versions of a story of a man named Joshua or Jeschu who was born, probably out of wedlock, to a young woman named Miriam and one Joseph Pantzer or Pandera, possibly a Roman soldier. This Joshua ben Pandera early in life joined a community of Essenes or Therapeutae in Egypt. The Essenes were a mystical offshoot of Judaism that practiced ascetic living, strict cleanliness and purification, vegetarianism, daily prayer and meditation, the avoidance of all clothing of animal origin, the abjuration of all oaths, and sharing of property in common. In these features they closely resembled the Pythagorean mode of life and according to Busenbark, they were organized into hierarchies of bishops, priests, and monks residing in churches and monasteries.[91] Like the earlier Pythagoreans, they seem to have been primarily influenced by the Egyptian mystery-tradition and, as the Dead Sea Scrolls attest, many of their ideas and practices found their way subsequently into Christianity. They possessed immense reputations as healers which is why they were called Therapeutae, or Physicians, in Egypt. These Therapeutae were especially remarkable for their emphasis on the contemplative life. Though Essenic communities were sprinkled throughout Palestine and Egypt, they were never more than 4,000 strong. The young Jeschu ben Pandera, i.e., "Jesus, son of the Panther," came under the tutelage of an Essene teacher named Ben Perachia, and when he left Egypt in his middle years, he was evidently considered a master of the mystic sciences. Ben Pandera traveled through Palestine, teaching, healing, and performing myriad "wonders." Because of this, he was arrested by Jewish authorities, tried, convicted of practicing "magic," and hanged on that account on the Passover at Lydda in 70 B.C. when he was 50 years of age.

One tradition states that Jeschu was related to Salome, the queen of King Jannaeus, who protected him during the course of his ministry from the heavy hand of Jewish law. However, she died in 71 B.C., whereupon the sacerdotal enemies of Jeschu speedily seized upon the occasion to judicially do away with him. Thus, the Gospel allusion to the "kingship" of Jesus may have had a tinge of historical truth behind it, since he may have been related to the royal family of Judah. Other portions of the New Testament seem to echo the Talmudic traditions concerning Jesus. In the opening chapter of Matthew, Mary, the mother of Jesus, is portrayed as an unwed mother, a consistent theme in the Talmudic accounts of Jeschu ben Pandera. In Matthew 2:13–15, we see that the Holy Family spent an indeterminate amount of time in Egypt, which squares with traditions concerning Jeschu ben Pandera's life there. The affirmation of Acts that Jesus was hanged from a gibbet on the Passover corroborates Jeschu's death at the same occasion and in the same manner reported in the Talmudic records. In sum, the Talmudic Jeschu stories appear to be our best track to the historic Jesus. These traditions represent the most plausible history we have of a man who was evidently a great teacher and healer, a veritable Physician as one of the Therapeutae, and he remains our best candidate for the historical Jesus.

If we accept Jeschu ben Pandera as the historical Jesus, it is then clear that the vast savior and resurrection mythos—originating in the dim mists of pre-historic lacustrine East Africa then codified and perfected in the lower Nile Valley—crystallized around him to create Jesus Christ, the putative founder of Christianity. This transmogrification was not the first such welding of man, myth, and divinity. The obscure pharaoh Zer of the 2nd Dynasty became identified with Osiris and in after-centuries, pious Egyptians made pilgrimages to his tomb, venerated as the burial place of their resurrected Divine Man, Osiris. The great Egyptian sage and polymath, Imhotep, was eventually identified with the pre-existing Egyptian deity Iu as Iu-em-hept, "he who comes in peace." Guatama of the Sakya clan of northern India was linked with prior black Buddhas, of whom he became the eighth avatar. Even Pythagoras was said to have been of divine parentage and was considered the human incarnation of the Greek god Apollo. In each instance, an extraordinary mortal man, whose exemplary purity of life seemed to waken the inner seed of deity, came to personify the presence of the Divine on earth. The followers of Jeschu ben Pandera who kept his teachings alive apparently saw him as just such a man and united his qualities with an established mythic savior, the Christ, i.e., Osiris the Karast.

The Christ as the Karast, whether as Osiris, Horus, Iu, or Jesus, is the "ever-coming one" and the "ever-resurrecting one." Instead of "Second Comings" there are Perpetual Comings, a concatenation worked out millenia ago and writ into the heavens in the cycle of the Great year. This schema is mythical, but it is human also, because man and myth fuse at crucial points and myth then becomes concrete in history. In this way, the man Jesus was welded to the mythic Christ, the Christ who ever comes, *ad infinitum.*

Appendix

CHRISTIANITY AND THE PISCEAN AGE

The linkage between Christianity and the Piscean Age, which ties it and presumably other religions to astrological cycles, has been an idea entertained by only a few antiquarians whose writings have for the most part remained obscure. Such a notion flies in the face of religious orthodoxy; it also runs counter to the grain of the scientific skepticism and critical scholasticism that characterize the present age. But recently Martin Bernal, author of *Black Athena*, a work of controversial but erudite scholarship, has acknowledged the relationship between the precessional shift into the sign of Pisces and the advent of Christianity. This is noteworthy because his book has received significant if wary attention from the ranks of established classicists and his ideas are being critically discussed in academic forums.

While the larger themes of Bernal's book are concerned with the evolution of the conflict between what he terms the Ancient (Afroasiatic) versus the Aryan (Indoeuropean) model of interpreting the sources of Greek history and culture, a short section in Chapter II of his book, entitled "Christianity, Stars, and Fish," deals with the connection between the onset of the Age of Pisces and the Messianism that led to the emergence of Christianity:

> ... the Messianism between 50 B.C. and 150 AD, and the idea that a new age was dawning, were not restricted to Jews ... Another element was the astrological change from the age of Aries to that of Pisces.[1]

Bernal also infers that the relatively close concordance between the beginning of the Piscean Age after 70 B.C. and the beginning of a new Sothic cycle around 139 A.D. made a profound impression on the Egyptian priesthood and accounts for the startling suddenness with which the Egyptian people, almost in a body, converted to Christianity in the 2nd century. As he says,

> ... the Egyptian priesthoods, who were closely tied to the stars, were given a double message of the end of an epoch.[2]

What is striking is that Bernal's perspective of the relationship between Osiris and Jesus closely mirrors our own, to wit,

> Whether or not Antinoos (the favorite of Hadrian) was meant to be the new savior for the new age can only be a matter for speculation. There is no doubt ... that the Christians saw their new Osiris, Jesus, in this way.[3]

Our own assertion that early Christianity evolving in Egypt was *the* religion of the Piscean Age is also echoed by Bernal:

> ... Christian representations of the fish first appear at the beginning of the 2nd century in Alexandria ... the early Christians saw themselves, and were seen by others, as followers of the new religion of the new Piscean Age.[4]

Finally, Bernal says,

> ... at the level of church organization and doctrine, all Christianity—not just that Egypt—was deeply permeated by Egyptian religion.[5]

Here we have in capsule an almost complete corroboration by an eminent modern classicist and linguist of the broad themes of this chapter. It appears that a new breed of scholar is emerging to re-think the cozy certitudes of received historiography.

Appendix Notes

1. Bernal M, *Black Athena: The Afroasiatic Roots of Classical Civilization*, London: Free Association Books, 1987, p. 125.
2. Ibid., p. 127.
3. Ibid.
4. Ibid., p. 128.
5. Ibid., p. 130.

Notes

1. Devisse J, *The Image of the Black in Western Art*, Volume II, Part 1, translated by William Granger Ryan, Cambridge: Harvard University Press, 1979, pp. 149–208, passim.
2. Massey G, *Ancient Egypt*, Volume II, New York: Samuel Weiser, 1970, pp. 727–906, passim.
3. Plutarch, "Concerning the Mysteries of Isis and Osiris," reprinted in Mead GRS, *Thrice Greatest Hermes*, Volume I, London: John M. Watkins, 1906, 1949.
4. Frazer JG, *Adonis, Attis, and Osiris*, Volume II, New Hyde Park: University Books, 1906, 1961, p. 85.
5. Plutarch, op. cit., p. 346.
6. Frazer, op. cit., 90; cf. also Budge EAW, *Osiris: The Egyptian Religion of Resurrection*, Volume II, New Hyde Park: University Books, 1911, 1961, pp. 24–5.
7. Plutarch, op. cit., p. 284.
8. Ibid., p. 268.
9. "Nor did they make libation of it (wine) as a thing dear to the Gods, but as the blood of those who fought against the Gods—from whom, when they fell and mingled with the earth, they think the vines came, and that because of this wine-drenching makes men to be out of their minds... in that... they are filled with the forefathers of its blood" (ibid., pp. 268–9). Plutarch, in this passage, is quoting the opinion of the fourth-century Egyptian-trained astronomer Eudoxus. The interpretation is garbled but the passage is significant for pointing out the symbolic connection between blood, wine, and the ancestral spirits.
10. Ibid., p. 320.
11. Ibid., p. 321.
12. Ibid., p. 320.
13. Ibid., p. 346.
14. Ibid., pp. 318–9.
15. "... every now and then at certain festivals they (Egyptians) humiliate it (Typhon) dreadfully and treat it most despitefully—even to rolling red-skinned men in the mud, and driving an ass over a precipice... because Typhon was born with his skin red and ass-like.... And on the Feast of Offerings of the Sun, they pass the word to worshippers not to wear on the body things made of gold nor to give food to an ass" (ibid., p. 305).
16. Luke 1:32–33.
17. Matthew 1:20–21.
18. Matthew 2:1.
19. Matthew 2:2–13; Luke 2:13–14.
20. Luke 1:78–79.
21. Mithra was the Persian solar deity born in a cave on December 25th. See Cumont F, *The Mysteries of Mithra*, New York: Dover Publications, Inc., 1903,

1956; cf. also Graves K, *The World's Sixteen Crucified Saviors*, New York: Truth Seeker Company, 1875, 1960, for details on other savior-types whose histories parallel that of Jesus.

22. The ecliptic is the apparent path of the sun—viewed at noon—relative to the horizon over the course of six months from solstice to solstice. At the winter solstice the sun rests at its nadir near the horizon; at the summer solstice it sits almost directly overhead.

23. Origen, Tertullian, Jerome, and Eusebius were all Christian Fathers who asserted that Jesus was born in a cave. See Doane TW, *Bible Myths and Their Parallels in Other Religions*, New York: Truth Seeker Company, Inc., 1882, 1948, pp. 154–5.

24. Busenbark E, *Symbols, Sex, and the Stars in Popular Beliefs*, New York: The Truth Seeker Company, Inc., 1949, p. 116.

25. Ibid., p. 126.; cf. also Carpenter E, *Pagan and Christian Creeds*, New York: Harcourt, Brace, & Co., 1921, p. 26.

26. Luke 2:7.

27. "Because the date of Christ's birth was unknown, it was combined, until about the year 354, with a baptismal feast which was celebrated January 6th in Rome on the date of an old pagan festival. After that time his birth was generally observed on December 25th... there was no officially fixed date for the celebration of the Nativity by the Roman Church until about the year 530 A.D., when, at the request of the Pope, the Scythian monk Dionysius Erigas, a poet and an astromer, fixed the date as December 25th" (Busenbark, op. cit., p. 118).

28. Matthew 2:2–3.

29. Carpenter, op. cit., pp. 29–30.

30. Ibid., pp. 39–46.

31. Massey G, *Lectures*, New York: Samuel Weiser, 1974, p. 167.

32. Ibid., p. 6.

33. The Bennu is the Heart of Osiris and the Soul of Ra. See Budge EAW., *Gods of the Egyptians*, Volume II, New York: Dover Publications, Inc., 1904, 1969, pp. 97; 371.

34. Plutarch, op. cit., p. 283.

35. Matthew 21:5–9; Luke 19:28–38.

36. Carpenter, op. cit., p. 48.

37. See Higgins G, *Anacalypsis*, Volume I, New Hyde Park: University Books, 1833, 1965, pp. 181–2; 801. That Herod Agrippa sought to cast himself as the expected Messiah is adduced in Robert Graves's historical novel, *Claudius, the God*.

38. Carpenter, op. cit., p. 48.

39. Plutarch, op. cit., p. 269. It is possible that the two fishes of the sign of Pisces derive from the double veneration of the Fish—as a "self-sent messenger"—in the Egyptian nomes of Oxyrhynchus on the one hand and Syene on the other.

40. Ibid., p. 270.

41. Luke 24:42–43.

42. See Massey, *Ancient Egypt*, Volume II, op. cit., p. 860.

43. Budge EAW, *The Book of the Dead: The Theban Rescension*, New York, E. P. Dutton & Co., 1928, p. 515.

44. Luke 11:29–32.

45. Luke 5:1–4.

46. Griaule M and Dieterlen G, *The Pale Fox*, translated by Stephen C. Infantino, Chino Valley: Continuum Foundation, 1965, 1986, p. 157.

47. Ibid., p. 181.
48. Luke 21:25–27.
49. John 8:58.
50. Busenbark, op. cit., pp. 149–50.
51. Acts 5:30–31.
52. See Frobenius L, *The Voice of Africa,* Volume I, translated by Rudolph Blind, New York: Benjamin Blom, Inc., 1968, pp. 204–27 and Beier U, *Yoruba Myths,* London: Cambridge University Press, 1980, pp. 20–32, for accounts of the Shango myth.
53. The hatchet or axe is the symbol of the deity (neter) in ancient Egypt. We might also note that Shango's zootype, the ram, connects him the Egyptian Amon, the Greek Zeus, and the Norse Thor.
54. Concerning Jesus, the canonical Apostle's Creed states, "He descended into Hell, on the third day he rose again from the dead..."
55. Maspero G, *Popular Stories of Ancient Egypt,* translated by A. S. Johns, New Hyde Park: University Books, 1915, 1967, pp. 147–8.
56. Budge, *Osiris...,* Volume I, op. cit., p. 64.
57. Budge EAW, *The Book of the Dead: The Papyrus of Ani,* New York: Dover Publications, Inc., 1895, 1967, p. 268.
58. Budge, ... *The Theban Rescension,* op. cit., p. 405.
59. Ibid., p. 132.
60. Ibid., p. 133.
61. Budge, *Osiris...,* Volume I, op. cit., p. 79.
62. Ibid., pp. 79–80.
63. Budge, ... *The Papyrus of Ani,* op. cit., p. cxxxix.
64. Carpenter, op. cit., p. 211.
65. Ibid., p. 202.
66. The Egyptians never believed in the resurrection of the mortal body; the re-arising body was the Sahu or spiritual body and Osiris was the Sahu personified.
67. John 19:38–42.
68. Budge, ... *The Theban Rescension,* op. cit., pp. 319–35.
69. Matthew 26:6–13.
70. Budge, op. cit., p. 448.
71. John 6:51–57. This chapter of John is replete with eucharistic imagery, wherein Jesus repeatedly calls upon his followers to eat his body to ensure eternal life. These Johannine passages are essentially no different from the so-called "Cannibal Hymns" of the Pyramid Texts where the re-arisen king, Unas, feasts upon the bodies of the gods.
72. Budge, op. cit., p. 258.
73. Ibid., p. 585.
74. Ibid., p. 605.
75. Ibid., p. 302.
76. Ibid., p. 372.
77. John 12:35–36.
78. Budge, op. cit., p. 262.
79. Bonwick J, *Egyptian Belief and Modern Thought,* Indian Hills: The Falcon Wing Press, 1956, p. 111.
80. Massey G, *Natural Genesis,* Volume II, London: Williams and Norgate, 1883, p. 417.
81. Luke 3:4–5.

82. Budge, op. cit., p. 474.

83. John 19:26–27.

84. "... those who worship Serapis likewise are Christians, even those who style themselves Bishops of Christ are devoted to Serapis" (cited in Massey, *Ancient Egypt,* op. cit., p. 756; also cf. Doane, op. cit., p. 342). Hadrian was emperor from 117 to 138. Authentic Christian communities, separate from Judaism, probably did not appear until the beginning of the second century, just prior to Hadrian's reign.

85. Budge EAW, *From Fetish to God in Ancient Egypt,* London: Oxford University Press, 1934, pp. 199–203; cf. also Bernal M, *Black Athena,* London: Free Association Press, 1987, pp. 116–7.

86. Begg E, *The Cult of the Black Virgin,* London: Arkana, 1985, pp. 13–5.

87. The first of the four canonical gospels, the one attributed to Mark, is thought to have been written between 70 and 80 A.C.E.; the last of the four, that of John, not until 120–130 A.C.E. However, there were at least a dozen gospels circulating from the second century on; the four in the New Testament were canonized in the fourth century. See Mead GRS, *Did Jesus Live 100 B.C.?.* London: Theosophical Publishing Society, 1903, 1949; also Willis Barnstone, editor, *The Other Bible,* San Francisco: Harper & Row, 1984, passim.

88. There is an apparent reference to Jesus in the *Antiquities* of Josephus: "Now, there was about this time, Jesus, a wise man, if it be lawful to call him a man, for he was a doer of wonderful works,—a teacher of such men as receive the truth with pleasure. He drew over to him both many of the Jews, and many of the Gentiles. He was (the) Christ; and when Pilate ... had condemned him to the cross, those that loved him at the first did not forsake him for he appeared to them alive again the third day, as the divine prophets had foretold ... the tribe of Christians, so named from him, are not extinct at this day" (Whiston W, translator, *Josephus: Complete Works,* Grand Rapids: Kregel Publications, 1867, 1981, p. 379). This would seem to be the most direct statement testifying to the historical existence of Jesus in the first century from that era's most important Jewish historian, except for one thing: the passage is entirely spurious. These words could never have issued from the pen of a pious Jew such as Josephus; the passage is so transparent a forgery that not even conservative exegetes use it to prove the historicity of Jesus. Thus, Josephus never wrote that paragraph; it was inserted into the text by a later Christian redactor to bolster the case for the historical existence of the Gospel Jesus. Bypassing this apocryphal passage by a late "pseudo-Josephus," we can still say that there is no authentic reference in the works of Josephus to any events remotely echoing the Gospels.

89. Mead, op. cit., p. 48. Mead's book is one of the most erudite commentaries on the early textual evidence concerning the life of Jesus and the first appearance of Christianity. He refers to Suetonious's mention (c. 95–100 A.C.E.) of some "Christiani" tortured by Nero (r. 54–68 A.C.E.), but Mead thinks that these were probably dissident Jews, possibly of an Essene persuasion. In any case this quotation by Suetonious is not unequivocal because there is almost no evidence that "true" Christians had appeared in numbers large enough to cause any political ripples in the time of Nero. Moreover, in referring to these "Christiani," Suetonious makes no mention of Jesus. Another point is that the early followers of Christ did *not* call themselves "Christians"—it was a somewhat derisive name bestowed upon them by non-believers. The term "Christian" denoting an organized body of worshippers, does not seem to have come into common usage until the second century.

90. "The garbled condition of the Talmudic records makes it impossible to determine the details with any degree of certainty, but they leave no doubt that there was a Jesus ben Pandera or Stada; that he was taken to Egypt; that he practiced magic and was crucified about one hundred years [actually 66 years—CSF] before the date given for the birth of the Biblical Jesus" (Busenbark, op. cit., p. 327).
91. Ibid., p. 366.